Spirituality in Action

Chris,

With prayers for you and your family,

Jim Bacik

Spirituality in Action

James J. Bacik

Sheed & Ward
Kansas City

Sheed & Ward™ is a service of The National Catholic Reporter Publishing Company.

Library of Congress Cataloguing-in-Publication Data
Bacik, James J., 1936-
    Spirituality in action / James J. Bacik.
       p.   cm.
    ISBN 1-55612-958-0 (alk. paper)
    1. Spirituality--Catholic Church. 2. Christian life--Catholic authors. I. Title.
    BX2350.2.B29   1997
    248--dc21

                      97-25338
                      CIP

Published by: Sheed & Ward
                 115 E. Armour Blvd.
                 P.O. Box 419492
                 Kansas City, MO 64141-6492

To order, call: (800) 333-7373

www.natcath.com/sheedward

Cover design by Emil Antonucci.

Contents

Introduction vii
Chapter One
Spirituality in Action 1
  1. Roots of the Problem 2
  2. Overview of the Problem in Christian History 3
  3. Retrieving Wisdom from the Hebrew Scriptures 8
  4. The Example of Jesus 9
  5. The Pauline Witness 11
  6. The Letter of James 12
  7. Augustine of Hippo 13
  8. Benedict of Nursia 14
  9. Hildegard of Bingen 15
 10. Francis of Assisi 18
 11. Dominic Guzman 20
 12. Thomas Aquinas 21
 13. Beghards and Beguines 22
 14. William of Ockham 23
 15. Catherine of Siena 24
 16. Desiderius Erasmus 25
 17. Martin Luther 27
 18. Ignatius of Loyola 28
 19. Teresa of Avila 30
 20. Francis de Sales 32
 21. Isaac Hecker 34
 22. Maurice Blondel 36
 23. Teilhard de Chardin 38
 24. Lay Spirituality 40
 25. Pope John Paul II 43
 26. Liberation Theology 44
 27. Karl Rahner 46

Chapter Two
Finding Meaning in Work and Leisure 57
  1. Christian Perspectives on Work 57
  2. Rediscovering Leisure 62
  3. Labor Day Blues: Searching for Genuine Leisure 66
  4. Peter Paul Rubens and the Catholic Imagination . . . 70
  5. Pablo Picasso and the Mystery of Life 74
  6. El Greco and the Power of Grace 78
  7. The Christmas Crib: A Call To Reflection And Action . . 82
  8. Christmas: A Celebration of Hope 86
  9. The Christmas Season: A Celebration of Beauty 90
 10. Lent and Structured Prayer 94
 11. The Metaphysics of Baseball 97
 12. Cal Ripken and Loyalty 102

13. Al Kaline: A Worthy Hero 105
14. Baseball and the Virtue of Eutrapelia 109
15. The World Series: A Rich Cultural Symbol 113
16. The World of Sports and the Search for
    Transcendence 117
17. The Olympics and Healthy Competition 121
18. The Olympics and Fortitude 125
19. Managing Our Burdensome Tasks 129
20. A Retreat by the Ocean 133
21. Reading Classic Books 136
22. Humor: A Clue to the Spirit 140
23. Finding Meaning in Arduous Tasks 144
24. Riding the Subway: an Encounter with an
    Unfamiliar World 150

Chapter Three

Christian Hope: Dealing with Time, Suffering and Death 154

1. Christian Hope and The Last Things 154
2. A Meditation on Time 158
3. The Problem of Procrastination: Advice from
   Gandhi and Jesus 161
4. Finding God in Natural Disasters 167
5. Responding to Ecological Dangers: Prophetic and
   Mystical Approaches 171
6. The Oklahoma City Bombing 175
7. My Father's Death: Grieving Alone 179
8. An Anniversary Meditation 183
9. Constructive Grieving 186
10. Remembering the Community Builders 191
11. Honoring a Peacemaker 195
11. Celebrating the Life of a Compassionate Priest . . . 198
12. John Savage: a Profile of Practical Charity 202
13. The Murder of a Student 207
14. Cardinal Bernardin: Befriending Death 212
15. Advice on Grieving 215
16. Inspiration from Grieving Parents 219
17. Enduring Physical and Spiritual Suffering 224

For my brother, David Lee Bacik
(April 23, 1943 – April 15, 1953)

Silent witness to the Gracious Mystery
Passive recipient of unstinting parental love
Active member of the Communion of Saints.

Introduction

Spirituality in Action

As we move toward the new millennium, popular interest in spirituality continues to gather momentum. A decade ago, in my book, *The Gracious Mystery*, I wrote about a growing number of individuals seriously engaged in a quest for meaning in the midst of absurdity, for an ultimate purpose which transforms the dullness of life and for a personal integrity which pulls together a fragmented existence. Today I encounter even more people who speak openly about following the will of God, finding the Lord in daily life and tapping the power of the Spirit within. Signs of this spiritual quest abound. Collegians around the country attend liturgies and retreats in large numbers. Spiritual books, like *Care of the Soul* by Thomas Moore, have made the best seller lists and recordings of Gregorian Chant have appeared on the popular music charts. Many adults participate regularly in small groups which have a broadly spiritual orientation. Enlightened business leaders speak openly of the spiritual needs of workers.

Many people today pursue the spiritual quest without any explicit relationship to organized religion. Some believe that spirituality and religion are antagonistic or mutually exclusive. Others are simply unaware of the spiritual core of religious traditions or know little about the spiritual wisdom they offer. Even active church members sometimes find their real spiritual nourishment, not from the liturgy or other parish programs, but from extra-parochial sources, such as support groups or self-help books.

However, individuals who pursue spiritual growth without benefit of traditional religious wisdom are in danger of adopting faddish approaches or muddling along without a clear goal or a disciplined regimen. Even those who seem to be making good spiritual progress may be missing opportunities for even greater personal growth.

This book is part of a broad effort to overcome the estrangement between spirituality and religion. It is important to demonstrate that the rich Christian tradition can indeed illumine and guide the spiritual quest today. We need to retrieve specific insights and advice from our religious heritage which can help us find greater meaning and purpose in everyday activities.

Chapter One begins by analyzing the historical roots of the split between prayer and daily life which threatens the spiritual health of so many Christians today. The Christian tradition has given a prominent place to the contemplative life and celebrated the monk as the great model of Christian perfection. Until recently, theologians and spiritual masters gave surprisingly little explicit attention to a spirituality for persons living active lives in the world. And spiritual guides who did address this issue often advised lay people to live like monks by following the kind of regimen and ascetical practices common to life in a monastery. This history helps explain why some serious Christians today seek spiritual nourishment and guidance outside the institutional church.

As the first chapter goes on to indicate, the Christian tradition does contain important resources for constructing a contemporary spirituality which unites prayer and action in a fruitful synthesis and provides a realistic model of sanctity for people living active lives in the world. The Bible teaches us that we meet the great God in and through the events of daily life. Jesus Christ expended himself in doing good, but still managed to find time for refreshing periods of reflective prayer. Concentrating on the Western tradition of Christian spirituality, the chapter gathers ideas for an integrated spirituality from great saints, such as Augustine of Hippo and Catherine of Siena, and from important scholars, including Maurice Blondel and Teilhard de Chardin.

This initial chapter concludes by placing these diverse insights retrieved from the tradition into a framework established by the great Jesuit theologian, Karl Rahner. Rahner understands contemplation and action not as competing activities, but as complementary dimensions of a full Christian life. Sanctity is rooted in the life of charity. The contemplative life and the active life are not ends in themselves, but means to promote the good of charitable living. As means, they are relative and not absolute. It is a fundamental error, according to Rahner, to say the contemplative life is intrinsically better than the active life in the world. It is wrong to assume that monks are automatically holier than married Christians immersed in secular activities. For Rahner, action is a broad term, which includes all the ways we express ourselves in the external world. From this perspective, prayer and contemplation appear as human actions, as do work and play. Rahner's broad understanding of action also includes death, which he sees as a definitive act of freedom exercised by the whole person.

The second and third chapters of this book contain short essays which draw on the Christian tradition to respond to various challenges faced by people living active lives in the world. These essays were originally circulated privately to promote personal reflection. Some were subsequently published for use in parishes. I have revised and organized them thematically for this book. Chapter Two examines the spiritual dimension of work and leisure activities. The individual articles invite reflection on the deeper meaning found in common activities, such as visiting an art museum, celebrating Christmas, watching the Olympics, riding the subway and reading good books. Following Rahner's broad notion of action, Chapter Three looks for signs of hope in our experiences of time, suffering and death. The essays examine the significance of disasters and tragedies, such as Hurricane Andrew and the Oklahoma City bombing. They probe the mystery of time and the problem of procrastination. A number of them record my own reactions to the death of loved ones and friends. My list includes unrecognized saints, like my godmother, as well as the universally admired Cardinal Joseph

Bernardin. Above all, I pay tribute to my deceased father, who remains for me a great source of pride and inspiration.

All of the essays in this book reflect the theological conviction that we can find God and achieve personal fulfillment precisely in and through our common human activities. My hope is that the material will resonate with active persons and prompt deeper personal reflection.

Chapter One

Prayer and Action: Developing an Integrated Spirituality

One of the great challenges for Christians today is to develop an integrated spirituality which is prayerful and reflective as well as active and involved in earthly affairs. We need a spirituality which combines prayer and action and creates a fruitful synthesis between liturgy and life. As Christians we need to cultivate the inner life so that we can find meaning in our external activities. By the same token, our life in the world should take us back to prayerful reflection. Busy persons have to find God in their productive work as well as their restful leisure. Active individuals are searching for a route to holiness which passes through the external world of action and leads to a state of inner peace. Married couples want their often demanding family lives to bring them closer to the Lord. Social activists need to develop a rich interior life which sustains their struggles against injustice. We need models of holiness for persons bearing heavy secular responsibilities, who can only snatch brief moments of prayer out of their overflowing schedules. The call to holiness must include Christians active in the world as well as contemplative monks in a monastery. Lay persons with worldly responsibilities need solid spiritual guidance and encouragement just as much as priests and sisters serving the faith community. In short, we all need to develop a spirituality which is, on the one hand, mystical and contemplative, and on the other, prophetic and active.

1. Roots of the Problem

The problem of relating action and contemplation is deeply rooted in Western history. Classic Greek culture prized the contemplative life and despised many aspects of the active life. In that society, slaves did the hard manual labor and women took care of domestic chores, so that free men could do philosophy, enjoy the arts and participate in the political life of the city-state. The philosophers did not esteem the activities of artisans and craftsmen because they did not promote contemplation of the beautiful, but simply produced what was necessary and useful. For Plato, the good life was represented by the philosopher who escapes from the illusory world of ordinary human activity in order to contemplate the unchanging world of ideal forms. An important task of Plato's philosopher-king was to create a political situation which would foster the contemplative life. Aristotle distinguished the inferior realm of human activity, which involved busy engagement in the changing world, from the superior realm of quiet contemplation, which rested in the truth and beauty of the unchanging eternal cosmos. For Aristotle, the good life included involvement in the politics of the city – a free activity which created the conditions for pursuing excellence, beauty and a type of earthly immortality. Aristotle simply assumed that no man who had to work for his livelihood could be a free citizen or lead the good life. This outlook developed by Plato and Aristotle generally prevailed in Hellenistic culture. By the third and fourth centuries after Christ, Plotinus, and other Neoplatonists, still exalted contemplation as the means of achieving union with the Deity. Their approach, however, further widened the gap between contemplation and action, because they no longer included political involvement among the highest human activities.

Classic Roman culture also suffered from the essential split between the active life and the contemplative life, but reversed the Greek position by putting greater emphasis on the active life. The Romans were even more reliant than the Greeks on slave labor, although some of the slaves were able to prosper and participate in the world of culture and education. Roman leaders were interested in the establishment and extension of their empire. Their genius was for political legislation and practical organization, especially on a large scale. While celebrating the active life, Roman culture did little to bridge the gap between action and contemplation.

2. Overview of the Problem in Christian History

Throughout its history, Christianity has had difficulty overcoming the destructive dichotomy between activity and contemplation characteristic of Greco-Roman culture. In the early centuries, Christian spirituality gave a primacy to contemplation which tended to devalue worldly activity. This outlook originated in the conviction of the early Christians that the end of the world was rapidly approaching, when Christ would return and complete his work of establishing the kingdom. Given this expectation, Christians had little motivation to be actively involved in the affairs of the world. As Paul's First Letter to the Thessalonians suggests, some disciples were neglecting the most common human activities, such as working and getting married, because they were expecting the return of the Lord. Even those Christians who were committed to an active life of charity did not think in terms of transforming the world or challenging its evil structures. Paul instructed the Thessalonians to carry on with their ordinary activities, because the end time was unknown. But he did not encourage them to change the world or overthrow the institution of slavery.

The Fathers of the Church also tended to place a higher value on contemplation than action. Origen (ca. 185-ca. 254), the most influential of the eastern Fathers, played a crucial role in this development. In the Egyptian cultural center of

Alexandria, he encountered Neoplatonic philosophy, which advocated a regimen of study and mortification in order to ascend from immersion in the material world to contemplative communion with the One. Origen incorporated this philosophy into a Christian framework, creating in the process a new theological paradigm which exalted the contemplative life over the active life. According to Origen, Jesus himself expressed the superiority of the contemplative life by praising Mary for choosing to sit and listen while her sister Martha was busy about many things. Origen's interpretation of this story had tremendous influence on both Eastern and Western spirituality. In the West, Augustine adopted a similar interpretation, as did Gregory the Great, who insisted that the active life is good, but the contemplative life is better. A more negative appraisal of the active life had been previously introduced into Christian thought by Tertullian (ca. 160-ca. 225). Although heavily influenced by Roman political philosophy, he claimed that the affairs of public life as well as the pursuit of philosophical knowledge are totally alien to the interests of the Christian community. His insistence that Jerusalem has nothing to do with Athens has reappeared periodically throughout Christian history.

Another Eastern Father, Gregory of Nyssa (335-395), promoted a type of contemplation which tended to widen the gap between prayer and earthly activities. He understood the spiritual life as a journey into contemplative darkness, which brings the believer into a loving union with God, who remains incomprehensible, beyond all thoughts and words. Pseudo-Dionysius, presumed to be a Syrian monk who died in the early 6th century, further developed this negative way or "apophatic" approach to the contemplative life in his short treatise, *The Mystical Theology*. After his work was translated into Latin in the ninth century, the negative way of contemplation became more important in the West, especially through the work of Meister Eckhart (1260-1327) and the unknown author of the fourteenth century classic, *The Cloud of Unknowing*. In our own century, Thomas Merton brought this form of contemplation to the attention of a wider audience. In all its various forms, apophatic mysticism carries the danger of devaluing the everyday activities of ordinary Christians, who cannot even aspire to such spiritual heights.

Other more affirmative forms of mystical contemplation also flourished in the West, including the warm, personal, intimate union with Christ described by Bernard of Clairvaux (1090-1153) and the prayer of quiet which led to the visions and raptures experienced by Teresa of Avila, the sixteenth century Spanish mystic.

The preference for the contemplative life expressed by all these influential spiritual masters took concrete form in the monastic movement. For the early Christians, who had to endure persecution, martyrdom was the great sign of total commitment to Christ. Many heroic Christians longed to follow the path of discipleship by giving their lives for the faith. The martyr became the supreme model of heroic virtue and the saintly Christian life. When the Roman emperor Constantine (ca. 288-337) ended the era of persecution and granted certain privileges to the church, sincere Christians were faced with the question of how to practice heroic virtue and demonstrate their total commitment to Christ. Anthony of Egypt (ca. 251-356) sought to imitate the simplicity and poverty of Jesus by becoming a hermit and retiring into the desert. Other Christians seeking perfection came to him for spiritual guidance and eventually joined him in a life of asceticism and withdrawal from the world. We can see in these desert hermits, gathered in Lower Egypt, the forerunners of the monastic movement, which eventually spread through the Christian world. In the West, Benedict of Nursia (ca. 480-540) founded a large monastery at Monte Cassino, near Naples, and wrote a rule which set the tone and style for monastic life in Europe. The Benedictine rule calls individuals to seek perfection in a stable common life, apart from ordinary worldly activities. Ideally, obedience to God's will, as mediated through religious superiors, promotes cohesion and collaboration within the community. Regular periods of silence enable the monks to listen to the voice of God. Ascetical practices foster a hunger and thirst for things divine. Spiritual reading, meditation and prayer in common open the mind and heart to deeper communion with the Lord.

The monastic movement produced a new ideal of sanctity. The monk replaced the martyr as the model of Christian perfection. If Christians were no longer called to die for their faith, they could still manifest their deep commitment to Christ by withdrawing from the world in order to seek holiness in a monastery. Monks, who left behind the pleasures and temptations of the world, represented the highest form of Christian discipleship. The monastic ideal of sanctity reigned supreme until the advent of the more active mendicant orders in the twelfth century and has continued to influence Catholic spirituality right up to our own time. We get some indication of the enduring power of this ideal in the remarkable popularity of the Trappist monk, Thomas Merton, who has helped shape contemporary spirituality through his voluminous writings.

In the history of Christian spirituality, it is remarkable how little is said about lay spirituality in the world. When the Fathers of the Church and the medieval theologians, including Thomas Aquinas, took up the question of the relative merits of the active life and the contemplative life, they were comparing priests serving congregations with cloistered monks and not lay people with members of religious orders. They simply did not include lay life in the world in their discussion of the various paths to perfection. Their assumption was that the struggles of daily existence precluded the kind of moral purity and contemplative repose needed for the ascent to sanctity. Only monks cloistered from the world could hope to reach the highest stages of spiritual development. Since there were no recognized guidelines or determined paths for a distinctive lay spirituality, lay persons serious about advancing in the Christian life had to adopt the ideals of monasticism and strive to imitate the practices of monks. For example, the Beguines and Beghards of the late medieval period tried to keep the traditional monastic vows while living as lay persons in the world. Others joined the Third Orders of the Franciscans and Dominicans in a search for spiritual perfection. The vast majority of Christian lay persons in the medieval world settled for a piety which tried to avoid damnation through fidelity to popular devotions and their annual Easter communion.

Lay spirituality did not fare much better during most of the modern period. By the mid-twentieth century, popular piety had generally accepted a wide chasm between the contemplative life reserved for a chosen few and the active life of most Christians living in the world. No clear theological solution to the long-standing dichotomy between contemplation and action appeared. Most believers assumed that priests and nuns were holier than lay persons, who had to contend with the evils and temptations of the world. Very few Christians thought of their daily work as a path to sanctity. Popular piety put greater emphasis on extraordinary religious experiences, such as appearances of the virgin Mary, than on finding God in ordinary activities. The path to holiness appeared to many as an escape route from the world. The cloister seemed to provide the best climate for growth in sanctity.

It is a great irony of history that the followers of Christ came to uphold the monk as the highest model of Christian perfection. After all, Jesus himself chose the path of an itinerant preacher in the world, rather than the stable life of an Essene monk in the monastic setting of Qumran. It is strange that the followers of Jesus, himself a layman, would assume that clergy are holier than lay persons. It is odd that Christians should neglect or despise a created world and a common humanity shared by Christ. It is inconsistent for disciples of the carpenter from Nazareth to disconnect their work from their quest for sanctity. Finally, it is intriguing that believers, dedicated to the Christ who went about doing good, came to assume the superiority of contemplation over action.

Underneath these questionable developments in Christian spirituality, we find the fundamental problem of the split between contemplation and action. Much to their credit, the Catholic bishops, assembled in the 1960s for the Second Vatican Council, recognized the centrality and the gravity of this problem. In the Pastoral Constitution on the Church in the Modern World, the bishops identified the split between the faith of believers and their religious lives on the one hand and their earthly concerns and daily lives on the other as "among the more serious errors of our age" (N. 43). The Council went on to exhort Christians to avoid "a false opposition between professional and social activities" and the life of prayer. Following the example of Christ, Christians should "gather their humane, domestic, professional, social and technical enterprises into one vital synthesis with religious values, under whose supreme direction all things are harmonized unto God's glory" (ibid.).

3. Retrieving Wisdom from the Hebrew Scriptures

In following the call of the Council to develop a more integrated spirituality, we can retrieve important perspectives and insights from our long and rich Judeo-Christian tradition. The Hebrew Scriptures presume that the Israelites met their God in the historical process. Through the Exodus, Yahweh freed his people from the yoke of the oppressor and gave them political, economic and social freedom. Israel was bound to Yahweh by a covenant of love which assured the Jewish people of divine guidance and support in their earthly journey. God gave Israel the Law to guide every aspect of daily life and to provide a framework for following the divine will in ordinary activities. Although Judaism had an elaborate system of ritual sacrifice, the prophets constantly reminded the people that religious ritual must lead to the works of justice and to caring for the widows, the orphans and the aliens. Good Jews did not flee from the world to some transcendent realm, but immersed themselves in real life with the guidance of the Torah. Later Jewish mysticism, especially eighteenth-century Hasidism, spoke of hallowing everyday life and transforming the most mundane activity into a sacred ritual. Following an authentic impulse of the Hebrew Scriptures, Jewish mystics believe they can lift up everyday activities, such as eating, drinking and working, into the spiritual realm by dedicating them to the service of their God. Christian spirituality which remains in dialogue with its Jewish roots is less prone to create a gulf between contemplation and action, and more likely to find God in everyday activity.

4. The Example of Jesus

The New Testament portrays Jesus as the fulfillment of the highest ideals and expectations of Judaism. He combined in himself the mystical and prophetic strains of the Hebrew Scriptures. Jesus was a man of prayer. Especially in Luke's Gospel, we see him going off by himself to be in prayerful union with his Father. He encouraged his disciples to pray and taught them a prayer which addressed God as Father. This prayer no doubt reflected his own deepest religious perceptions, which were rooted in his Abba experience of intimate union with God.

For Jesus, prayer and action were essentially intertwined. Strengthened by prayer, he resisted temptation and went about doing good. He prayed before critical decisions, such as choosing his inner circle of disciples. His prayer in the garden before his arrest prepared him for the supreme act of freely handing over his life for the cause of God and humanity. Reflecting his Galilean peasant background, Jesus presented himself within the prophetic tradition of Israel, epitomized by Moses and the Exodus experience, rather than the priestly tradition centered on worship in the Jerusalem Temple. As Mark's Gospel indicates, Jesus was himself a carpenter, a man who earned his living in his home town of Nazareth by working with his hands. In his public life Jesus carried on the mission of John the Baptist, but lived a less austere lifestyle and preached a more positive message. While John was in the desert preaching a baptism of repentance, Jesus moved among the people, reminding them of God's mercy as well as divine justice. In his teaching Jesus insisted on the essential connection between love of God and love of neighbor. He played down messianic expectations, while emphasizing concrete acts of charity toward those in need.

The New Testament also presents Jesus as a great teacher of wisdom who instructed the people by word and deed. Jesus is the wisdom of the Father and a sage greater than Solomon. He not only taught the Beatitudes, but exemplified them in his own character and behavior. He was poor in spirit and single-hearted in doing God's will. He was a peacemaker who showed mercy to others and endured persecution for holiness' sake. Jesus was a master teacher who shared his wisdom through proverbs and parables. His whole life of active service to others was a great parable of God's love for the human family. His healings and exorcisms manifested the presence of the kingdom and the power of the Spirit. He taught his disciples about love of neighbor by reaching out to sinners, sharing meals with outcasts, including women in his company and responding to the needs of Gentiles. He reinforced his teachings on serving others by washing the feet of his disciples. By cleansing the Temple, Jesus challenged the authority of the chief priests, elders and scribes (mostly Sadducees), who benefited economically from the religious activities centered in Jerusalem. By actively recruiting followers and preaching to the people, he drew suspicion from the Romans who feared insurrection, especially at the time of major festivals in Jerusalem.

Jesus was not a monk who spent most of his time in prayer and contemplation. He was an itinerant preacher who went about doing good; a spiritual guide who imparted wisdom by word and symbolic action. He balanced his active life of preaching, healing and community-building with regular prayer and periods of quiet reflection. He sent his disciples out to carry on the work of the kingdom, reminding them of the importance of prayer and fasting.

As we try to work out a viable spirituality today, Jesus stands as our primary exemplar and inspiration. By his example, the carpenter from Nazareth reminds us of the essential dignity of human work. His lifestyle suggests that the ordinary activities of life can bring us closer to God. His great emphasis on community-building indicates that the journey to holiness can be undertaken in the company of family, friends and colleagues. The way Jesus related preaching and prayer challenges the traditional assumption that the contemplative life is separate from and superior to the active life. Jesus remains the supreme model for all of us who are trying to deepen our spirituality while living active lives in the world.

5. The Pauline Witness

The Apostle Paul carried on the active tradition of Christ, who called him to discipleship. He had his own trade as a tent maker and expended his energy preaching the gospel of Christ, crucified and risen. Although he insisted that good works could not merit heaven, Paul also taught that life in the Spirit should issue in the deeds of the Spirit. Those conformed to Christ through baptism and nourished by the Eucharist must walk "in newness of life." The new life of the Spirit, already available to Christians here and now, does not lift us out of the world, but transforms all of our ordinary relationships and activities. The love shared by husbands and wives, for instance, takes on a deeper significance for believers by functioning as a sign of the love of Christ for his church.

After the death of Paul, his disciples continued the task of adapting the Christian message to the changing circumstances of the late first century Greco-Roman world. The Second Letter to the Thessalonians reminds Christians that the day of the Lord's return is unknown, and admonishes them to avoid idleness, because now is the time for "every good deed and word." The Epistle to the Colossians challenges Christians to avoid actions contrary to the Gospel and to live out their participation in the death and resurrection of their Lord. Ephesians emphasizes that believers have already been enlightened by Christ and must now "live as children of light," producing deeds of goodness, righteousness and truth. The Pauline epistles do not challenge the existing social structures, but they do call on the faithful to act in good conscience and to carry out their responsibilities "in the Lord."

Some Christians have used the letters of Paul to justify a quietism which exalts complete passivity and abandonment to God, while demeaning all human effort, including acts of virtue and ascetical practices. As even our brief survey suggests, however, Pauline theology actually promotes a healthy balance between union with Christ and living out this reality in everyday life. The indicative of grace leads to the imperative of virtuous action. Far from justifying quietism, Paul encourages us, by example and teaching, to manifest the fruits of the Spirit in everyday life.

6. The Letter of James

In the New Testament, the letter of James serves as a primary witness to the importance of the active life of practical charity. Exhorting his readers to follow the wisdom of God, James insists that believers should match their words with action. Faith which does not lead to acts of charity is empty. Those who store up abundant wealth by exploiting workers will be condemned. True religion is to "care for orphans and widows in their afflictions" (1:27). Those blessed abundantly by God should give "generously and ungrudgingly" to others. Faith demands that we love one another and avoid discrimination. Following the example of Abraham and Rahab, our faith must issue in effective action. The Christian community should be an example to the world of just relationships and practical charity for the needy. James puts great emphasis on the proper use of speech, a powerful human capacity which is so difficult to control. "The tongue is a small member and yet has great pretensions" (3:15). Verbal praise of God is essentially linked to practical care for human beings. Authentic discourse reflects deep faith. Recognizing that speaking is an action which can produce disastrous consequences, James warns against various kinds of inappropriate speech: slander, swearing, arrogant boasting and useless complaining. We should use our voices to pray for the suffering and to sing praise to God, always confident of the power of prayer.

In striving for a contemporary spirituality of action, we do well to meditate on the letter of James. It does not directly attack Paul's teaching on faith and works, nor does it opt for a spirituality of action divorced from prayer and contemplation. It does, though, advocate a living faith which leads to authentic speech, practical charity for the needy and consistent efforts on behalf of justice and peace.

7. Augustine of Hippo

With these scriptural insights in mind, we can turn to important theologians and spiritual masters for further help in overcoming the split between contemplation and action. Concentrating on Western Christianity, we begin with the great fountainhead of that tradition, Augustine of Hippo (354-430). Although he gave primacy to contemplation in the spiritual life, Augustine retained a healthy respect for the active life. For him the process of spiritual growth does culminate in the serene contemplation of the triune God; but the process necessarily includes keeping the commandments, working for justice, living out the beatitudes and performing charitable acts. Participating in the trinitarian life of God does not excuse Christians from active involvement in the world, but calls us to transform the world into the city of God. Because we experience the healing touch of Christ, the divine physician, we must be compassionate to others. As we grow in the spiritual life and become more authentic images of the triune God, we will naturally reflect divine love in our daily activities. Augustine never let his esteem for the contemplative life lead to a disdain for the active life. Augustine's balance is evident in this paraphrase of one of his typical aphorisms: we should not be so caught up in contemplation that we forget the needs of our neighbors; and we should not be so involved in worldly activities that we do not have time for contemplation.

Augustine clearly played a decisive role in shaping a spirituality which celebrates the contemplative life. But we cannot blame him for the unfortunate split between prayer and daily activities which plagues us today. On the contrary, his theology contains important insights which can help us achieve a more fruitful synthesis of contemplation and action.

8. Benedict of Nursia

As we saw, the monastic movement in both the East and the West, encouraged idealistic Christians to seek sanctity by withdrawing from the world of action and concentrating on the contemplative life of prayer and discipline. Benedict of Nursia, the patriarch of Western monasticism, did indeed help establish a new model of Christian perfection which demands a set routine of regular spiritual exercises. But Benedict's rule also exhibits a great sense of balance and moderation. It encourages a healthy combination of prayer and work. The daily routine includes the office in common, private prayer and manual labor, which nourish the soul and the body. All of these carefully scheduled activities are for the glory of God and the sanctification of the individual.

The Benedictine ideal of balancing prayer and work proved to be remarkably effective. Benedictine monks helped preserve Western civilization. The monasteries functioned as centers of learning and culture. During the Dark Ages they provided stability and security. The monks cared for the environment by working hard to clear the land and to improve sanitation. The monasteries were self-sufficient economic units and often functioned as focal points for both the secular and religious activities of the surrounding populace.

Benedictine spirituality has valuable resources for a contemporary spirituality of action which attempts to meet the challenges of the postmodern world. It calls busy people to carve out time for daily prayer which nourishes the soul. It counters the hedonistic trends in our consummerist culture with moderate asceticism and discipline, designed, not to punish the body, but to liberate the soul. In our noisy bustling world, it encourages us to find places of solitude and moments of silence, which enable us to hear the voice of God.

Benedict's enduring advice is to seek spiritual growth through the regular and steady repetition of moderate spiritual exercises, while avoiding the fads and quick fixes favored by our culture. His rule demands good stewardship which means treating the simple and ordinary things of this world with the same respect accorded the vessels used in the liturgy. It suggests that we develop an interior stability, a center point which enables us to cope with the inevitable transitions of our mobile society. Finally, Benedictine spirituality reminds us of the importance of forming supportive communities of faith for Christians who are active in the world.

9. Hildegard of Bingen

We find a great example of the creative power of Benedictine spirituality in the life and thought of Hildegard of Bingen (1098-1179). She was the tenth child of aristocratic parents, who sent her, when she was only eight years old, to live in a tiny, strictly cloistered house attached to a Benedictine monastery. In her late teens she took her vows as a Benedictine nun and twenty years later became the superior of a small group of sisters. At the age of forty-two, she had a profound religious experience, a spiritual awakening which unleashed a remarkable surge of creative energy. She saw a heavenly vision bathed in "the greatest brilliance" and heard the voice of the "Living Light" telling her to "speak those things which you see and hear." Very aware of her own frailty and limited education, she sought advice about the authenticity of her visions from others, including her friend, Bernard of Clairvaux. He eventually brought the matter to the attention of Pope Eugenius III, who gave his approval. Encouraged by this affirmation, Hildegard spent ten years dictating her understanding of the vision to her secretary, a man by the name of Volmar, who put the material into grammatically correct Latin for publication under the title *Scivias* (*Know the Ways*).

By the time she was fifty, Hildegard was well known as a spiritual guide. Many people sought her advice, including the German emperor Frederic Barbarossa and King Henry II of England. After she succeeded in moving her convent to a new site near Bingen, she experienced a new burst of creative energy. She wrote nine books, including a trilogy of commentaries on her visions and scientific books dealing with nature and popular remedies for health problems. Hildegard had a special passion for music, which has the power to arouse "sluggish souls to watchfulness," and soften hard hearts for the gift of the Spirit. For her, music was a metaphor for God: "O Trinity, you are music, you are life." Creation itself is "a song of praise to God" and "symphony of the Holy Spirit which is joy and jubilation." She saw herself as "the lyre and harp of God's kindness" and believed that we all should be musical instruments of the Spirit. Music unites us with the saints in heaven, who praise God with "a pleasant and fine symphony of sounds."

Hildegard herself composed a whole cycle of original chants and songs for the liturgical year. Recent recordings of her rather sophisticated chants have proven to be quite popular. She also wrote a musical drama, called "Play of the Virtues," which depicts various virtues that bind the devil and strengthen the soul for making wise choices. The recent revival of this morality play is another sign of the current interest in Hildegard's work and suggests something of the spiritual hunger prevalent in our culture.

Hildegard's creativity also emerged in her distinctive use of feminine imagery for God. She speaks of *Sapientia,* or Lady Wisdom, who is "as terrible in regard to fear as lightning is menacing" and "as soft in regard to goodness as the sun is bright." In her visions she saw a beautiful young woman identified as Love. "She has her tent in eternity" and "it was from her that all creatures proceeded, since love was the first. She made everything." Hildegard addresses *Sapientia* in exalted terms: "O moving force of Wisdom, encircling the whole of the cosmos, encompassing all that is, all that has life in one vast circle." She sees a female figure assisting in the symphony of creation: "O burning light of the stars – You are arrayed as a high-ranking woman with neither stain or fault. And you are the playmate of the angels, a companion of the holy ones."

Hildegard's creative activities were crucial to her physical and emotional health. Before she began to write at the age of forty-two, she was often sick and "felt pressed down" by self-doubt and the bad advice of men calling her to a false humility. But once she allowed her creative energies to emerge, she "received the strength to rise up" from her sickbed. When she was free to record her visions, compose music, write poetry and offer spiritual advice, Hildegard enjoyed an amazing flow of energy and experienced a great sense of personal integration. For her, creative activity was therapeutic and life-giving. Through her personal struggles she came to realize that "wisdom resides in all works of art."

In 1158 Emperor Frederic Barbarossa invited Hildegard to undertake an unprecedented public preaching tour in order to further the cause of church reform. For the next twelve years, she traveled all over Europe preaching in great cathedrals and numerous monasteries to the clergy as well as the laity. Through her public preaching, she was able to share her profound spiritual insights with a much wider audience. Exhausted by her arduous missionary journeys and some unfortunate conflicts with church authorities, Hildegard died at peace with God and the church on September 17, 1179.

Hildegard of Bingen invites us to reflect on the connection between the interior life of prayer and creative activity. We need to be attentive to the deepest well-springs of our energy. We function best when our actions flow smoothly and spontaneously from the depths of our souls. It is helpful to recognize and purify our motives. The Holy Spirit, who inhabits the center of our being, is the true source of creativity. Discipline and asceticism are designed to liberate and facilitate the flow of creative energy. Personal integration leads to a greater zest for life. We are more effective when our actions reflect the love in our hearts, rather than the convictions of society or the expectations of others. Our energy level increases when we are in tune with the symphony of the cosmos and the wisdom of the Gospel.

Hildegard of Bingen often repeated the hope that her spiritual reflections would be useful to others. In our own time, she is once again offering the extremely practical advice that we should be more responsive to the Spirit within, who is the true source of creative energy.

10. Francis of Assisi

By the twelfth century, the practical task of integrating action and contemplation was rendered more difficult by the general malaise which prevailed in the church, including the ignorance and superstition of the laity, the poor education and worldliness of the parish clergy and the greed and sloth which characterized much of monastic life. The most successful and enduring efforts to reform this situation were carried on by the Mendicant Orders, the Franciscans and Dominicans, who revitalized the internal life of the church, while emphasizing the active life of preaching and practical charity.

As a young man, Francis of Assisi (1182-1226) enjoyed the good life of social status and worldly pleasure – a lifestyle made possible by a lucrative family business. At the age of twenty he fought in a local war, was captured and spent a year as a prisoner. After his release, he found himself more interested in a life of prayer, penance and charity. This conversion process was focused in a grace-filled encounter with some lepers, which transformed his negative attitude toward them into compassion and led to a life of service, directed especially to the outcasts of society. Throughout his life, Francis responded to his deep religious experiences not by withdrawing from the world into a monastery, but by living in the world according to the "form of the Holy Gospel."

Answering a call of the crucified Christ to rebuild the ruined chapel of San Damiano, Francis raised the money by selling some valuable cloth from his father's store – an illegal act which led to a trial and a dramatic renunciation of his patrimony. At the Lord's command, he began to preach publicly and soon attracted a small group of followers. Exercising strong leadership, Francis secured papal approval for his group, recruited new members and sent them to preach throughout Italy and beyond, even to the Near East. This was the beginning of an extremely significant spiritual movement, the establishment of a new type of religious order which combined contemplation and service in a fresh dynamic synthesis.

In his later years, Francis, suffering from poor health, resigned his leadership position in the community and spent long periods in prayer and reflection. In 1224, a profound meditation on the suffering Lord produced in his body the stigmata or wounds suffered by the crucified Jesus. Shortly after this remarkable religious experience, Francis composed his *Canticle of Brother Sun*, which celebrates the organic unity and beauty of the whole created world. For him, the world is sacramental, reflecting the goodness and beauty of the Creator. Francis called on his followers to give praise to the Creator God, not only in words, but also in deeds, especially service to the poor and dispossessed of this earth.

Authentic Franciscan spirituality has always recognized the essential connection between the created world and the great God, represented especially by the suffering Christ, who illumines the deepest truths about human existence. This spirituality calls us to move from a prayerful recognition of the God dwelling within to the mission of loving the world and all people through concrete acts of charity. In his classic work, *The Soul's Journey into God*, Bonaventure of Bagnoregio (ca. 1221-1274), who served as a general minister of the Franciscans for seventeen years, shows how we can move from contemplating the divine presence in the created world and in the human heart to union with God through the crucified Christ. Bonaventure encourages a method of visual meditation, which prayerfully pictures the events of the life of Jesus, in order to attain a deeper awareness of God's presence and greater compassion for those in need.

Franciscan spirituality has continued to inspire creative approaches to living the Gospel in the contemporary world. For example, Leonardo Boff, a liberation theologian steeped in the Franciscan tradition, insists that practicing charity on behalf of the poor today demands that we challenge the unjust structures and systemic evils which imprison so many people in the hellish circle of poverty. Imitating the compassionate Christ in the contemporary world means taking seriously his role as liberator of the oppressed. Genuine charity, inspired by honest reflection, seeks justice for those in need.

A contemporary spirituality which reflects Franciscan ideals will strive for sanctity by combining love of God with compassionate care for those in need. It will not seek escape from a sinful world, but will follow a path through created reality which leads to the Source of all truth, goodness and beauty.

11. Dominic Guzman

The decisive shaping event in the life of Dominic Guzman (1170-1221) was not a mystical experience or an ecstatic moment of prayer, but had to do with pastoral practice. It occurred when he was a 36-year-old canon regular traveling with his bishop from Spain to Belgium. In southern France, they encountered a large retinue of Cistercian legates of Pope Innocent III, traveling with great pomp and splendor. They were preaching a message of conversion to the people caught up in the Albigensian heresy, but with very little success. Dominic and his bishop convinced the papal legates that their preaching would be much more effective if they abandoned their luxurious lifestyle and reinforced their message with a simpler life of poverty. Dominic did not merely criticize the legates, but joined them in the new pastoral approach, which combined poverty and preaching. Eventually, he received permission from Rome to found the Order of Preachers and spent the rest of his life establishing priories and devoting himself to study and preaching. He did not write a separate rule for his order, but left them with the apostolic mission to preach the Gospel.

Historically, religious orders were founded for the purpose of promoting the holiness and salvation of their members. The Dominicans were the first to take as their primary purpose the salvation of others. Dominic insisted on the importance of personal study and established priories in Paris and Bologna so that the friars would have access to the great universities in those cities. For him, theological study was not an end in itself, but rather, the essential preparation for effective preaching. An early constitution of the Order gave the superior the right and duty to dispense the brethren from anything which hindered their study and preaching. It went on to say "our study ought to tend principally, ardently and with the greatest striving to the end that we might be useful to our neighbors' souls."

Dominican spirituality reflects the conviction that love of God and love of neighbor are essentially connected and are not at cross purposes. The common life rooted in contemplation and liturgical prayer should nourish the active life of teaching, preaching and caring for others.

We see this spirituality reflected in the great Dominican scholars and saints, including Albert the Great, Thomas Aquinas, Catherine of Siena and Meister Eckhart. They stand as living reminders that a life of active service to others can be an authentic and effective path to holiness.

12. Thomas Aquinas

In his explicit discussion of the relative merits of the active life and the contemplative life, Thomas Aquinas (1225-1274) stayed within the traditional framework. Following Aristotle, he lauded the intellectual pursuit of wisdom as the most noble human activity. With Augustine, he recognized contemplation of God as the highest form of human perfection. But true to his Dominican heritage, he held that a contemplative life which flowed into apostolic activity was superior to one that remained self-contained. In his treatment of this question, Aquinas did not take up the issue of lay spirituality or the value of ordinary activity in the world.

The major contribution of Aquinas to the ongoing discussion of the relation between action and contemplation is more indirect. His magnificent synthesis of Aristotelian philosophy and Christian faith affirmed the inherent value and fundamental goodness of the created world. Grace does not destroy the natural order, but perfects it. There is an essential harmony between reason and faith, philosophy and theology, the secular and the sacred. This organic and balanced theology challenges the type of monastic spirituality which fostered contempt for the world. If human nature as a whole is fundamentally open to divine grace, then we cannot ignore or demean our bodily existence. If the soul possesses a natural desire for God, then we should not simply dismiss the passions and emotions which color our daily existence. If the finite material world reflects the infinite power of the Creator, then we dare not disdain our earthly home as nothing more than a source of temptation. By solidly establishing the essential goodness of the created order, Thomas Aquinas has provided us with an essential building block for a viable spirituality of action in the world.

13. Beghards and Beguines

Although medieval theologians, including Thomas Aquinas, did not develop the topic of lay spirituality, groups of lay people did form during the Middle Ages in order to pursue a life of holiness. For instance, during the twelfth century in the Low Countries, groups of men, known as Beghards, and women, called Beguines, gathered in small communities to pray together and perform works of charity, while supporting themselves through their skilled labor.

The Beguines made especially important contributions to the religious life of the late Middle Ages. They grew rapidly during the thirteenth century, attracting middle class, urban women, who sought spiritual growth while living celibate lives, sometimes singly, but more often in small groups. They did not join a religious order or live in a cloister, but remained active in the world, serving those in need or doing ordinary secular work, such as producing textile goods. Thus the Beguines were remarkably independent of the traditional male authority exercised in family life and in the church. These women did not fit well into medieval society, since they were neither wives nor nuns. Some church leaders supported the Beguine movement as an appealing alternative to heretical groups of Cathari or Albigensians, who were attracting women by welcoming them into the highest ranks of perfection and leadership. Pope Honorius III (d.1227) initially offered an informal approval of the Beguines, but later refused to make it official. After that the hierarchy and many theologians, including scholars at the University of Paris, detected heretical tendencies in the movement and came to view it as a threat to established authority. The Beguines survived the official condemnation of the Council of Vienne in 1312, but in greatly reduced numbers. They experienced a revival in the early part of the nineteenth century, when more than 1,700 Belgian women joined the movement. Although not as widespread today, Beguine groups still exist, primarily in Belgium.

The Beguines, along with their male counterparts the Beghards, testify to the enduring desire among some lay people to strive for greater holiness. They also remind us of the need for a lay spirituality which does not merely imitate monastic life, but finds its own distinct path to sanctity through the world of action.

14. William of Ockham

William of Ockham (ca. 1285-1347), a Franciscan scholar who exercised great influence on the later Middle Ages, proposed a philosophical system, known as Nominalism, which indirectly challenged the traditional monastic model of sanctity. In opposition to Thomas Aquinas, who insisted on the power of the intellect to discern the universal structures of a divinely ordered world, Ockham emphasized the will and the arbitrary character of the world. He denied that universals existed, either in created reality or the divine mind, and claimed that all of creation is totally dependent on the will of God, who could have created a very different kind of world. He had little appreciation of mystical experience and was leery of theological speculation about the nature of God. His influential thought led to a spirituality which emphasizes freely responding to the will of God in all the circumstances of life. This outlook effectively challenged the medieval assumption that only monks could achieve holiness. Thus Ockham set the stage for a new model of holiness open to any individual who responds generously to the call of God.

Although Ockham encouraged all Christians to strive for holiness in obedience to God's will, he denied that there are degrees of Christian perfection. He admitted that people experience contemplative union with God, but insisted that such experiences occur only through divine initiative and not through any monastic regimen or spiritual purification. Lay people active in the world could just as easily receive such a gratuitous blessing as monks following the ascetic path in a monastery.

The theology developed by Ockham introduced a type of relativism into Christian spirituality. His followers insisted that God does not call Christians to fit into a divinely ordered world with fixed hierarchies and unchanging moral principles, but rather to do the divine will in all circumstances, no matter how arbitrary it might appear. Personal salvation depends not on following a prescribed code of behavior, but on responding to the summons of God, who addresses us as unique individuals. The moral imperative for all Christians is to live a virtuous life and to respond generously to the divine initiative.

Ockham's fundamental theological position opens up the possibility of including lay people in the search for Christian perfection. On the other hand, his theology undercuts the Thomistic synthesis of grace and nature which provides a firm foundation for appreciating the positive value of human activity in the world. Today, Ockham's thought is more helpful in challenging lingering assumptions about the primacy of the monastic ideal than in constructing a viable spirituality of action.

15. Catherine of Siena

Catherine of Siena (1347-1380), who was declared a Doctor of the Church in 1970, combined a rich contemplative life with a life of public service to church and society. As a young girl, Catherine spent many hours in prayer and was blessed with some profound religious experiences. Despite pressure from her family to get married, she became a lay member of the Order of Saint Dominic and continued a life of prayer in the family home. At the age of twenty-one, she heard a call from Christ to undertake an active life of service. She responded by devoting herself to caring for the sick and ministering to prisoners facing execution. She wrote public letters and preached sermons on significant issues of her time, ranging from the low moral standards of the clergy to the importance of launching a crusade against the Turks. Despite great demands on her time, she maintained a deep contemplative prayer life. During an especially vivid vision of the crucified Christ, she received the stigmata. Not long afterwards, she negotiated a treaty between Florence and the papacy and met with Pope Gregory XI at Avignon, France, to persuade him to return the papal court to Rome.

In her book, *The Dialogue,* dictated during an ecstatic religious experience, Catherine indicates that the love of God manifested in Christ involves a tremendous responsibility to serve others and to care for the world. This lofty teaching took on flesh and blood in her own life, as she allowed her deepest religious experiences to propel her into a productive life of public service. Through her words and especially her deeds, Catherine of Siena reminds us that an authentic spirituality of action must be rooted in prayer and concern about the common good.

16. Desiderius Erasmus

Desiderius Erasmus (1466-1536) played an important role in developing a Christian humanism which celebrates the active life in the world. After living the monastic life for six years and studying scholastic theology for two years, Erasmus took the advice of Thomas More and devoted himself to studying the Bible and the Church Fathers. These studies, combined with his broad knowledge of the Greek and Latin classics, enabled him to become one of the great leaders of the Renaissance and a champion of church reform. Reflecting important Renaissance themes, Erasmus insisted that prayerful contemplation and speculative thought should lead to the practice of the moral virtues and the search for a fulfilled human life in the world. Especially through a classical education, human beings can realize their potential and develop their talents in order to live wholeheartedly in society. It is not necessary to practice renunciation in a monastery in order to move toward perfection. Christian lay persons can seek holiness by living virtuous lives in the world. Education should inspire young people to imitate saintly individuals, who achieved genuine self-knowledge and demonstrated practical wisdom in serving God and improving the human community.

The Renaissance provided Christianity with a new model of sanctity: the Christian humanist who is well educated and fully engaged in the affairs of the world. At its best, Christian humanism keeps a healthy balance between prayer and action. It invites believers to imitate Christ and the saints by using their gifts in the service of others. It is open to all Christians, including lay persons, who want to consecrate their ordinary activities to God. Christian humanism provides an alternative route to holiness, beside the paths followed by the martyr, the monk and the mendicant.

In today's secularized world, it is vitally important to keep alive the very notion of Christian humanism, because atheistic humanists tend to co-opt and redefine the term within their limited framework. Believers must insist that atheists and agnostics do not have a monopoly on the ideal of human fulfillment. On the contrary, the Christian claim is that obedience to the will of God is the true foundation of self-fulfillment. Belief in God does not preclude effective involvement in the world, but grounds and inspires the active life. Following Christ does not stifle human development, but unleashes our true potential. The ideal of Christian humanism remains a valuable component of a contemporary spirituality of action.

17. Martin Luther

A century after Ockham, Martin Luther (1483-1546), the Augustinian friar who led the Protestant Reformation, directly attacked the medieval monastic ideal from another angle. Guided by his central insight that salvation is a free gift accepted by faith and not earned by merits, Luther insisted on the universal priesthood of all Christian believers and the holiness of secular pursuits in the world. All the baptized have direct access to God and are open to receive God's justifying grace. Even the most rigorous monastic practices cannot earn divine favor and are not necessarily more pleasing to God than secular activities. Contrary to popular understanding, Luther did not oppose good works, but did insist that they flow from justifying grace and are not the precondition for receiving grace. Christians must participate in the continuing battle against Satanic forces at work in the world, but always under the impulse of grace.

Lutheran spirituality is rooted in Word and Sacrament. Baptized believers find strength and guidance for exercising their universal priesthood by reading the Bible and listening to sermons as well as by participating in the communal celebration of the Lord's Supper and receiving Christ truly present in the Eucharist. Luther was convinced that scholastic theology had gone fundamentally wrong by accepting the ethical system of Aristotle, who advocated the systematic cultivation of virtues in order to control the extreme inclinations of human nature. The radical solution of Luther was to reject philosophy as a source of truth and to rely on Scripture alone. Thus Luther attacked the great synthesis created by Thomas Aquinas, which insisted that faith and reason were essentially compatible and that grace builds on nature, rather than destroying it.

In dialogue with Martin Luther, a contemporary spirituality of action should maintain a dialectical posture by affirming some of his insights and rejecting others. Surely we must reject the dichotomy between grace and nature, which tends to deny the essential goodness of human activity. On the other hand, Luther reminds us of some essential Christian truths which are important for an integrated spirituality of action: the universal priesthood of all the baptized; the value of secular pursuits in the quest for holiness; the normative character of the Scriptures; and the primacy of divine grace and the gift of faith in the Christian life. We can appropriate these teachings, as did the Second Vatican Council, without denying the traditional Catholic synthesis between nature and grace.

18. Ignatius of Loyola

In response to the Protestant Reformation, the Catholic church in Europe experienced a remarkable explosion of spiritual energy. Great saints arose to lead a massive reform movement within the church. For our purposes, Ignatius of Loyola (1491-1556) deserves special prominence because he developed a comprehensive and integrated spirituality of apostolic service, which provides a clear alternative to traditional monastic spirituality. Born into a noble Basque family, Ignatius lived the life of a courtier and gentleman soldier until the age of thirty. While convalescing from a battle wound, he underwent a profound religious conversion, which led to a year of prayer and mortification at Manresa, near the Benedictine monastery of Montserrat. During this time he experienced both great desolation of spirit and deep religious insights, which formed the basis of his classic work, *Spiritual Exercises*, a record of his own religious journey, designed to guide others along a similar path. After a brief pilgrimage in the Holy Land, Ignatius spent the next ten years studying at various places, including the University of Paris where he immersed himself for seven years in the thought of Thomas Aquinas. During his Paris years, he gathered a group of students who became the original nucleus of the Society of Jesus. The group eventually vowed to commit themselves to undertaking any apostolic service, anywhere in the world, at the request of the pope. By the time Ignatius died in 1556, about a thousand Jesuits were already involved in a great variety of apostolic works, including education, retreats and missionary endeavors.

The Ignatian focus on service is rooted in solid theological convictions. The Gospel calls Christians to imitate Christ, who went about doing good for others. In the *Spiritual Exercises*, Ignatius invites reflection on the activities of Jesus: choosing disciples, multiplying wine at Cana, driving the sellers out of the Temple, preaching sermons, calming the storm, walking on the water, sending forth the apostles to preach, converting Mary Magdalene, feeding five thousand, raising Lazarus, going to Jerusalem, preaching in the Temple, celebrating the Last Supper and carrying his cross. This series of meditations, which puts so much emphasis on imaginatively recalling the deeds of Christ, has the cumulative effect of encouraging a life of active service. From Thomas Aquinas, Ignatius learned a proper appreciation of the essential goodness of human activity, which grounds the effort to find God in all things. Near the end of the *Spiritual Exercises* he says: "In all creatures on the face of the earth God works and labors for me."

The Ignatian approach encourages Christians to achieve a healthy outlook on life by combining a fundamental indifference to the world with a loving care for it. Ascetical practices clear the mind and purify the heart so that we can reject Lucifer and follow Christ, who sends us into the world "to spread his sacred doctrine" and "to help all human beings." According to Ignatius, authentic faith leads to service and true love manifests itself "in deeds rather than in words." As later Jesuit writers phrased it, the goal of Ignatian spirituality is contemplation in action. Prayer and service are essentially linked.

Ignatius did not want members of his society to say the office together in common, and he warned against forms of prayer that would divert them from helping their neighbor. Time should be set aside for prayer, but always in order to prepare for service. Apostolic action is not a distraction from prayer, but a prayerful way of finding God in all things and enjoying "the Lord in many places and duties." Ignatian spirituality fosters a new form of asceticism imposed by a life of dedicated service which requires self-sacrifice and the willingness to go where needed to perform "any work of charity."

Ignatian spirituality has great resources for all those who want to find deeper meaning in their everyday activities. Any Christian can profit by employing the methods suggested in the *Spiritual Exercises* to discern and follow the divine call. By giving primacy to the active life of service, Ignatius created a new ideal of holiness which can guide and inspire lay people living ordinary lives in the world. If God can indeed be found in all things, then everyday activities can serve as a catalyst for spiritual growth. By developing a fundamental indifference to earthly realities, Ignatian spirituality frees people to use the good things of life responsibly and wisely in service to the reign of God. Christians in all states of life can benefit from the critical self-examination encouraged by the *Spiritual Exercises* – a process well designed to help us recognize and heal the psychological wounds inflicted by life in the modern world. Ignatian spirituality suggests an alternative model of Christian sanctity: the contemplative in action, who follows God's will intelligently and generously in all the particular circumstances of life. God blesses us not only with holy monks, but also with saintly homemakers, factory workers, corporate managers and lawyers. We can find exemplary virtue in men and women; married couples and single individuals; young and old; educated and uneducated. No one is excluded from the call to holiness. Martyrs, monks and mendicants do not have a monopoly on sanctity. Ignatius of Loyola bids us to heed this summons to sanctity by maintaining a contemplative spirit in the midst of our demanding daily activities.

19. Teresa of Avila

Teresa of Avila (1515-1582) exemplifies the close connection between contemplative prayer and the work of church reform. The first three decades of her life gave little indication of her future greatness. She enjoyed a generally happy childhood in a large well-to-do family. At the age of twenty she entered a Carmelite convent in Avila. Plagued with illness and depression, she made little progress in her spiritual life, despite being generally faithful to a life of prayer. Just before turning forty, she read Augustine's *Confessions* and experienced a striking religious conversion while praying before a statue of the suffering Christ. From then on she was blessed with an even richer interior life, including visions and mystical experiences centered on the humanity of Christ and friendship with God. In her masterpiece, *The Interior Castle*, she describes her own spiritual development as a journey through seven mansions leading to the innermost core of the soul where she was united with God in a spiritual marriage.

Teresa's mystical experiences propelled her into an extremely active life of church reform. Dissatisfied with the distractions of life in her large convent, in 1565 she established a smaller house of dedicated nuns who were more faithful to poverty and contemplative prayer. She went on to establish fourteen other reformed convents. In 1567, Teresa met a newly ordained Carmelite priest, later known as John of the Cross, who became her protégé. She got him and others to collaborate with her on a reform of the Carmelite friars, leading to the establishment of an independent province of those more deeply dedicated to poverty and prayer. Convinced that personal holiness was the key to a more vigorous and effective church, Teresa poured herself into reforming the Carmelite order. She traveled incessantly, wrote books, mediated political disputes, raised funds and did spiritual direction – all while battling health problems. As her interior life deepened, her zeal for church reform expanded. Her rich prayer life fueled her active life of service. Reflecting her own pragmatic impulses, she insisted that contemplation is not an end in itself, but should lead to love of neighbor. Doing good works facilitates spiritual development because such acts purge our imperfections and develop virtues. Contemplatives also participate in the apostolic mission of the church through their fidelity to the hidden life of prayer. Named the first woman doctor of the Church in 1970, Teresa of Avila stands as a marvelous witness to the essential unity of the mystical and prophetic dimensions of the Christian life. Her simple advice for all those interested in spiritual growth remains relevant today: trust God and act charitably.

20. Francis de Sales

In France, the Catholic quest for a post-Reformation spirituality took two very different directions. French Catholics associated with Jansenism, Quietism and the French School, led by Pierre de Berulle, developed an indifferent and even contemptuous attitude toward secular activities. Driven by a one-sided sense of the corruption of human nature and the sinfulness of the world, they put great emphasis on ascetical practices, self-abnegation and detachment from earthly things.

The devout humanism espoused by Francis de Sales (1567-1622) took French spirituality in a much more positive direction. Born of a noble family in Savoy, Francis received an excellent classical education, studying both theology and law at the university of Padua. Shortly after completing his studies, he was ordained a priest and later was consecrated as Bishop of Geneva in 1602. Francis was totally devoted to a life of pastoral service, especially as a spiritual director for individuals serious about following Christ. In 1609, he published his great work, *Introduction to the Devout Life*, which remains a major contribution to the development of a more inclusive spirituality of action in the world. In the Preface, Francis points out that almost all previous spiritual writing was directed to those withdrawn from the world; while his purpose was "to instruct those who live in town, within families, or at court, and by their state of life are obliged to live an ordinary life as to outward appearances." He went on to say that it was a mistake and even a heresy to banish the life of holiness from "the manual laborer's workshop," "the homes of married people" and "the soldier's camp." God calls all Christians to follow Jesus wholeheartedly. The whole created order, especially the world of personal relationships, reveals the love of Christ. The human heart has an innate capability to receive and to radiate the pure love of God manifested in the humble and gentle Jesus. Christians discipline themselves, not to inflict suffering on themselves, but to transform human desires into a passionate longing for God.

The *Introduction to the Devout Life* reflects the character and virtues of Francis himself – his sensitivity and balance, his warmth and integrity, and especially, his total dedication to Christ, the humble and gentle Lord. Francis frequently advises his readers to "live Jesus." The call to imitate Christ is not confined to those who live a cloistered life in a monastery, but extends to all Christians who are living ordinary lives in the world. All Christians have the name of the meek and humble Jesus engraved on their hearts, and thus bear the responsibility of submitting to God totally and treating others gently. The example of the compassionate Jesus guides all disciples in all their activities and relationships. The *Introduction* is filled with an "inspired common sense" and solid practical advice for imitating Christ in all the circumstances of life. Francis, who once described himself as "human as could be," had a remarkably integrated sense of human nature. Out of his own deep religious experience, he knew that God speaks to our hearts, touching our emotions as well as our intellects. Jesus calls each one of us by name to be as fully human and fully Christian as possible. Francis, known as the gentleman saint, assumed that both men and women were called to a life of devout humanism. He himself formed a close friendship with a young widow, Jane Frances de Chantal (1572-1641). She shared his spiritual vision, but retained her own distinctive religious sensibilities, rooted in her experience as a wife and mother. Together they founded the Visitation Sisters in 1610. Francis hoped that these women would form an unenclosed community, devoted to serving others, especially through visiting the poor. Although the Visitation Sisters soon became a cloistered community, their founding superior, Jane Frances, kept before them the image of the gentle Jesus, which is at the heart of a truly devout humanism.

St. Francis de Sales, the master spiritual director, has a personal message for all of us: be truly human; follow the example of the compassionate Jesus; seek holiness in and through daily activities; and do it all with a joyful sense of God's abiding love.

21. Isaac Hecker

Isaac Hecker (1819-1888) is an important figure in the quest for a distinctively American spirituality which combines a contemplative spirit and a life of action. Hecker reflects the great optimism which prevailed in the United States in the nineteenth century as well as the passion of the age for comprehensive explanations of human existence. In his own life Hecker combined a deep mystical sensibility with a practical desire to make a difference in the world. His contemplative spirit was formed by his deeply religious Methodist mother, nurtured by his contacts with the Transcendentalists at Brook Farm and channeled by his conversion to Catholicism and his ministry as a priest. He studied the great Spanish mystics: John of the Cross, Teresa of Avila and Ignatius of Loyola, and developed his own theology rooted in the conviction that the Holy Spirit living in our souls is the true source of life and vitality. At the same time, he lived an active life as a public lecturer, a pastor of a New York parish, the founder and editor of the journal *Catholic World* and the co-founder and superior of the Paulist Congregation. He was also a world traveler, devoted to spreading his vision of a renewed Catholic Church which would evangelize the United States and the whole world. Hecker's life manifests the power of a fruitful synthesis of contemplation and action.

In a sermon preached in 1863, entitled "The Saint of Our Day," Hecker expressed his views on the type of active spirituality needed in the modern world. Each age, he insisted, has its distinctive form of spirituality and sanctity: martyrs in the early church; hermits of the fourth and fifth centuries; monks of the early middle ages; soldiers of Christ of the post-reformation period. Hecker claimed that nineteenth century Americans, who prized freedom and intelligence as the means for human progress, needed to find God not in the desert or the cloister, but in "busy marts, in counting rooms, in workshops, in homes" and in all the situations which constitute human society. Christians must construct "the pillars of sanctity" out of "the cares, toils, duties, afflictions and responsibilities of daily life." Recognizing that most people of his day would not find perfection through martyrdom or the monastic life, Hecker called for "heroic Christians" who would use "a fully enlightened intelligence and an entire liberty of will" to realize the great goals of finding God and achieving perfection. In this sermon, Hecker proposed, as a model of spiritual perfection for his age, St. Joseph, who was "no flower of the desert or plant of the cloister." On the contrary, he carried "God with him into the workshop" and "found the means of perfection in the world," which he consecrated to God "by making its cares and duties subservient to divine purposes."

Hecker often emphasized the active role that the Catholic laity should play in fighting the "public corruption" and "private immorality" evident in American culture. To resolve these social problems, we need apostolic witness from "honest men in commerce, unbribed legislators, upright lawyers, just judges, honest mechanics." Hecker was absolutely convinced that Catholicism had the needed resources to help the United States reach its potential. He urged Catholics not to withdraw from society, even if it appeared to be hostile, but to collaborate on the great task of reforming it.

During his lifetime, Isaac Hecker generally enjoyed the respect of his fellow Catholics, including the American hierarchy, who felt no need to condemn his distinctive theological vision. But when the 1889 translation of Walter Elliot's biography of Hecker appeared in France, a great controversy erupted over some of Hecker's ideas, including his emphasis on the internal guidance of the Holy Spirit, his celebration of personal freedom and his support for American political institutions. Critics also challenged his celebration of natural virtues and his supposed preference for active virtues over the passive virtues honored by a previous age. In 1899, Pope Leo XIII issued an apostolic letter, *Testem Benevolentiae*, which condemned some of Hecker's supposed positions under the heading of the Americanism heresy. The pope rejected a position which relied so much on the internal guidance of the Spirit that it neglected the external teaching authority of the Church. He also suggested that those who lauded natural virtues were implying that nature alone was stronger than nature transformed by grace. Furthermore, the pope denied the distinction between passive and active virtues by recalling that Aquinas considered all virtues to be active.

Americanism has been called a "phantom heresy." Cardinal James Gibbons of Baltimore, and other defenders of Hecker, insisted that the heresy described by Pope Leo never existed. Nevertheless, the pope's condemnation had a devastating effect on Catholic intellectual life in the United States for over a generation. It left a cloud of suspicion over those who shared Hecker's passion for a distinctive American spirituality. With the more open climate created by the Second Vatican Council, there has been a renewed interest in the life and thought of Hecker. Although his tremendously optimistic spirit seems out of tune with our more somber postmodern mood, we can still learn a great deal from Isaac Hecker's great dream of an energetic Catholic laity devoted to finding God in daily activities and committed to transforming society.

22. Maurice Blondel

The French philosopher Maurice Blondel (1861-1949) provides us with a profound analysis of human action with important consequences for contemporary spirituality. Blondel, a committed Catholic layman, was passionate about overcoming the dichotomy between nature and grace which characterized the dominant theology of his time. This theology, which envisioned divine grace as a superstructure sitting on top of the natural world without penetrating it, made it difficult for ordinary Christians to achieve an integrated spirituality and to find supernatural significance in their daily activities. Blondel analyzed this problem in his brilliant doctoral dissertation completed at the University of Paris and later published in 1893 under the title, *L'Action.* He proposed a radical solution based on a philosophical analysis of human action which reveals its essential orientation to the divine. Although his writing is dense and his argument subtle, Blondel offers profound insights, often expressed in felicitous phrases, which can guide and inspire our spiritual quest.

For Blondel, human action includes all our decisions and everything we do that determines our being and destiny. In poetic terms, he lauds good and free action, which "makes our heart beat," reveals "the most intimate secrets we hide from ourselves," enables us "to participate in an infinite power," creates "a secret nuptial" between our will and the divine will, and initiates us into a "nascent mysticism." Through human action, we encounter our God.

Constructive activities are like "laboratory tests" which facilitate our personal growth. They "set the whole of our being into motion," create a unity between ideas and feelings and deepen our self-knowledge. They galvanize "our diffused energies," make us conscious of our freedom and vivify our intentions, while unifying our soul and body into "a natural whole."

Our actions propel us out of ourselves and link us to other people and the larger world. In an ever widening circle, we move from family to friends, to neighborhood, to country and, eventually, to a global solidarity with the whole human family. Through our legitimate activities, we "impress ourselves on the world and "stamp our imprint on the milieu where we live." Through loving actions, we "transport the center of our being" into "intimate union with others." The love that we share creates a "fount of energy" and is reflected back to us "in a warmer and more concentrated way." Action on behalf of others is "the social cement" and the "soul of life" which creates genuine community life. Human actions done well are "a public service" and "contribute to a great work," often beyond what we can perceive or imagine. Through acts of love we risk our security and entrust ourselves to the universe, relying on the Infinite Power who inhabits the depth of our being. Lovers "taste the interior life" of one another and in the process encounter the "Fecund Infinite" hidden in the beloved. Human love keeps expanding outward in search of the infinite God.

As Blondel insists throughout his work, profound reflection on human action is the key to overcoming the extrinsic notion of grace, which inhibits personal growth. In and through the ordinary activities of life, we meet God and move toward greater maturity. Blondel did recognize that some human actions are sinful and destructive. Out of his own experience, he knew that the cross is part of ordinary life. His philosophical analysis of human action demonstrates that human beings have an inexhaustible yearning for a self-fulfillment which transcends personal limitations. By refusing to accept any earthly accomplishment as final and by choosing openness to the infinite, we deepen our spiritual lives and prepare ourselves to hear the Christian message in a faithful way.

By overcoming the dichotomy between grace and nature, Maurice Blondel set the stage for the positive contributions of European Catholic scholars such as Karl Rahner and Teilhard de Chardin. Although Blondel's thought is not well known in the United States, it does resonate with the American pragmatic spirit, which insists that actions speak louder than words. Blondel invites us to reflect more deeply on the ways that our ordinary activities can bring us closer to God.

23. Teilhard de Chardin

The Jesuit scientist and theologian Teilhard de Chardin (1881-1955) devoted his life to developing a religious vision which celebrates human action. In his spiritual classic, *The Divine Milieu*, first written in 1927, Teilhard argued with great passion that we can sanctify all our activities because in and through them "the divine presence is upon us and seeks to enter our lives."

Most Christians, according to Teilhard, lead a double life in which their natural concern about worldly activities seems to diminish or undercut their supernatural love of God. In the years following his ordination as a priest, Teilhard experienced a wrenching conflict between his passionate desire to pursue his scientific interests and his longing to love God wholeheartedly. Traditional Christian spirituality, which emphasized the moral dangers presented by involvement in the world, simply intensified the problem for him. The standard advice to offer up daily activities for the honor of God struck him as an inadequate solution to the fundamental problem. It is surely fitting and helpful to purify our intentions in order to carry out our daily responsibilities in tune with the divine will. A good intention, according to Teilhard does pour "a priceless soul into all our actions; but it does not confer the hope of resurrection upon their bodies." In other words, this approach does not touch the question of the inherent value of our activities or their permanent validity.

Teilhard's more radical solution is rooted in his theology of creation and incarnation. For him creation is not a once-for-all event of the past accomplished by God alone, but rather an on-going process, which demands our active cooperation with God in bringing the evolving world to its fulfillment. From this perspective, all legitimate and constructive human actions have intrinsic and everlasting significance because they participate in God's creative activity.

Teilhard developed his distinctive perspective on the incarnation through reflection on the Pauline texts (Rom. 8:19-23; Col. 1:15-20; Eph. 1:9-23), which describe the universal Christ as the center of the universe, the goal of the evolving world and the personal reconciler of everything on earth and in the heavens. The cosmic Lord is incarnate in the world, drawing it forward and upward into final union with himself. The presence of the Word-made-flesh animates the whole material world, creating a divine milieu charged with creative energy. The Incarnation will be complete only when all the spiritual power locked into matter is released and gathered by the universal Christ.

Human beings share in this task of building up the body of Christ and completing the incarnation. All of our legitimate activities help to form the kingdom inaugurated by Christ. Even our humble tasks and ordinary activities help to divinise the world. This means that human action possesses an intrinsic value and a lasting significance. As Teilhard insists, God is present "at the tip of my pen, my spade, my brush, my needle – of my heart and of my thoughts." The divine presence "sur-animates" all honest work, rendering it holy and full of meaning. Nothing authentically human is profane for those who view the world with the eyes of faith. Liturgy and private prayer remind us of "the knitting together of God and the world." Encountering the risen Christ at Mass prepares us to meet him in our daily activities. In the liturgy we offer to God not only the consecrated host, but also all the joys and burdens of our efforts to transform the world. Private prayer attunes us to the divine presence which burns at the center of the earth, illuminating and energizing all human endeavors. Prayer helps us persevere in the burdensome tasks of life and enables us to express gratitude for the activities which bring joy and satisfaction.

Today, Christians who are keenly aware of personal imperfections and societal contradictions may find Teilhard's grand vision overly optimistic. His positive assessment of human action strikes some believers as utopian and unrealistic. Theologians have criticized him for failing to appreciate the pervasive power of original sin and the destructive consequences of the social sin which infects institutions. Nevertheless, Teilhard has made an enduring contribution to a contemporary spirituality of action by insisting on the intrinsic value and permanent significance of all constructive human endeavors. The path to holiness does indeed pass through the world of action. Our work is not a spiritual encumbrance, but a participation in the divine creativity. By meeting our daily responsibilities, we spread the kingdom and build up the body of Christ. These faith convictions, which have validity apart from Teilhard's distinctive theological vision, are essential to a viable spirituality of action.

24. Lay Spirituality

Developments in lay spirituality since the Second Vatican Council remind us that active involvement in the world is a genuine route to holiness. We are more conscious today of the distinctive calling of the laity to bring Gospel values to daily life in the family circle and at the work site. A growing number of lay persons now recognize that their secular activities can be a catalyst for spiritual growth.

Throughout Christian history, most baptized persons have maintained their ordinary lives in the world. In the early church there were no clear distinctions between clergy and laity. Even after a distinctive group of ordained clergy appeared in the third century, influential authors, including Tertullian, Origen, Chrysostom and Augustine, continued to insist on the priesthood of all baptized persons. Lay persons have played influential roles in the development of spirituality; for example, Anthony of Egypt, who sought God in the desert in the fourth century. It is remarkable, however, how little explicit attention has been given throughout Christian history to a distinctive spirituality for lay persons, who remain active in the world. After the monk replaced the martyr as the great model of Christian holiness, ordinary people had little guidance or incentive for pursuing holiness through their daily activities. As we saw, lay groups serious about the spiritual life, such as the Beguines, sought holiness by trying to appropriate the practices of monks. Medieval theologians and spiritual writers largely ignored the distinctive challenges faced by the laity. The great Thomistic synthesis has little explicit guidance for lay Christians who want to pursue holiness through their daily round of activities.

Only in the nineteenth and twentieth centuries did theologians such as John Henry Newman, Yves Congar and Karl Rahner explicitly address the distinctive challenges and contributions of the Christian laity. Drawing on the work of these theologians, the Second Vatican Council officially addressed the question of the status and role of the laity for the first time in the history of the Catholic Church. The Bishops reaffirmed the traditional teaching that lay people participate in the priesthood of Christ. All baptized persons have a fundamental equality and a responsibility to use their gifts for the common good. Every member of the church is called to "the fullness of Christian life and to the perfection of charity." The universal call to holiness prompts lay people not only to participate actively in the church, but also to transform society according to Gospel values. Lay people have a special duty and responsibility, which cannot be performed by anyone else, "to infuse a Christian spirit into the mentality, customs, laws and structures of the community" in which they live. Recognizing the serious threat posed by a piety which separates faith from daily life, the council's Pastoral Constitution calls for an integrated spirituality, which gives witness to Christ in all the activities of life. Christians should infuse their secular enterprises with religious values so that all things can be harmonized in a great hymn to God's glory.

Since the council, lay spirituality has flourished as never before in the history of the church. Some people concentrate on ministering within the church in various capacities, including catechists, liturgical ministers and pastoral leaders. Other lay persons put their efforts into service to the world, witnessing to the reign of God in their work and civic activities. These dedicated people are living out a spirituality of action. They are in the process of creating a new model of holiness to the benefit of the whole church. They remind us that it is possible to find a path to sanctity through the complexity of the secular world. The call to holiness is indeed universal, and not the exclusive vocation of monks, priests and members of religious orders. Collectively, dedicated lay people are accumulating a valuable treasury of wisdom on worldly spirituality. Busy people have found ways to incorporate regular prayer into hectic schedules. Committed individuals have learned to find God in their work, even when it is tedious and burdensome. Married couples have developed creative approaches to keeping the Gospel alive in the family circle.

Dedicated lay people deserve encouragement in their struggle to lead a life of holiness in the world. They need a theology which resonates with their experience and illumines their journey, and a model of sanctity which calls them to carry on their secular activities with deep commitment and prayerful reflection.

25. Pope John Paul II

In dialogue with contemporary philosophy and modern culture, Pope John Paul II has made important contributions to a spirituality of action. His important book, *The Acting Person: A Contribution to Phenomenological Anthropology* (Reidel Publishing Dordrecht, Hollen 1979), first published in Poland in 1969 when he was bishop of Cracow, examines human activity as the key to understanding the fundamental structures of the human person. He distinguishes between passive events that merely happen to us and human actions which engage our freedom and manifest our essential nature. We all experience situations of genuine freedom, in which we may perform a particular action, but need not do so. As a theologian, John Paul recognizes that we belong entirely to God, but at the same time, he insists that we must be in possession of ourselves in order to choose a course of action and to determine the direction of our lives. We possess the root power to govern ourselves and to judge our own actions.

For John Paul, we find our fulfillment as persons through our free actions. Our activities propel us outside of ourselves and enable us to make an impact on the external world. But they also leave a lasting residue in our souls and help shape our moral character. Every action plays a role in the quest for genuine self-fulfillment. Again as a theologian, the pope knows that happiness derives from communion with God, but he also insists that we find our happiness on this earth through a life of activity which respects reality and seeks the truth.

Through our actions, we also express ourselves as self-transcendent creatures. We are more than all of the factors that determine our lives and all of the forces that restrict our freedom. We have goals that exceed our grasp and experience longings that cannot be fulfilled on this earth. As spiritual beings, we can choose a course of action in response to a call from beyond ourselves. In our self-transcending activities, we function as integrated persons, who have at least an intuitive sense of the essential unity of body and soul.

In the final part of *The Acting Person,* John Paul shows that mature persons exercise freedom, find fulfillment, experience transcendence and achieve integration only by participating in community life. As social beings and members of diverse communities, we are bound by the law of love which remains the norm and guide for all human activity.

Throughout his pontificate, Pope John Paul has drawn heavily on his philosophical anthropology in writing his encyclicals, especially on social questions. In *Laborem Exercens,* for example, the pope approaches the contemporary discussion of capital and labor by emphasizing the dignity of workers. Human beings who do intellectual or manual work do not act as mere instruments of production, but function as true creators. Through their labor, workers not only help create a better world, but also achieve their fulfillment as human beings. Work enables individuals to participate in community life by founding families and contributing to the common good. Our labor should bring us closer to God and enable us to share in the divine creativity. By patiently enduring arduous toil, we share in the cross of Christ and the promise of his resurrection. By meeting our daily responsibilities, we participate in the great spiritual task of transforming and reconciling the human family. John Paul's encyclical on human work adds an authorative voice to important themes already developed by other authors, including Blondel and Teilhard.

26. Liberation Theology

Contemporary political and liberation theologians have insisted that liberating activities directed to creating a more just society are essential to an authentic Christian spirituality. Dedicated discipleship calls for active involvement in fighting against institutional evil and systemic injustice.

Borrowing a Greek term, used originally by Aristotle and more recently by Marxist scholars, liberation theologians speak a great deal about *praxis,* which indicates purposeful social action designed to free people and transform society. Christian faith is not merely a matter of affirming creeds and dogmas, but necessarily involves active engagement in the task of overcoming injustice and prejudice. A concern over orthodoxy, or correct beliefs, must be balanced by an even more fundamental concern for *orthopraxis*, or correct conduct in imitation of Christ. The Hebrew Scriptures focus on the Exodus, the story of a people freed from political, economic and social bondage by their God. The Gospels witness to Jesus Christ the liberator, who frees the captives and preaches the good news of salvation to the poor. Christ calls his followers to share in his liberating activities.

From this perspective, theology is the interpretation and transformation of Christian *praxis*. Liberation theology gives a primacy to practice over theory. The actual practice of the faith by Christians contains an implicit theory, which theology brings to conscious awareness. Theology must be prepared to criticize and challenge not only the injustice in society, but also the contradictions and hypocrisy within the community of faith. Theology offers this critique from the perspective of the liberating activity of Jesus and from within a particular historical and cultural context.

A spirituality of action which takes liberation theology seriously finds God in working for peace and justice in the world. Genuine Christian faith is both mystical and prophetic. It is rooted in a life of prayer which issues in concrete action on behalf of the poor and oppressed of this world. Fighting the great battles against social ills, such as consumerism, racism and sexism, drives Christian believers back to prayer and reflection. This spirituality recognizes, along with the American pragmatic tradition, that actions do speak louder than words. Our actions reveal the depth and content of our beliefs. The imitation of Christ demands personal discipline and social witness. Charitable activities must include intelligent efforts to transform unjust structures and oppressive systems, as well as compassionate care directed to individuals. Christian action, understood as *praxis*, combines theory and practice, prayer and prophecy, justice and charity, personal compassion and institutional transformation. This rich understanding of *praxis* challenges the traditional supremacy of contemplation in the spiritual life and suggests a more balanced approach to Christian discipleship.

27. Karl Rahner

The influential German Jesuit, Karl Rahner (1904-1984), provides a solid theological foundation for constructing a viable spirituality of action. His theological anthropology, or fundamental understanding of human existence, invites us to rethink the essential relationship between the active life and the contemplative life. His comprehensive and integrated theological system offers a framework for understanding and organizing the insights of the spiritual masters we have already discussed. But Rahner's theology is not the only way of establishing a foundation or framework for a contemporary spirituality. We could also turn to the work of Hans Urs von Balthasar or build on the key insights of political and liberation theology. But for me, and many other pastoral ministers, Rahner continues to offer the most helpful guidance for the spiritual quest.

Rahner's whole theological system is rooted in his understanding of the human person as spirit in the world. As spiritual persons, we have infinite longings and are positively oriented to the Mystery we call God. We hunger and thirst for a love that is imperishable and for knowledge that exceeds our grasp. We have the ability to reach out to others and to withdraw into the solitude of our own hearts. As bodily creatures, we walk the paths of this world. Our pilgrim journey brings us a diverse mixture of pleasure and pain, success and failure, satisfaction and disappointment. Along with our infinite longings, we experience our overwhelming finitude. We know physical fatigue, emotional upset, moral failure, intellectual limitation and religious dryness. In all aspects of our lives, we experience both the power of divine grace and the threat of sin and guilt. In our better moments, we hear a call to develop our potential, to deepen our relationships and to serve the common good. As Christians we believe that God calls us to put on the mind of Christ and to be more responsive to the promptings of the Spirit.

Rahner believes that we answer this call and fulfill our nature by a healthy alternating rhythm of activity in the world and withdrawal into the sanctuary of our inner life. Through our actions we develop our potential and shape our environment. The external world creates an open space where we can grow spiritually and practice virtue. Just as the body is the extension of the soul, so our external actions extend our interior sentiments into the world of time and space. For Rahner, there are no purely internal acts. Since we are embodied spirits, the deepest stirrings of our souls always resonate in our bodies. The most speculative thoughts are accompanied by images in the brain. Our fundamental spiritual attitudes get translated into our daily actions. From this perspective, we can see contemplation and prayer as types of action.

The world of action is like a laboratory where we can test our theories and develop our potential. Rahner agrees with Pascal that we learn to be humble people by practicing acts of humility. We come to a genuine knowledge of the great human realities, such as love, truthfulness, loyalty, trust and hope, not by speculating about them, but by acting on them. Action is the basis of knowledge. We discover the truth through trial and error. Theory gets tested and justified by activity in the real world. The world of action provides a path which can lead us to wisdom as well as virtue.

With all of his emphasis on the role of action in the spiritual quest, Rahner never loses sight of the importance of prayer and contemplation. Prayer is a fundamental act of human existence which gives expression to the depths of our being. In prayer we place ourselves as whole persons before the divine presence, while recognizing our total dependence on the Creator of all. Prayer comes as an unearned gift from the Spirit within us. Under the influence of the Spirit, we can offer fitting praise, thanksgiving and petition to the Gracious Mystery. From this perspective, prayer is an end in itself, and requires no other purpose to justify itself.

But prayer is also functional. A rich prayer life helps facilitate healthy personal development. Prayerful contemplation enables us to gain perspective on our actions in the world, so that we see them as part of a larger divine plan. Prayer provides motivation for acting in accord with the divine will and energy for pursuing our highest ideals. Contemplation helps us appreciate the divine grace that permeates our whole being. It also reveals the ambiguities in our active life and the sinfulness that threatens to distort our earthly activities. Quiet reflection enables us to hear the promptings of the Spirit to love God and our neighbor as ourselves. A lawyer friend of mine once told me that he could not survive in his profession and maintain his ethical standards without daily prayer. He speaks for many who know both the temptations of the world and the power of prayer.

For Rahner, however, action and contemplation are not simply two separate activities or realms of human existence. They need not exclude or diminish one another. On the contrary, they are meant to exist in a fruitful synthesis, mutually conditioning and fructifying one another. The rigors and demands of daily life send us back to prayer for wisdom and strength to continue the struggle. Prayer reminds us of our responsibilities in the world and prepares us to meet them. All Christian believers find elements of both action and prayer in their lives. A contemplative monk is engaged in action; a busy married woman with a career snatches a few moments of prayer. Christians serious about spiritual growth must strive to find a healthy balance between action and contemplation or, more precisely, to cultivate a fruitful synthesis which embraces both. There is no mathematical formula to determine this mixture. Rahner says it is wrong and dangerous to think that every Christian must possess both prayer and action in equal and full measure. Finding the right mix is an important part of spiritual discernment. One or the other will predominate, but each must receive its due, and neither can be totally neglected. Surely the common problem for Christians active in the world is to find time for prayer and contemplation so that they will not be overwhelmed by the demands of daily life. The ideal of balancing work and prayer is as important for lay people raising a family as it is for monks in a monastery. We must all find a healthy balance for ourselves, which takes into account the need to nourish our souls and to meet our daily responsibilities. That mix will no doubt change over the course of a lifetime. A retired man now spends longer periods of time in quiet reflection than he did when he was working fifty hours a week and snatched a few brief moments of prayer from his busy schedule. All Christians must guard against collapsing the dialectic between work and contemplation and destroying the fruitful tension which enables each to flourish. Prayer should not be an escape from earthly responsibilities; and daily activities should not overwhelm our prayer time.

Action and contemplation do not simply represent two distinct ways of life. Rather, they are modes or dimensions of human existence, which should interact to produce a healthy Christian life. Most Christians express their commitment to the Lord through an active life in the world. Some express their discipleship by withdrawing from the world into the contemplative life of the cloister. The church needs both in order to function as a credible sign and effective instrument of the reign of God. Contemplatives who live a regimented life of prayer and reflection give witness to the deepest source and ultimate goal of all earthly activity. They remind us that we all move toward the final renunciation and surrender we call death. Those active in the world manifest the Christian conviction that God can be found in all things and that the whole of creation is destined to share in the final victory.

Rahner argues that we cannot say that the contemplative life is simply better than the active life, or vice versa, for that matter. The perfection of the Christian life consists in authentic love of God and neighbor. Charity is the greatest virtue, and the most sublime Christian activity. It is not a mere attitude of mind, but involves concrete action in the world. It engages our whole being and represents our total achievement. Rahner periodically expressed reservations about the Vatican II statement that the liturgy is the summit of the

Christian life. For him, the life of charity represents the highest achievement of Christian discipleship. God's grace often manifests itself more radically and definitively through charitable acts than liturgical celebrations.

Love of God and neighbor are essentially connected. To claim love of God, while ignoring the neighbor in need, is fundamentally deceitful and contradictory. Genuine love for other human beings implies love for the Creator of all people. In an age threatened by cynicism, love of neighbor takes on special significance, because it has an inherent power to make the Christian claim more credible. Christians actively engaged in serving others proclaim the core of the Christian message through their deeds. Disciples dedicated to transforming unjust institutions and dehumanizing systems give witness to the enduring power of Jesus Christ the liberator. Christian compassion points to a God who loves all human beings unconditionally.

If Christian perfection consists in charity, then no one state of life can claim to be the highest form of discipleship. There is no intrinsic reason why a married person active in the world cannot be as holy as a monk spending long periods of time in prayer each day. The contemplative life and the active life are not ends in themselves, but rather means directed to the goal of love of God and neighbor. Means are not absolutes, but are relative to particular personal needs and external circumstances. As means, neither the active life or the contemplative life can claim an essential supremacy over the other. Their value as a means depends entirely on how effective they are in helping individuals become better lovers of God and neighbor. Traditionally, the church assumed that the cloister created a space for sanctity, while the world overwhelmed believers with temptations. The church's official list of canonized saints includes very few married people who lived active lives.

The theology of Karl Rahner effectively challenges this understanding of sanctity, which has been dominant in the church from the third century to our own time. If a particular state of life is only a means to the end of charity, then there is no inherent reason why the monk should be seen as the highest model of Christian perfection. The list of canonized saints, dominated by martyrs, monks, virgins and clergy, does not reflect the true history of Christian charity. The universal call to holiness proclaimed by the Second Vatican Council reminds us of how many lay Christians throughout history felt excluded from that invitation.

In challenging this dominant tradition, Rahner found support in Clement of Alexandria (ca. 150 - ca. 215), a cultured man of his time, who wanted to reconcile the Christian faith with Greek philosophy. Because he put such great emphasis on the innermost attitudes of Christians as the true foundation of any state of life, Clement understood that a secular life of marriage and activity in the world could bring believers closer to God. He encouraged lay persons to serve the Lord well in human affairs and to bring the world back to God. Rahner also drew on the preaching of John Chrysostom (ca. 349-407), who continually called Christian lay persons to a life of perfection. He insisted that the Sermon on the Mount is addressed to all Christians, not just monks, and that all baptized persons need to pray and read Scripture in order to grow in charity. Neither Clement nor Chrysostom developed a complete theology of lay asceticism and holiness, but they kept alive the valuable insight that growth in charity is the path to perfection for all Christians. In our own century, Rahner was able to incorporate this insight into his comprehensive spiritual theology and make it available to the whole church.

Although Rahner emphasizes the graced character and potential revelatory power of legitimate worldly activities, he also recognizes that they remain threatened by sin and distortion. We can get so absorbed in earthly pursuits that we lose sight of the kingdom of heaven. Constant immersion in secular activities can absorb our attention and distract our souls. Daily activities can occupy our time and energy, leaving no room for prayer. The routine and boredom of everyday life can dull our spiritual sensibilities. Work can be an escape from intimate relationships and personal reflection. Achievement can lead to false pride. The essential ambiguity built into human activity means that we must be alert to distortions and open to improvement. Prudence dictates that we learn from mistakes and make needed corrections. The virtue of fortitude prompts us to follow our conscience and act decisively even in ambiguous situations. A spirituality which effectively resists evil learns from the example of Jesus, who was fully engaged in the world without succumbing to its temptations. Our confidence is finally in the Holy Spirit, who gives ultimate meaning to all our virtuous activities.

Not only does Rahner provide a theological framework for a spirituality of action, but he also suggests ways of finding greater meaning in particular activities. Our work offers us the opportunity to develop our God-given potential and to help spread the kingdom in the world. Leisure activity, including play, has the power to lift us out of ordinary time and to reveal the transcendent dimension of life. One of Rahner's great contributions is his insistence that we can find God in the ordinary activities of life. Living in a culture which prizes the spectacular, we need his reminder that simple activities can be filled with deep meaning and bring a quiet joy. While the media and influential televangelists highlight striking conversions and extraordinary gifts of the Spirit, Rahner advises us to listen attentively to the Lord, who whispers good news in and through the events of everyday life. In a private conversation, I once asked Rahner about his own deepest religious experience and he told me that it was "immersion in the mystery." When I pressed him for details, he explained that he was not referring to a specific mystical experience, but to the general experience of the mystery dimension of ordinary life. Out of this deep experience, he has written insightful and inspiring articles on finding God in the most common activities, such as moving about, sitting down, seeing, laughing, eating, sleeping and praying. Through his immense influence on twentieth century spirituality, Rahner has encouraged many other Christians to appreciate the mystery dimension of ordinary activities and to mine the riches of daily life.

Rahner has given special attention to the profound experience no one escapes, the mystery of death. Reflecting a key insight of his teacher, Martin Heidegger, he insists that a proper attitude toward death is essential to living an authentically human life. At a popular level, Christians generally think of death as a passively endured event, in which the soul is separated from the body and continues to live on for an infinitely long period of time, known as eternity. Convinced that this common perception is not only wrong, but harmful, Rahner challenges it at a number of points. Drawing on reason and revelation, he insists that death is not a passive event that we undergo, but rather, a free activity in which we dispose of ourselves in a definitive way. Death is the moment of maximum freedom. It offers us the opportunity to hand ourselves over to the gracious God in a final free act, which is irrevocable. Death is not a separation of soul and body, but an action of the whole person. As embodied spirits we surrender our whole being to our Creator. We Christians believe in both the immortality of the soul and the resurrection of the body. Together these two perspectives suggest that we live on as whole creatures, body and soul, happy with God forever. According to Rahner, eternity is not a very long period of time. It is rather the ultimate fulfillment of time, the validity of our existence, the irrevocable culmination of our freedom and the definitive realization of all our hopes. An indefinite continuation of life as we know it would indeed be hell, as the Russian philosopher Berdyaev noted. Death leading to eternal life is the only possible way to escape this hell.

For Rahner death is an action which brings into focus all the limitations of human life. In dying we know the weakness of the flesh and the diminishment of our physical power. Our freedom runs up against external forces and uncontrollable circumstances. Dying is an especially intense combination of free activity and passive suffering. The doctrine of hell reminds us that it is possible to refuse to surrender to God and to die in the self-contradictory posture of selfishly clinging to our own autonomy. Despite all the darkness of death, Christians find hope in the resurrection of Christ, which vindicated his life and gave ultimate meaning to his death. The resurrection proclaims to us the most important truths: God is trustworthy; love is stronger than death; and all of our virtuous activities in the world have ultimate meaning and abiding validity.

Karl Rahner's integrated theology offers radical solutions to the problems which have plagued the historical development of a spirituality of action. His positive assessment of all legitimate human effort challenges the bias of the classic Greek philosophers against manual labor and the work of craftsmen, while affirming their appreciation of philosophical contemplation and political involvement. Rahner also challenges the longstanding assumption that, after the martyr, the monk represents the highest model of Christian perfection. By insisting that sanctity comes from following the example of Jesus through a life of charity, Rahner opens up the path to holiness to all Christians in any state of life. By pointing out that contemplation and action are interrelated components of a healthy personality, he encourages us to bridge the gaps which plague modern spirituality: between liturgy and life; between love of God and love of neighbor; and between clergy and laity.

Furthermore, Rahner's comprehensive theology provides a framework for assimilating important insights of spiritual masters throughout history. Most of all, he encourages us to follow the example of our supreme spiritual guide, Jesus of Nazareth, who expended himself doing good for others, but also found time to withdraw into prayerful solitude. From the Rahnerian perspective, the distinctive New Testament spiritualities of both Paul and James appear as essential components of an integrated Christian life. Rahner encourages us to appropriate the specific spiritual insights of great saints: Augustine, who cautions us not to neglect prayer or avoid action; Benedict, who calls for a balance between prayer and work; Hildegard, who demonstrates the connection between contemplative prayer and creative activities; Francis of Assisi, who helps us see God present in the beauty of creation and the faces of the needy; Dominic, who insists that prayerful study leads to active service of others; Aquinas, who teaches us about the essential goodness of an active life rooted in prayer; Catherine of Siena, who exemplifies the connection between spirituality and public service; Ignatius, who admonishes us to find God in all things and to serve others wholeheartedly; Teresa of Avila, who reminds us that effective church reform must be rooted in personal conversion; Francis de Sales, who encourages us, no matter what our state in life, to imitate the gentle Jesus in our activities and relationships. Rahner's theology of action reflects the insights of these influential spiritual guides and directs our attention to the diverse ways they have related prayer and human activity.

Rahner's organic theology preserves and corrects valuable ideas from authors who have contributed to a spirituality of action. His open approach encourages us to carry on the tradition of Christian humanism espoused by Erasmus and other Renaissance figures, while guarding against a mere humanism which ignores or denies the transcendent dimension of human existence. He can accept Luther's teaching on the universal priesthood and the value of secular activity, while challenging his theology that creates a gap between nature and grace. His system can affirm all the marvelous insights of Blondel on the value and significance of human action, while maintaining the necessity of prayer and reflection for a balanced life. Rahner's sober realism can embrace Isaac Hecker's call for the Catholic laity to transform American culture, without falling into a naive optimism or excessive nationalism. His theology of grace provides a solid foundation for Teilhard's grand religious vision of the divine milieu which divinises all human activities, but it also offers a strong corrective to Teilhard's utopian tendencies. His theology of the laity supports the marvelous growth of lay involvement in the church since Vatican II, while reminding lay persons not to neglect their vocation to transform the world. Finally, Rahner's theological anthropology can incorporate and apply the personalistic philosophy of Pope John Paul II, but will move it in a more inclusive and universal direction.

Some theologians insist that Rahner's system cannot integrate the perspectives of liberation and political theology. His theological anthropology, the critics claim, fails to take into sufficient account the concrete social, political and economic situations of particular human beings. In responding to this criticism, which he took very seriously, Rahner admits that he did not say enough about the social situation of people today, but insists that his theological anthropology recognizes the need for social analysis and is open to the insights of political theologians. The theological debate between Rahnerians and liberationists will go on as theologians search for more adequate ways of expressing the Christian faith in a postmodern world. But at the practical level, Christians today cannot ignore the major insights of liberation theology. A consistent spirituality of action must be both mystical and prophetic. We are called to fight against social sin and to promote peace and justice in our world. Prayer is not a private affair, but should attune our ears to the cries of the poor. Liturgy is not an escape from reality, but a community celebration which alerts us to the structural injustices and systemic evils which banish so many people to the margins of society. Orthodoxy should promote *orthopraxis*. It seems to me that Rahner's theology can affirm all these themes, while calling attention to the essential interplay between the mystical and prophetic dimensions of an authentic Christian spirituality of action.

Chapter Two

Finding Meaning in Work and Leisure

1. Christian Perspectives on Work

Can we honestly say that our work is fulfilling and brings us closer to God? Although some integrated believers can answer with at least a qualified affirmation, many others, reflecting the common tendency to divorce belief from everyday life, are forced to respond more negatively. An unemployed man who has been looking for a job for years describes his feelings of inadequacy and failure, adding that he often finds himself angry at God over his plight. A mother of three youngsters declares that she does not work (evidently meaning that she does not have a paying job outside the home), but that she seldom thinks about God when she is so busy around the house. A factory worker says that his job is boring and has little to do with God whom he meets mostly in church and in private prayer. A middle manager for a large corporation states that she likes some aspects of her job and hates others, but that none of it has much to do with God or religion. A highly successful salesman of luxury items acknowledges that he finds no intrinsic meaning in his work and that, therefore, it seems impossible to relate his work to his religious convictions. A doctor who is totally dedicated to her patients and finds work extremely fulfilling does not recognize any clear links between her work and her spiritual life. A workaholic, in a rare moment of honesty, admits that his compulsive work habits are really an escape, not only from his family responsibilities, but also from facing his God. These examples suggest the great difficulties that many religious people today have in relating their work to their faith in God. Perhaps the following considerations can help close this unfortunate gap between sacred beliefs and secular activities.

1. As a society, we must place a high priority on creating new jobs with adequate pay and decent working conditions. Meaningful employment is crucial to self-realization and providing for material needs. Unemployed people often feel worthless and suffer from psychological damage even if they continue to have sufficient food and adequate shelter. All sectors of society, including labor, business, government and voluntary associations, should cooperate to produce more jobs, especially ones that are long-term and contribute to the well-being of society. Unemployed individuals who get decent jobs are in a better position not only to achieve greater self-fulfillment, but also to develop a deeper appreciation of a God who is the source of material as well as spiritual blessings.

2. Work includes all purposeful planned activities designed to achieve something worthwhile. It is destructive to equate work with a paying job. Mothers working full time in the home, for example, are doing some of the most important work known to the human family. Some have estimated that this work is worth about $45,000 a year, but the deeper truth is that these demanding domestic efforts are really invaluable. Individuals doing volunteer work often make extremely significant contributions which are easily overlooked or taken for granted. Meaningful work cannot be entirely determined by a paycheck. The Lord can be found in the kitchen as well as the factory or the office.

3. For those caught in jobs which they experience as meaningless or dehumanizing, the answer may be in finding new employment. A very successful salesman who found little satisfaction in his high-paying job quit and went back to school to prepare to be a counselor. He now makes far less money, but feels much better about his service to others. Individuals dissatisfied with their jobs could benefit from reading *What Color Is Your Parachute?* by Richard Boles, a guide to discovering one's own talents and gifts as the basis for finding a fulfilling job. Sometimes we meet the God of our longings along new and unmapped paths.

4. We should try to transform the burdensome and toilsome aspects of our work. One constructive approach is to strive for a broader perspective and a more positive attitude. Some find it helpful to offer up their toil for a higher cause. Thus, a mother does her housework for the sake of providing a pleasant atmosphere for her family. An employee in a fast food restaurant regularly offers his work to Christ, his personal Savior, who carried a more difficult cross. A waitress finds meaning in a job often considered to be demeaning by thinking of it as a sort of art form carefully designed to please her diverse customers – an approach with the added incentive of increased tips. A church worker who must go to many meetings considers these often tedious gatherings as part of her ministry. A truck driver puts up with his daily grind by remembering that it earns a paycheck which puts bread on the table and helps educate his kids. Furthermore, burdensome work can be transformed by allowing it to teach us important lessons about real life. Thus it instructs us in patience and acceptance. It reminds us that there are no easy solutions to many of our pressing problems and that we must trod the path of life with determination and perseverance. Toil can give us a sense of sober realism, countering the temptation of uto-

pian thinking which assumes that we can have success without effort and resurrection without the cross. The project of transforming toil should be accompanied by efforts to reduce it. Learning to delegate is often helpful. A heavily burdened advertising man found some relief by giving an intern a welcomed chance to do some necessary background research on a project. Performing unpleasant tasks quickly and getting them out of the way can reduce stress. Healthy attitudes and constructive approaches can turn toil into a manageable, if difficult, part of a larger and more meaningful work project. Carrying the cross of burdensome work surely offers one of the better opportunities for an encounter with the crucified and risen Lord.

5. We can use our work as a catalyst for learning and personal development. An elementary school teacher took a course on new methods for teaching reading which enhanced her skills in the classroom and brought her a greater sense of work satisfaction. A manager read a book on communications and now deals better with some of his co-workers. A trial lawyer attended a conference on legal procedures and now does a better job of representing her clients in the courtroom. A factory worker enriched himself by taking a course provided by his company. When work fosters personal growth, it seems to take on an added significance. In this process the eyes of faith can detect the God who calls us to develop to the fullest all the talents we have received.

6. We should cultivate a proper attitude toward the money we are paid for our work. Decently paid workers should feel a healthy sense of pride in being able to meet their own material needs and those of their loved ones. A reasonable desire to improve one's earning power in order to be a better provider and to contribute to the common good can be seen as legitimate and fitting in the light of the overall thrust of the Gospel. On the other hand, ma-

terialistic concerns over money can get out of bounds. Individuals can be consumed with making more money. The desire for a higher salary can represent a destructive competitive urge to surpass others. Some workers, such as teachers, nurses and social workers, may find it better for their mental health to concentrate on the satisfactions they find in serving others rather than dwelling on the inequities in salary scales. Our worth before God is not dependent on how much money we make. In our society, healthy attitudes toward money are hard to achieve, but remain crucial to the task of finding greater fulfillment and of integrating our work into our spiritual life.

7. According to the Judeo-Christian tradition, we possess a special dignity as workers. The *Book of Genesis* pictures God as working six days to make the world. The first human beings were given the task of tending the garden even before they sinned. Thus, work is an essential dimension of human existence and not merely a punishment for sin. All legitimate human work has an intrinsic goodness and possesses a special dignity. This positive outlook was clearly represented by Jesus of Nazareth, the son of a carpenter, who took up his father's trade. When he returned to Nazareth to preach, the people could not accept him as a special prophet because they knew him as an ordinary carpenter, a man who labored with his hands. Furthermore, Jesus labored diligently and responsibly at the difficult task of establishing the reign of God. His preaching drew on examples of ordinary workers, such as farmers, day laborers and women in the home. While classic Greek culture despised manual labor as fit only for slaves and women, the Bible, written in an agricultural milieu, recognizes all types of legitimate labor as intrinsically worthwhile. From this perspective, work appears as a mirror through which we can gain a glimpse of the God whose image forms the core of our being.

In summary, our work can serve as an effective catalyst for self-fulfillment by drawing us out of our laziness and selfishness into responsible and enriching activities. It is precisely in and through these very ordinary but extremely significant activities that we encounter the Gracious Mystery who sustains our efforts and gives permanent meaning to all our legitimate work.

2. Rediscovering Leisure

Beth is serious about spirituality. She recognizes the need for greater balance in her life as a basis for personal growth. For years she has struggled to incorporate more leisure into her work-dominated life. Teaching full-time and raising three children by herself makes overwhelming demands on her time and energy. She estimates that she has about a half hour of time for herself during an average workday after she gets the kids off to school, drives to the university, teaches her classes, drives home, cooks dinner, runs the children to their activities, prepares classes and tries to put some semblance of order into the house. Frequently, the weekends feel even more hectic when she has to catch up with small jobs around the house and manage all the children's activities. Sometimes Beth feels like a slave chained to her tasks. She is imprisoned in a world of work which saps her energy and threatens to crush her spirit.

The arrival of the summer has often intensified her frustration. For her, summer represents a different way of living, characterized by a more leisurely pace and fun-filled activities. Her mind is filled with previous memories of relaxed afternoons at the beach, pleasant family vacations, and easy-going hours of aimless activity. She longs for the sense of repose and integration she felt in those days. Her spirit cries out for the recreating power of spontaneous fun and a leisurely schedule. Unfortunately, summers seldom afford her the opportunity for the genuine leisure she craves. She usually teaches during the summer session to make ends meet financially. Odd jobs around the house, delayed for months, demand attention. Her children are involved in a number of summer activities and she often has taxi duty. A few years ago it dawned on Beth that there was little escape from her year-round hectic schedule. If she was going to make progress in her spiritual life, it would be in the midst of the daily demands on her time.

No doubt many of us, myself included, can identify with Beth's inner struggle, if not the details of her situation. Too much work and not enough leisure dulls the spirit. "Busyness" has become a national disease which threatens our ability to live fully human lives. A society which judges individuals according to economic success inevitably exalts work over leisure. A culture which retains a strong sense of the Protestant work ethic tends to equate hard work with goodness and the divine favor. Given these pressures, it is not surprising that individuals begin to identify themselves with their work, losing in the process a proper sense of the role of leisure.

Those of us wrestling with this kind of problem need to examine our fundamental perspective. Long ago, Aristotle offered an alternative view of the good life in which work was for the sake of leisure. For him, leisure activities included enjoying play and music as well as engaging in philosophical discussions and creative political activity. Aristotle insisted that these activities were intrinsic to the happiness which all seek. In our century, various authors, sensing the destructive character of our exclusive preoccupation with work, have tried to revive the Aristotelian vision. In his classic work, *Leisure, The Basis of Culture* (1952), Josef Pieper insists that a healthy culture must give primacy to leisure over work. Leisure makes us human, develops a proper sense of freedom, and enables us to discover the transcendent in the ordinary. We must learn to be silent, to become more receptive, and to appreciate the good things found in our daily existence. The life of leisure is furthered by education in the liberal arts, which emphasize the pursuit of truth for its own sake as well as the development of the whole person. For Pieper, genuine leisure is rooted in divine worship, which should be seen as a worthy end in itself. As a byproduct of such education and worship, we will develop an inner calm and contemplative spirit which will enable us to counter the dehumanizing tendencies of the work ethic.

This radical reversal of our usual way of relating work and leisure calls into question the fundamental attitudes and assumptions which undergird the dominant work ethic. Many of us are in danger of understanding ourselves exclusively as workers whose worth is determined by being able to achieve particular goals. This attitude can create a compulsive controlling approach to all of life, including personal relationships. Workers are tempted to apply the fast-paced, goal-oriented approach required on the job to their leisure time activities, thus reducing leisure to a deadening extension of work. In the United States, it is difficult to escape the illusion that life is nothing more than a series of short-term goals to be attained by hard, purposeful work. Perhaps the radically different approach to work and leisure espoused by Aristotle and his followers can cut through our false consciousness and free us for more creative solutions to the problem.

The Aristotelian perspective also helps us understand some of our common feelings about summer. Our longings for more serene summers should not be dismissed as a nostalgic desire to return to the pleasures of childhood. They represent, rather, a common search for a more complete human existence which celebrates the spontaneous and aimless aspects of life as well as the planned and purposeful. All of us need activities which tend to be enjoyable and meaningful in themselves to counter-balance those which are performed primarily for external goals. From this viewpoint, our summertime longings appear as a genuine cry for wholeness which should be heeded.

A spirituality which is truly viable in the age of transition must find God's peace in the real world of job and family. Most of us cannot suddenly alter our lifestyles to provide for long hours of play and contemplation. We can, however, try to develop a more contemplative spirit which will enrich our work and lighten our burdens. In order to move in this direction, we should choose leisure activities which compensate for the rigors, demands and drains of our particular work.

Following these perspectives and principles, Beth has introduced some helpful changes into her life. Securing the cooperation of her children, she has delegated more of the household chores, thereby gaining some precious time for her own personal needs. She now takes a walk by herself after dinner while the kids do the dishes. The time alone is calming and the exercise helps her sleep better.

She has begun to do fifteen minutes of mantra or centering prayer meditation each morning, designed to create a sense of serenity as she begins her day. This meditation, made possible again because the children are taking greater responsibility for themselves in the morning, is already producing results as she reports more energy and clearer focus throughout the day. While Beth formerly felt half guilty watching escapist entertainment on TV, she now watches her favorite programs with an easy conscience on the theory that it helps quiet her jangled nerves. In the past, vacations involving travel have produced a good deal of stress. This summer, the family is going to stay in the city and spend some time leisurely exploring the local parks and points of interest. Sunday Mass has become for her an important resource in cultivating a more contemplative spirit. Often distracted by her ushering duties, she dropped that responsibility and now concentrates on participating in the liturgy in a relaxed and receptive fashion. She finds that the Mass often does provide enlightenment and inspiration which help her find deeper meaning in her daily activities.

Beth's effort to achieve a healthier balance between work and leisure is instructive for all of us wrestling with similar problems. We can begin with an honest examination of how much the dominant work ethic has influenced our fundamental perspectives and attitudes. It helps to identify the precise ways our work affects us physically and spiritually so that we can choose leisure activities which enhance the positive potential in our work and compensate for the dehumanizing tendencies. To do this we need to recognize the intrinsic value of leisure and find realistic ways of incorporating more of it into our daily lives. Regular spiritual exercises are crucial to achieving a healthier balance. They enable us to bring a more contemplative spirit to the inevitable demands of daily life.

3. Labor Day Blues: Searching for Genuine Leisure

Labor Day, which signals the end of summer, produces some surprisingly strong emotional reactions in a good number of Americans. Although many simply enjoy the day as part of a smooth transition from summer leisure to autumn routines, others experience darker sentiments. One woman told me that she got depressed just thinking about summer ending so soon. A boating enthusiast was upset because he had not gotten in as many hours on the water as he would have liked. For me, the holiday this year brought some melancholy feelings which have prompted further reflection on the cause and deeper meaning of Labor Day blues. Since my intuition is that these feelings are connected with fundamental attitudes toward leisure time, I want to explore this notion by recalling a few of my summer experiences.

In many ways this summer was more relaxing and refreshing than usual. For the first time in many years, I was not faced with the pressure of meeting a deadline for a writing project. Actually, I did have an August deadline for a book tentatively entitled *Life in the Church*. As I began to revise the manuscript, however, it became clear to me that it would be better to reshape the whole project into a book on renewing parish life. This conviction was strengthened during the annual meeting of the Catholic Theological Society in St. Louis, when it dawned on me that theologians have written very little on the parish, despite the fact that parish life is such a crucial factor in handing on the faith and in shaping distinctive Catholic sensibilities. I became convinced that a book which combined theological perspective and practical suggestions could be a valuable contribution. Since this shift in approach made it impossible to meet the deadline, I placed the task into a longer time frame and adopted a more relaxed posture. I found support for my mellow mood in Karl Rahner's sage advice that if something is impossible to do, we are not required to do it. With pressures reduced, I was able to enter more wholeheartedly into the summer activities. My two-and-a-half week teaching stint at Fordham proved to be an especially rich opportunity for the renewal of my spirit. The fifteen students in my graduate course on "The Spiritual Quest with Guidance from Karl Rahner" were not only bright, enthusiastic and hard working, but also brought a wealth of practical experience to the discussion. The chemistry was special, making the mutual exchange even more fruitful. The amazing power of Rahner's theology to guide and inspire the spiritual search of educated Westerners was evident once more.

Since my class met for just three hours in the morning, I had more free time than usual for leisure activities. Walks in the nearby Bronx botanical gardens stimulated some prayerful reflection. The Broadway play *Les Miserables* intensified my passion for the works of justice. A Mozart flute concerto featuring Jean-Pierre Rampal touched some latent tender feelings. A concert commemorating Duke Ellington's first appearance at Carnegie Hall spoke to my heart and reminded me that discipline can foster spontaneity. A weekend visit with my sister and her family on Long Island enabled me to experience anew the power of a home Mass to unleash deep emotions and to inspire fruitful dialogue. The visit also provided an opportunity to enjoy the simple pleasures of family life with people who mean so much to me.

All these leisure activities combined to form a nourishing mix for body and soul. They functioned like a holistic retreat touching often neglected dimensions of my being. There were even periods of relaxation when my Type A personality surrendered to the demands of the moment, enabling my deeper self to know something new about the nature and value of genuine leisure. We are not merely workers nor is productive effort the only source of satisfaction in life. Leisure brings a self-contained joy and allows the spirit to soar and expand in harmonious ways.

Unfortunately, the pursuit of leisure is not always such an integrating and satisfying experience. It can degenerate into frenzied and stressful activity. For me, the game of golf represents many of the things that can go wrong with leisure activities. Of course, for some people golf is a truly relaxing game which enables them to enjoy the outdoors, the fellowship and the occasional good shot. They come home in a good mood, refreshed by their experience on the links. They are able to savor the game because they have come to terms with their limitations. For example, they lay up short of the creek on a par four hole, very content to reach the green in three instead of the standard two. They have a fairly accurate idea of what score they will shoot; and if they do better they are pleased, and if worse, it is not a big deal. They engage in a healthy competition with their realistic potential.

It is all so different for me. I experience a round of golf as a struggle which produces frustrations and tensions. My body maliciously wars against my mind, preferring to lunge erratically at the ball, rather than swinging smoothly through it. Despite repeated efforts to follow the example of golfers who play within their capabilities, I have been unable to accept my realistic limitations. Most times that I venture onto the course, I expect to play better than I actually do. A thousand times and more I have figured out the game and gotten my swing into theoretical working order only to find that something else has gone wrong. The harsh truth is that each year my game gets a little bit worse. The golf demon, which has a secure place in my psyche, refuses to accept this reality, insisting instead that imagined skills will magically produce an acceptable round. Real golf courses, however, have trees and traps. Bad shots multiply, the score balloons, my concentration wavers, the round is ruined and frustration takes over. In the midst of these woes, I do not care about beautiful scenery, well-manicured fairways, bright sunshine or even fellowship for that matter.

All of this would perhaps be merely a tolerable waste of leisure time if it ended with the last putt on eighteen, or even the nineteenth hole in the clubhouse. But, alas, the demon also controls my rerun equipment, which specializes in replaying poor shots. I seldom recall the good shots, and if they do come to mind, they produce only mild satisfaction. It is as though they are the expected result of following a simple procedure. The bad shots, especially those which cost extra strokes or affect the match, are another story. They have an amazing power to resurface and even to affect my general mood.

The golf demon has had a field day with one particular shot from this summer's galaxy of bloopers. It occurred in the Bacik Open, a prestigious tournament which I longed to win for many years. Playing for once even beyond my expectations, I found myself leading the tournament by three strokes after sixteen holes. It took only one spastic swipe at the ball, however, to ruin the dream. As my drive on seventeen hooked to the left over a road and out of bounds, a sinking feeling took over my being. Perhaps it was my mental state which accounted for the ensuing series of ugly shots adding up to an eight on the hole. Losing the tournament by one stroke was not so bad; it was how I lost it which motivated the mood-altering reruns.

Golf is my lens for detecting leisure gone bad. Any activity which inspires such bodily tension, mental stress or emotional frustration cannot achieve the important goals of genuine leisure activity.

Can this personal account of summer past shed any light on the depths of the Labor Day blues? People who spend most of their waking hours working hard on planned, purposeful, stressful and draining activities both desire and need genuine leisure which is spontaneous, purposeless, relaxing and re-creating. Summer symbolizes the possibility of satisfying this craving. Labor Day highlights the limitations of our leisure activities and poses questions about their quality and effectiveness. Have jangled nerves been soothed enough to withstand the increased pressures ahead? Did any of the summer activities nourish our spiritual lives as might a prayerful walk or inspiring concert? Did supposed leisure activities such as vacations, trips, tours and gardening degenerate into stressful moments like a golf game out of control? Perhaps the end of summer is inevitably dark because we can never get enough of activities which integrate and refresh and because we recognize failures to make the most of leisure opportunities.

If so, the answer is not simply to survive. We need to find ways of maintaining a leisurely attitude in the midst of our work day. It will help if we can learn to relax even when the demands are heavy. A balanced life will incorporate leisure activities into the weekly routine. The foreboding connected with the end of summer is really an invitation to develop healthier attitudes toward both work and leisure.

4. Peter Paul Rubens and the Catholic Imagination

In 1994, "The Age of Rubens," a major exhibition of over 125 paintings by seventeenth-century Flemish artists, including thirty important works by Peter Paul Rubens, drew almost 220,000 people to the Museum of Fine Arts in Boston and more than 230,000 to the Museum of Art in Toledo, Ohio, it's only other venue. Those of us who were fortunate enough to see it enjoyed a sumptuous visual banquet as anyone with even a vague sense of Rubens' art can imagine. The work of Rubens takes us back to the world of seventeenth-century Flanders, a strategically important part of northwest Europe, later divided among France, Belgium and the Netherlands. It was the era of the Catholic Counter Reformation, during which the Church responded aggressively to the attacks of the Protestant reformers. The reform in the Catholic Church inaugurated by the Council of Trent (1545-1563) produced a large number of great leaders and saints: the ascetic Pope Pius V (d. 1572), who restructured the church bureaucracy and published the official Tridentine catechism; the spiritual master, Ignatius of Loyola (d. 1556), who founded the Jesuit order to spearhead the reform movement; the great mystics, Teresa of Avila (d. 1582) and John of the Cross (d. 1591), who renewed their Carmelite orders; the courageous Jesuit missionary Francis Xavier (d. 1552), who carried the faith to India, Indonesia and Japan; and the saintly bishop of Geneva,

Francis de Sales (d. 1622), who fostered a spiritual renewal in his diocese which influenced the larger church.

The Catholic Reformation also set the stage for one of the Western world's greatest painters, Peter Paul Rubens, who lived from 1577 to 1640. He was baptized a Catholic in Flanders, an area historically torn by conflicts between Calvinism and Catholicism. Under economic and political pressure, his own father had converted from Catholicism to Calvinism and then back again to Catholicism. Already in his early teens, young Rubens felt called by God to be a painter. In the year 1600, at the age of twenty-three, he made the long journey to Italy where he studied the works of the great Renaissance painters, such as Michelangelo and Raphael. He creatively assimilated the newly emerging Baroque style with its grand scale, dynamic energy, heroic figures and highly emotional content. In Rome he received the first of his many major commissions to produce three large paintings for the Chapel of St. Helena.

In 1608, Rubens returned to Antwerp to attend to his ill mother, but she died before he arrived. Though sometimes characterized as a Christian Stoic who held his emotions in tight check, Peter Paul grieved deeply over his mother's death and went to a monastery for a time to deal with his intense sense of loss. He emerged from his retreat into an Antwerp filled with opportunity for a superbly gifted artist. Warring factions signed a peace treaty in 1609 which facilitated a major revival of economic and cultural life in the battle-scarred city. Rubens became the court painter for the Catholic Archduke, Albert, and his wife, Isabella, who represented the Spanish throne in Flanders. He received numerous commissions to do altarpieces and hangings for new and refurbished churches and chapels. The income from his painting enabled him to build a palatial home, which included a magnificent studio where he employed many artists to assist him in fulfilling the growing demand for his work. Having established such an effective setting for following his artistic vocation, Rubens was content to remain in Antwerp until his death in 1640.

Peter Paul Rubens exemplified the classic ideals of the Renaissance. He was an intelligent, balanced man with far-ranging interests. He enjoyed a happy family life and was blessed with eight children. His knowledge of Greek and Latin literature and art was unsurpassed in his time. He used his renowned diplomatic skills to make important contributions to the cause of peace. In 1630 he successfully negotiated a cessation of the conflict between England and Spain.

But he is celebrated today for his vast output of great paintings. Working with his large and well-organized team of artists, he produced an average of about one painting a week for forty-one years, many of them considered major masterpieces. Art critics have called him one of the greatest colorists in history and have compared his dramatic skills as a painter with the story-telling genius of Homer.

As a painter, Rubens cannot be understood or appreciated apart from his Catholic faith and heritage. He was a devout Catholic who attended Mass daily. Many of his paintings deal directly with religious subject matter and make generous use of biblical and theological symbols. He had an intuitive grasp of the deeper meaning of Scriptural scenes and a keen appreciation of the distinctive characteristics of the Catholic tradition. Even his vast output of secular paintings, including mythological scenes, portraits and landscapes, reflected a highly developed Catholic imagination which sees reality as coherent, intelligible and open to the transcendent. Above all, Rubens presented in brilliant and dramatic fashion the great themes of the Catholic Reformation. He made the teachings of Trent come alive in visual image. He defended the traditional faith through his paintings as Ignatius and Teresa did through their writings.

Many of his paintings express the Catholic Reformation's insistence on the real presence of Christ in the sacrifice of the Mass which reenacts the bloody sacrifice of the Cross. In "The Last Supper," one of thirty-nine ceiling paintings done for the Jesuit church in Antwerp, Rubens portrays Jesus giving communion first to Peter, who represents traditional Catholic teaching. At times Rubens used "disguised symbolism" to present the theology of the Eucharist. His grandiose work "The Adoration of the Magi," for example, depicts the baby Jesus on a wooden crate covered by a white cloth, representing the real presence on the altar of sacrifice. Rubens' dramatic work "Christ and the Penitent Sinners" graphically defends the Catholic understanding of the sacrament of Penance, which was denied by some of the Reformers. The painting places Mary Magdalene in a penitential posture, kneeling before the risen Christ with arms crossed over her breasts. In the background are three biblical characters who experienced forgiveness: King David, the Good Thief, and most prominently, the weeping Peter, who appears against the background of a rock symbolizing his own power to forgive sins. The central figure of the risen Christ extends his arms in a welcoming gesture which suggests his continuing offer of forgiveness and reconciliation.

The Blessed Virgin Mary plays a prominent role in Catholic Reformation theology and in Rubens' paintings. One of his greatest masterpieces, the "Assumption of the Virgin," which serves as the main altarpiece in the Antwerp Cathedral, portrays the traditional Catholic belief that Mary was taken to heaven, body and soul. Rubens has Mary borne aloft by numerous angels. On the ground some disciples are examining her empty sarcophagus, while the apostle John looks heavenward at the ascending Virgin. Thus Rubens presented the church with a marvelous imaginative portrayal of the traditional Marian doctrine centuries before it was officially defined in 1950.

Rubens made a great effort to portray the saints as intercessors and role models for all Christians. His large altarpiece, "Madonna, St. Gregory the Great and Saints," portrays Pope Gregory in liturgical vestments, holding a large volume of his writings. He is gazing upward at a famous icon of the Virgin. The dove placed above his head suggests that he faithfully proclaimed the truth of the Catholic faith in word and ritual through the power of the Holy Spirit.

At times Rubens' paintings took on a much harsher polemical edge. In 1626 he produced about twenty tapestries for a convent in Madrid on the theme of the "Triumph of the Eucharist." One of them, "The Victory of Eucharistic Truth

Over Heresy," portrays the mythical Father Time raising his daughter Truth over a battlefield strewn with defeated heretics, including Martin Luther and John Calvin, who are surrounded by fire-breathing monsters. The female personification of Truth is pointing to an inscription with the Latin words of consecration at Mass "Hoc est Corpus Meum" (This is My Body).

Peter Paul Rubens helped shape the Catholic imagination during the long period of strife between Catholics and Protestants which lasted all the way into our own century. But how do contemporary Catholics respond to his work today? Some Catholics, who recall the pre-Vatican II church, experience an ambivalent mix of recognition and dissonance. The emphasis on Eucharistic realism, the confession of sins, the intercessory role of Mary and the saints, and papal prerogatives is familiar. The accompanying symbols and images are part of the imaginative grid through which we still see the world. But we also join younger Catholics and our Protestant friends in sensing some dissonance or imaginative estrangement. The world of Rubens feels a bit unbalanced and far too polemical. Catholics tutored by Vatican II bring to the encounter with Rubens an imagination which is more Christocentric and ecumenical. We tend to see the role of Mary and the saints within the unique mediatorship of Christ. The important dialogues between Protestants and Catholics have produced general agreement on the nature of the Eucharist and the real presence of Christ. Many Catholics are rethinking the way they can best celebrate the Sacrament of Reconciliation. Vatican II adopted many of the reforms suggested by Martin Luther. The period of the Counter-Reformation was polemical and defensive; the postmodern age calls for dialogue and collaboration.

The art of Rubens, however, remains a classic expression of the Catholic imagination which celebrates tradition and recognizes the presence of God in the whole of reality. Encountering his work affirms our faith and challenges us to find appropriate ways to express it in our world.

5. Pablo Picasso and the Mystery of Life

In late September of 1980 my sister and I attended the Picasso Exhibit at the Museum of Modern Art in New York City. After driving into Manhattan from her suburban home on Long Island and miraculously discovering a parking spot nearby, we entered the museum and we found ourselves in a marvelously stimulating new world. The exhibit extended through forty-eight galleries housing more than 900 works of art by Pablo Picasso, the best known artist of our century.

As we leisurely wandered through this amazing exhibition of artistic talent, I was glad I had spent a bit of time recalling the highlights of Picasso's life: born in Spain in 1881; exhibited talent as an artist at an early age; moved to Paris in 1900; began the cubist movement in 1907; responded in 1937 to the brutality of the Spanish Civil War by producing his great painting "Guernica"; entered into many love affairs which produced four children; found great artistic inspiration from his mistress Marie-Therese; joined the Communist Party in 1944; lived as a recluse after World War II; and continued his vast outpouring of creative work until his death in 1973. This outline helped set a frame for viewing the whole exhibit of paintings, sculpture and ceramics, which was arranged in chronological order.

Allowing Picasso to direct my attention and engage my imagination was a fascinating experience. My reactions were mixed. I was thrilled to see the originals of well-known prints like "The Tragedy," which hangs in my office. The more representational, readily intelligible paintings gave me a renewed appreciation of the beauty of our world. A few of the very odd pieces made me think Picasso was putting me on or mocking artistic standards. I experienced a sense of satisfaction in deciphering some of his more abstract work, sometimes with the help of comments from art critics. When I encountered a piece which left me totally baffled, I took comfort in the comment of an artist friend that it had taken her years to learn to appreciate Picasso.

As a total experience, my three hours in the world of Picasso was wondrously exhilarating and stimulating. Even though I could really absorb only a fraction of the vast collection, this great creative genius managed to expand my horizons, touch my heart and enrich my spirit. We all bring our own interests to an encounter with classic works of art. I approached Picasso with theological concerns in mind. From this perspective, the exhibit served as a striking reminder of the power of the artist to open up hidden aspects of reality. There was very little explicit religious material in the exhibit. I recall only one crucifixion scene, completed in 1930, and a series of studies on Grunewald's famous "Crucifixion" done a couple of years later. I was struck, however, with the remarkable ability of Picasso to see beneath the surface of reality, to sense hidden connections, to disclose the depths of the human situation. Believers can discern a religious dimension in Picasso's art which prepares the mind and heart for a more explicit act of faith. Faith can be described as a way of seeing, an angle of vision, a type of consciousness. For the theist it means seeing meaning in the midst of absurdity, perceiving the extraordinary in the ordinary, discovering hidden depths beneath the surface, discerning benign mystery in and through daily life. For Christians, faith enables us to see the world through eyes formed by the teachings and example of Jesus of Nazareth. Good artists seem to descend intuitively into the deeper realms and are able to help us see something of their vision. They challenge our ordinary perceptions and move us to see in a new way. At his best Pablo Picasso draws us into a new world, challenges our assumptions and discloses new truths about reality.

In 1907 Picasso helped inaugurate a new artistic movement known as cubism, based on the insight that a particular object appears differently when viewed from diverse perspectives. The cubist painters made use of disconnected geometric forms in order to enable the viewer to see a given subject from various perspectives simultaneously. Cubism reminds us that reality is so rich and mysterious that it cannot be comprehended from one viewpoint or exhausted in a few traditional images. This fundamental perception, which had a profound effect on the artistic world, also developed within the world of theology. Today we recognize that the biblical authors portrayed the inexhaustible personality of Jesus in various ways according to their own perceptions and the needs of their community. The Eastern and Western Fathers of the church had very different understandings of divine grace. In the thirteenth century, Bonaventure's mystical understanding of the Christian faith complemented the intellectual synthesis of Aquinas. Theology today includes many different schools of thought, ranging from Karl Barth's neo-orthodoxy to Karl Rahner's transcendental Thomism. Contemporary theology looks and feels like a Picasso cubist painting.

Like all artists, Picasso had favorite themes and subjects. Monkeys, stringed instruments, acrobats, women, people suffering and sexual encounters kept reappearing in the exhibit. I reacted quite differently to his treatment of diverse themes. His portrayal of sex, for example, seemed mechanical, superficially erotic, and near the end of his career, totally inauthentic. I saw little indication of sex being rooted in relationship or connected with mutual love. On the other hand, I found myself moved and enlightened by the portrayals of human suffering. The many paintings with upturned heads, open mouths, teeth showing, distorted countenances, transported me back to encounters with grieving people and sharpened my awareness of the terrible suffering endured by so many people today.

The highlight of this theme and of the whole exhibit was his massive painting "Guernica," named after the Basque town decimated in 1937 by German and Italian bombers flying on behalf of Franco. Working very quickly, Picasso gave expression to his own pain over the war in his native country by painting distorted and broken bodies in an unrelieved scene of suffering. In the exhibit, a whole gallery is devoted to this painting and all the studies that went into it – the original sketches and the development of the details. Paul Tillich considered "Guernica" one of the greatest modern religious paintings because it discloses the depths of the human predicament with all of its estrangement and despair. The painting is clearly not religious in any explicit way. Nor is it religious, it seems to me, in the positive sense of suggesting some way of salvation or path to wholeness out of the brokenness of human tragedy. Its real religious function, however, is to open up the depths of reality, to help us appreciate the destructive tendencies in the human heart, to increase our empathy for suffering people, to know in a new way the absurd terrors of war. Thus Picasso at least raises the religious question of how we are to deal with human suffering. He sharpens our sense of our own inadequacies and our need for salvation from a power greater than ourselves. "Guernica," as well as Picasso's other works dealing with suffering, draw us into the world of tragedy and force us to face the dark side of human existence. From there, it takes eyes of faith to detect the light of hope shining in the darkness.

6. El Greco and the Power of Grace

In 1982 an exhibit of over fifty paintings by Domenikos Theotokopoulos, better known as El Greco, traveled to four sites including the Del Prado Museum in Madrid, Spain, and my home town, Toledo, Ohio. This remarkable exhibit highlighted the growing reputation of El Greco as a great painter with a remarkable spiritual vision of reality.

In order to appreciate El Greco's religious sensitivities, we must locate him in the context of the Catholic Counter-Reformation as it developed in late sixteenth century Spain. In that country, the Inquisition was especially cruel and oppressive in its attempt to preserve Christendom by insisting on the doctrinal orthodoxy taught by the Council of Trent in opposition to the teachings of Protestant reformers. We can get some sense of this oppressive religious climate by recalling that in 1577 St. John of the Cross was apprehended by traditionalist members of his own Carmelite order, taken to Toledo where he was imprisoned in a tiny cell, and beaten regularly by other friars in an effort to get him to renounce his efforts to reform the order.

It was in this very year, 1577, that Domenikos Theotokopoulos also came to Toledo, the center of the Counter-Reformation in Spain. He had been born in Crete in 1541 where he was influenced by Byzantine icon art; went to Venice in his late twenties where he assimilated the style of Titian, especially his creative use of rich and diverse color; and then moved on to Rome where he encountered the work of Michelangelo with its heroic treatment of the human figure. In his middle thirties, he decided to go to Spain, apparently to further his career, but after failing to secure the patronage of King Philip II, settled in Toledo where he remained for thirty-seven years until his death in 1614. In his adopted home he found patrons, mostly clergymen interested in religious orthodoxy, who commissioned him to produce paintings for religious institutions. Living at least periodically in luxury, he associated with the city's religious and intellectual elite. His duties included serving on an archdiocesan council which judged the religious orthodoxy of works of art. He wrote treatises on art and architecture, which unfortunately are lost. But most importantly, during his years in Toledo he produced some of the greatest religious art the world has known. The polemical atmosphere of the Counter-Reformation influenced El Greco's choice of religious themes and his treatment of them. Thus, the numerous paintings which depict Mary as a sinless recipient of God's grace (for example his Annunciation, Visitation, Nativity, Madonna, Pietà, Holy Family and Pentecost) are obvious responses to the Protestant attempts to downplay her role. The often repeated theme of the Purification of the Temple symbolized the attempt of the orthodox church to purify itself by casting out the heretics. The many portrayals of the penitents, Peter and Mary Magdalene, which bring out the reality of sin and the possibility of repentance and forgiveness, were designed to counter the Protestant objections to Confession, a point El Greco highlighted by depicting Peter holding the keys which symbolize the power to forgive sins. The various representations of St. Jerome holding the Vulgate (his Latin translation of the Bible) reminded Catholics that fidelity to this translation was a necessary safeguard for orthodoxy. His many paintings of saints reflected the Catholic insistence on their value as examples of the Christian life as well as their intercessory power, a teaching vigorously attacked by the Reformers. Clearly, zeal for orthodoxy was a major influence on the art of El Greco.

Through his painting El Greco preserved for us many of the stories and legends of the saints popular during the Counter-Reformation. For example: St. John was saved from the wrath of Domitian when the poisoned wine he was commanded to drink turned into a serpent; St. Luke the evangelist was also an artist and a physician; St. Ildefonso, the seventh century archbishop and patron saint of Toledo, received a chasuble from the Blessed Virgin; St. Sebastian, an officer in Diocletian's army, was shot with arrows for refusing to sacrifice to the gods; St. Lawrence was grilled alive for refusing to renounce his faith; St. Andrew died on an X-shaped cross; St. Martin, a well-do-do military man during the time of Constantine, cut his cloak in two and gave half to a beggar; St. Bernardino, a fifteenth century preacher, used a tablet inscribed with IHS as a visual aid and became known as a proponent of devotion to the Holy Name of Jesus; St. Bartholomew was flayed alive with a knife for maintaining his commitment to Christ. El Greco produced a magnificent "Visual Lives of the Saints" which not only preserves some marvelous stories but also provides us with inspiring examples of heroic virtue.

Entering the world of El Greco reminds us of the Counter-Reformation period which, in many of its aspects, lasted until the Second Vatican Council in the 1960s. It is a world dominated by defensive attitudes, polemical debates and arguments over doctrinal orthodoxy. Catholics emphasized a sinless Virgin, interceding saints, frequent Confession, authoritarian leadership and a suffering Jesus. Individuals who encounter El Greco's Counter-Reformation outlook generally respond according to their own religious perspective. Protestant Christians typically find his polemical paintings to be foreign to their own piety. Older conservative Catholics may experience a bit of nostalgia as they enter a familiar world, while progressives breathe a sigh of relief that a new ecumenical Christocentric era has dawned. Most younger Catholics do not understand or care about these disputes of the past.

The defensive posture of the Catholic Reformation, however, could not confine the genius of El Greco. In his case, adherence to orthodox teaching did not deaden his spirit but liberated his creativity. He was able to bring out the spiritual meaning and values which are at the core of the traditional symbols so prominent in his religious paintings. His severe portrait of the Grand Inquisitor, which brings to mind Dostoevsky's celebrated critique in *The Brothers Karamazov* of the oppressive character of the Inquisition, suggests that he did not espouse the excesses of Catholic Spain's reaction to Protestantism. El Greco's defense of orthodoxy was less harsh and more rooted in spiritual concerns.

The genius of El Greco is also manifest in his approach to the relationship between grace and nature, the divine and the human, the supernatural and the natural. Many of his especially religious paintings suggest the traditional theology which understood grace as a superstructure placed on top of nature forming a two-decker world. El Greco often placed angels, apparitions, heavenly life and ethereal light in the top part of his paintings while depicting in the lower part firm ground, brooding cities and human skulls. Thus he created a world which emphasizes divine transcendence. Grace comes from above and is directed downward toward a sinful suffering world. This familiar classical orientation invites us to gaze upward to find the omnipotent God.

In El Greco's religious art, however, grace is not merely a divine superstructure placed on top of the natural world. The best of his paintings suggest that grace and nature are essentially connected. Grace builds on nature, as Thomas Aquinas taught. The heavenly light penetrates and transforms the people who walk this earth, as El Greco's treatment of the saints graphically portrays; Mary is pure and sinless because she was called by God; Magdalene's face becomes serene because she was touched by divine mercy; Francis can peacefully cradle a skull because of his faith in the afterlife; Sebastian's sufferings have meaning because his sacrifice is accepted by God; Dominic can be totally immersed in prayer because he is alone with God; the apostles are ecstatic because the Pentecostal Spirit has descended upon them; the

Baptist is heroic because the lamb of God has appeared. In short, for El Greco, grace envelops nature and raises it to a higher state where it finds its true fulfillment.

Moreover, the human beings in El Greco's world seem to have an orientation to the divine, a propensity for the spiritual, a heart that searches out transcendence. The elongated figures, the upward gazes, the sensitive prayerful hands, the tenuous contact with the firm earth, the surrounding ethereal light, the deployment of clouds, all give the sense of a spiritual dimension, a thirst for the divine which constitutes the essence of true human existence. To move within El Greco's horizon is to know the best of the classical religious outlook where grace and nature are not opposed but are brought together in a higher unity.

Some modern scholars have insisted that El Greco was not a genuine mystic like his great Spanish contemporaries Teresa of Avila and John of the Cross. They see him more at home with the defenders of orthodoxy than the small bands of spiritualists who resided in sixteenth-century Toledo. It seems to me, however, that this major exhibit should prompt a reassessment of his work. El Greco may not have been a mystic according to the traditional definition, but he surely had a marvelous sense of human transcendence and the spiritual dimension of life. His paintings speak to the heart about a God whose love and power are manifest in the world. The grace which triumphs in the lives of the saints is available to all believers. The human heart does long for God. Traditional religious symbols reflect divine light and mediate divine blessing to us. El Greco invites us into a world charged with spiritual energy and religious meaning.

7. The Christmas Crib: A Call to Reflection and Action

The Christmas crib scene is an important instrument for transmitting our religious heritage. It has helped shape the Christian imagination ever since it was popularized by St. Francis of Assisi, beginning in 1223. The figures are all familiar: Mary, Joseph, three kings, a few shepherds, some animals and the baby Jesus wrapped in swaddling clothes lying in a manger. Nativity scenes are set up in homes where families gather and in churches where communities of faith assemble for worship. The combination reminds us that church and home are connected. Liturgy and everyday life are intertwined.

The Nativity scene is the Gospel in symbolic form. It represents the fundamental story of our salvation. It is the doctrine of the Incarnation expressed imaginatively. We may not be able to explain the doctrine to our own satisfaction, but we appreciate the symbol and know the story it represents. Caesar Augustus orders a census. Joseph and Mary must go to Bethlehem to register. Mary is pregnant, overshadowed by the Holy Spirit as the Scriptures put it. Joseph has decided to divorce his fiancee' informally, but is told in a dream to continue with the marriage process and to take Mary home as his wife. When the couple arrives in Bethlehem, the town of David, there is no room for them in the inn. Mary gives birth to her first-born son, wraps him in swaddling clothes and lays him in a manger. Shepherds living in the fields hear the good news from the angels and come to see the newborn Savior. Wise men from the East follow a star, and arrive in Jerusalem seeking information about the infant king of the Jews. King Herod sends them on to Bethlehem as part of his plot to kill his potential rival. The wise men, guided by the star, find the child and pay him homage, offering him gold, frankincense and myrrh. Then they foil the treacherous Herod by returning home by a different route.

The story is woven together from two separate accounts in Matthew and Luke. The composite is not totally consistent, but that does not matter. The story surrounding the Nativity scene is faithful to the message of the Scriptures and contains the essential truths of our faith. As the scripture scholars tell us, the infancy accounts are the Gospel in miniature.

In contemplating the crib, we know more theology than we recognize or can express. We know it intuitively and implicitly as we know the rules of logic when we argue logically. The Nativity scene teaches us that our God loves us unconditionally, with a maternal care beyond reckoning. It reminds us that we are important creatures, possessing a wondrous dignity. The scene instructs us in the meaning of the Incarnation. The Word has become flesh, pitched its tent in our midst, shared our joys and our sorrows, laughed and cried as one of us. A human being like us in all things but sin has gathered our best hopes and dreams and put them before the Creator God. This baby in a manger grows to manhood, becoming the best we have witnessed. He is so obedient, so open, so responsive to the divine gift and summons that it is true to say he is God personally present in our midst. In Him, God and humanity are joined in an unbreakable bond of love.

As a profound symbol, the crèche carries layers of meaning. We all appropriate it in our own way and at our own level. But the essential message has a power to reach the core of our being. Our God loves us and this divine care is focused for us in Jesus the Christ.

Crèches which fit comfortably in homes and churches are not so welcome on public property. The first amendment, which demands a separation of church and state, has served our nation well and enabled religious groups to flourish. It has also erected a wall of separation between religion and public life which has often been detrimental to both. The ban against crèches in the public square reminds us that we have a responsibility as believers to bring our faith commitments with us into the public arena. We may not be able to display the figure of Jesus, but we can bring his wisdom to bear on public policy questions. We function as both citizens and believers. The message of the Nativity scene is that the divine and the human are joined as one. Our task is to integrate all that we are as humans into our fundamental option for God. This prepares us to be constructive dialogue partners, promoting the common good and spreading the kingdom of peace and justice in the world. The absence of the crèche in the public square can be turned to advantage. It puts the responsibility on us to be instruments of the kingdom in public affairs.

The connection between the crib and family life is clearer and more direct. The Nativity scene symbolizes the intimacy that we treasure and the mutual love we desire. It reminds us of our responsibilities to be peacemakers in the family setting, to be bearers of good gifts for one another. In the family we learn the kind of sober realism and patient endurance represented by a long journey and a birth in a stable. Family life which reflects the Nativity scene teaches us that persons are more important than possessions and that we are fragile creatures who require loving care. It would indeed make a difference if the spirit of the crib could remain in our homes after the figures are put away.

As we reflect on the crib in our comfortable homes, we realize that many of our brothers and sisters around the world are homeless and hungry. Most Christians have an immediate, instinctive sense that trying to feed our hungry neighbors is a good and proper thing to do. Images of emaciated children trigger our compassion and perhaps our guilt. The Christmas spirit calls us to share our abundance with the less fortunate.

Meditation on the Nativity scene can strengthen this conviction. Luke says that Mary placed Jesus in a manger. The Greek word translated as manger really means "feeding trough," the kind used for animals. Some scripture scholars believe that Luke is deliberately suggesting that Jesus is given as our food and nourishment. Throughout his Gospel, Luke develops this theme. Jesus used table fellowship as a way of reaching out to others, including the despised and outcasts. He demonstrated compassion for the hungry by multiplying the loaves and fishes to feed the large crowds who gathered around him. At the Last Supper, Jesus hosted a meal which symbolized all of his efforts to nourish others. After the Resurrection, the disciples on the road to Emmaus recognized him in the breaking of the bread.

The Lord gave his disciples the task of carrying on his ministry of feeding people. As we know from chapter twenty-five of Matthew's Gospel, this is not a mere humanitarian gesture. Jesus has identified himself with those in need. To feed a hungry person is to feed Christ. Furthermore, our very salvation is dependent on how we respond to our suffering brothers and sisters.

Our celebration of the Eucharist gives focus to the ministry of feeding. We who are nourished by participating in the sacred meal have a responsibility to strengthen others. By sharing in the one bread and drinking from the same cup, we are formed into the one Body of Christ with the task of carrying on his mission of service. The sacred banquet symbolizes the solidarity of the whole human family and reminds us of our responsibilities to one another.

The baby Jesus in the feeding trough has become the risen Christ who gives himself as our food and nourishment. This same Christ is found in starving people. Reflection on the Nativity scene should strengthen our resolve to use our national abundance to help less fortunate people.

This general resolve must be carried out in a complex world. We need creative ways of helping other countries without falling into a new colonialism. Despite the negative attitudes toward the United Nations prevalent in the United States, we must work with other affluent countries in assisting developing nations. Even with good will and our national abundance, the United States alone cannot solve the immense problem of hunger which still plagues the human family. Moreover, our humanitarian efforts should not be disguised extensions of military policies.

The Incarnation does not erase the complexity of life. Christmas, which delights children, is also a feast for serious adults. The baby in the manger ends up on a cross. Nevertheless, the Nativity scene remains a powerful symbol of hope. The God present in Jesus will never abandon us and will reward all our good efforts.

8. Christmas: A Celebration of Hope

An authentic Christian celebration of the Christmas season must relate to life in the real world. We celebrate Advent against the backdrop of the busy days of December. The Christmas liturgies focus the hopes for peace in our hearts and our world. On the Sunday after Christmas we probe the significance of the Incarnation for family life. The feast of

Epiphany challenges the narrow exclusive attitudes which create division and discord in daily life.

In the United States we celebrate Christmas as the richest nation on earth. For a number of years economic indicators have been good, with low inflation rates and relatively high employment figures. The average American family shares more gifts at Christmas than most people in the world could even imagine. Our blessings are abundant indeed.

Considering the international scene, our celebration of Christmas includes gratitude for a long list of constructive developments: the collapse of the Soviet Union; the liberation of Eastern Europe; the dismantling of apartheid in South Africa; cessation of violence in Northern Ireland; a peace agreement between Israel and the Palestinians. The cause of freedom and democracy has made more progress than was even imaginable a decade ago.

But despite all these positive signs, the national mood remains strangely ambivalent. The genuine progress of the recent past has produced a measure of satisfaction, but it has not touched the core of our psychic life. We are grateful for our affluence, but many experience economic insecurity. We are glad the Cold War is over, but we do not feel much safer. In the depths of our being flows a darker stream of perceptions and feelings which have coalesced into a more somber mood. This is not to say that American optimism is completely dead. We still are blessed with persons who manifest a springtime piety and a culture which reveals bright moments of resiliency. Nevertheless, there is a darker mood exercising a powerful influence on the American psyche. We might think of it as a contemporary version of the dark night of the soul, which includes a profound feeling of insecurity as well as the classic sense of the absence of God. The current mood bears a family resemblance to the anxiety described by existentialists in the 1960s, but it centers less on meaninglessness and more on a radical sense of contingency or vulnerability. It involves a deep fear of uncontrollable chaos, random attacks and senseless violence. This mood is fueled by terrorist bombings, drive-by shootings and serial killings. Recent decreases in violent crime bring little comfort. The core of this somber mood is solidified by our inability to solve major social problems such as racism, poverty, drug addition and the breakdown of family life. We have lost something of the modern optimism which believed that reason and science could solve our problems and lead to a better life. The postmodern mood is much more aware of irrational forces and intractable problems that threaten and retard human progress.

European scholars often identify World War I as the initial attack on modern optimism. In the United States the shift of mood occurred at a much later date when President John Kennedy was assassinated in 1963. Something deep within the American psyche changed that fateful day in Dallas. Without any warning chaos suddenly invaded Camelot and unleashed new fears and anxieties. Unknown sinister forces can attack at any moment and we are powerless to ward them off. Even the best and the brightest with all their rational planning cannot create a secure world. We are not as much in control of our destiny as we once thought. Progress is not assured. We cannot count on reason and science to save us. Life may not be better for the next generation. The death of the young president, who symbolized the hope for a brighter future, opened up a great abyss which swallowed up all naive optimism.

Most Americans alive today are too young to have a direct memory of the Kennedy assassination, but they cannot escape the consequences of this national tragedy. The dark night of random chaos is now a permanent part of the American psyche.

Many subsequent events have reinforced this dark mood and acquainted more Americans with a fundamental sense of limitation and insecurity: the assassinations of Martin Luther King and Robert Kennedy; our failure to win the war in Vietnam; the prolonged detention of our hostages in Iran; the explosion of the space shuttle Challenger; the bombing of the Trade Center in New York; the Los Angeles riots; and the Oklahoma City bombing. The daily news constantly reminds us of how little progress we have made in overcoming poverty, crime and racism. Even the great international triumphs have manifested a dark side. The Soviet Union has collapsed, but ethnic strife and economic chaos are rampant. Eastern Europe has gained political freedom, but social problems have multiplied. Violence has increased in the occupied territories since the peace accords were signed between Israel and the Palestinians. The election of Nelson Mandela in South Africa has not solved the great economic problems of the black majority.

The dark mood created by random violence, intractable problems and tainted successes can itself function in ambivalent ways. It can, for example, teach us a healthy sense of limitation or drive us into a paralyzing despair. The dark night is like somber background music which can either inspire or depress us. Negative responses abound. Influential philosophers reflect the postmodern mood by denying any overarching meaning to life. The dark night experience leads some people to act as victims instead of free persons responsible for their own lives. It is common to blame our social problems on those "other people" who are different. It is even possible to blame God for inflicting chaos on our world and allowing random attacks on our security.

Christmas suggests a more positive response to the somber national mood. Our Christian celebration of the feast joyfully and confidently proclaims a fundamental truth which our troubled world desperately needs to hear: The great God has already reclaimed and transformed the dark night of random chaos. The Creator who wove an intelligent pattern into the fabric of the evolving world has once more touched the earth, definitively ordering all things for our good. The incomprehensible and inexhaustible Mystery of the cosmos has tenderly embraced our humanity, providing an unending source of comfort. The Word has become flesh, bringing all things human into the orbit of divine love. The Logos has pitched his tent in our midst, establishing an enduring center of meaning for our complex and ever-changing world. The Holy Spirit has overshadowed a virgin, transforming in the process the whole human family. A child is born in Bethlehem, focusing the power of love which embraces every human being.

Christmas announces in word and symbol that the bright light of divine love has already pierced the dark night of chaos. The Incarnation means that all apparently random events, good and bad, are part of a larger plan. The dark night of imminent danger has been transformed into the silent and holy night of divine presence. The witching hour has been taken over by a whole host of angels. A child is born and the light of hope shines in the land of gloom. The Word made flesh illumines the darkness, "a darkness that did not overcome it." In the large cosmic war between the light and the darkness as well as the daily struggles against chaos, Christmas insists that we place our hopes in the Light of the world.

This fundamental message of Christmas, however, is not easily appropriated. The dark night continues to send depressing messages. Societal contradictions still plague us. Our personal stories are often disrupted by irrational forces. Even in our more integrated moments we sense the threat of chaos. In the real world, betting against the darkness seems risky at best.

Only the eyes of faith can discern the transforming power of the Incarnation at work in the depths of our hearts and the unfolding of history. The liturgies of the Christmas season encourage and enable us to sharpen our faith vision. Advent calls us to glimpse with Isaiah the rays of light shining on the land of gloom: to ponder with Mary the overshadowing power of the Spirit: to join with the Baptist in disciplines which focus our vision on Christ the true light of the world. The Christmas stories featuring shepherds who see the glory of the Lord and wise men who follow a star alert us to intimations of the divine presence in our own lives. The feast of Epiphany teaches us that God has mysterious ways of transforming the most disruptive situations created by the rulers of the world into moments of grace. Faith instructed and enlivened by these Christmas celebrations can face the dark night, whatever its guises, with full confidence that the final victory is to Christ, the light of the world.

9. The Christmas Season: A Celebration of Beauty

The feast of Christmas contains an intrinsic core of beauty which shines through all of the crass commercialism threatening to darken the true meaning of the season. Not even the frenzied activities, which accelerate during the month of December, can totally eclipse the splendor which surrounds the coming of Christ. In our noisy world, it is still possible to hear enduring echoes of angelic voices proclaiming the glad tidings of the birth of the Messiah.

Our long celebration of Christmas does indeed place heavy demands upon us. Custom dictates that we buy gifts, send cards, wrap presents, decorate homes and attend parties. The pressures of the holiday season seem to mount as inevitably as the coming of the winter solstice, which the feast purposely accompanies.

Nevertheless, Christmas retains deeper levels of meaning which have a unique power to satisfy our spiritual needs. We need Christmas to make sense out of our lives and to manage the chaos that threatens us. The annual celebration of the Incarnation enables us to contemplate the blessings that have graced our lives and to find healing for the wounds and sadness accumulated during the year. We need a special celebration of the coming of Christ to gladden hearts depressed by the inevitable sorrows of everyday life. The birth of the Prince of Peace offers much needed hope that a glorious reign of justice will ultimately replace the institutional evils which oppress so many members of the human family.

Part of the wondrous power of Christmas to touch the depth of our spiritual needs comes from its impulse to beauty. We tend to associate Christmas with beautiful things. The essential message of the feast is attractive and luminous in its simplicity. The Christmas season unleashes a great deal of creative energy and calls forth artistic skills. We want to make the season beautiful and to keep alive the traditions which have lifted our spirits in the past.

This impulse takes shape in the neighborhoods where the annual appearance of carefully arranged lights performs the traditional Advent function of stirring memories and awakening hopes. Families take great care to keep treasured traditions alive by decorating their homes, sharing brightly wrapped presents and enjoying special meals together. In our churches, we replace the reflective mood of Advent with the festive celebration of Christmas. The crib scene, flowers around the altar, special decorations, the traditional hymns – all combine to create a beautiful ambiance with a remarkable power to raise our spirits and gladden our hearts. Our celebration of Christmas is indeed an artistic creation, an art form which speaks to our hearts and our imaginations.

Our desire to make the Christmas season beautiful reflects the deepest meaning of the feast we celebrate. In the great drama of human history, the eyes of faith detect a coherent plan with an overarching purpose and comprehensive meaning. The Supreme Artist has been at work composing a symphony of love which energizes the human spirit and promises fulfillment for the longings of our hearts. The great prophets were attuned to the divine music and caught glimpses of the gracious mystery unfolding in human history. The prophet Isaiah knew that when the time was right and the mountains were leveled and the valleys filled in, then the glory of the Lord would be revealed. Addressing the Creator of the Universe, Isaiah proclaimed: "We are the clay and you are the potter, we are all the work of your hands."

In the fullness of time, the finest work of divine hands appeared on the earth. With the birth of Jesus, the marvelous symphony of divine love achieved a fitting climax by combining the fulfillment of past promises with bright hopes for the future. The great drama of human history reached its defining moment with a guarantee of the ultimate triumph of good over evil. The coming of the Savior made irrevocable the presence of divine grace in human affairs.

The evangelist Luke tells us that an angel of the Lord announced the birth of Jesus to poor shepherds living in the fields around Bethlehem. The glory of the Lord shone around the shepherds and they were terrified by this manifestation of divine power. But the angel comforted them with good news: the Messiah, the Lord and Savior, had been born that day in the city of David. As warrant for these tidings of great joy, the angel offered a sign strikingly beautiful in its simplicity: "In a manger you will find an infant wrapped in swaddling clothes." After that a multitude of the heavenly host appeared, offering praise and glory to God. This time the divine splendor did not overwhelm the shepherds with fear, but gave them confidence to seek out the new born Messiah. Once they saw, they understood what had been told to them concerning the child. The shepherds returned to their fields, glorifying and praising God.

Luke's inspiring and instructive infancy narrative is an enduring contribution to the beauty of the Christmas season. It is a poetic reminder that the glory of the Father and the radiance of the Spirit were manifested concretely and definitively in the Incarnate Word. In Jesus we find a perfect balance and harmony between the infinite divine splendor of God and the human form manifesting it. He is the perfection of fulfilled humanity and the epiphany of God's love. Jesus preserves, fulfills and integrates all the beauty found in the created world and in the human family.

The impulse to make the Christmas season a beautiful celebration is rooted in the very meaning of the Incarnation as the supreme manifestation of the glory and splendor of God. The season does indeed provide a marvelous opportunity to recall and celebrate the beautiful moments that have brought joy to our hearts. Each Christmas, some people can look back and celebrate great blessings received during the year, such as getting married, having a baby and finding a job; while others can recall simple, but meaningful, experiences – a deep conversation with a friend, periods of harmony in family life, a small victory over injustice, moments of genuine prayer. Christmas invites us to express our gratitude to the glorious God who is the source of all good gifts, great and small.

With its nostalgic power to evoke deep emotions, Christmas can be an especially sad time for individuals who have experienced recent traumas; for instance, the death of a loved one, a divorce, the breakup of a relationship, the loss of a job or the discovery of a serious illness. But the beauty surrounding Christmas also has the power to heal wounds, manage chaos and transform sadness. The Incarnation teaches us that the marvelous plan of God encompasses all the darkness of life with the light of ultimate meaning. Jesus, who began his life in a manger and ended up on a cross, has conquered death and all the other dark forces that assail us. The risen Christ will one day complete the work of establishing the reign of peace and justice. This is wondrous good news and a grace beautiful beyond belief. Let us rejoice and be glad.

10. Lent and Structured Prayer

This year Bill is taking Lent more seriously than ever before in his life. At the Ash Wednesday Mass, the homily invited him to seize the opportunities provided by the Lenten season for developing a deeper prayer life. He was mildly surprised to hear that over 70% of Americans say they pray at least several times a week and felt comfortably included in the 55% who pray everyday. Most days he says an Act of Contrition before going to bed at night, a habit he picked up from his devout Catholic parents. The traditional Catholic blessing before meals has always been a part of his own family routine. But he knew the priest was right in suggesting that Christians who pray regularly need to pay more attention to the quality of their prayer. One good barometer is whether our daily prayer influences the way we live. Does it help us to be more obedient to the will of God? Does prayer help us act with greater compassion and charity? Does it attune us to the whisperings of the Spirit, echoing softly in and through our ordinary activities? For some unknown reason, these questions broke through Bill's usual benign inattention and exposed a large gap between the prayers he says regularly and the activities that fill his daily schedule.

Disturbed by the dawning awareness of this dichotomy in his life, Bill caught the significance of another line in the homily: Prayer is a lifeline for those drowning in the waves of busyness and confusion created by the contemporary world. There are some days when he feels like he is drowning and needs a lifeline. Pressures at work have multiplied over the years as he moved up the corporate ladder. It is not always easy to maintain his ethical standards in the highly competitive world of business. He is not totally immune from the pathologies of consumerism. Balancing time commitments to both job and family presents a continuing challenge. Personal time, devoted to his own interests and needs, has shriveled up to practically nothing. He worries a great deal about how to care for his ailing widowed mother. Raising teenagers is more difficult than he ever imagined. The Nike Company has convinced his fourteen year old son that he simply must have Air Jordan athletic shoes which cost $135, and so far, reasonable discussion on this topic has proven elusive.

All of these pressures and temptations are threatening to submerge Bill, as his energy to resist them steadily drains away. He needs prayer as a lifeline to keep from drowning. He needs to pray regularly to cope more effectively with the demands of daily life. Failure to maintain a daily regimen of serious prayer is like losing sleep; it creates a deficit which distorts our perceptions and depletes our energy.

Prayer can provide security and energy because it is a fundamental human activity which gives expression to our unquenchable thirst for the infinite and to our total dependence on a transcendent power. It is our way of offering praise, gratitude, petition and sorrow to the Source and Goal of our deepest longings. Through prayer we open our hearts to the promptings of the Spirit who lives within us. Regular prayer enables us to reflect on the life of Jesus and put on the mind of Christ. Liturgical prayer unites us with other Christians in offering fitting worship to God. Prayerful reflection enables us to keep our priorities straight and guides our efforts to live the law of love in our complex world. Finally, prayer keeps alive our hope that history will reach its appointed goal and that our deepest aspirations will one day be satisfied.

For the great spiritual masters, prayer is a deep and engaging activity. They speak about enjoying intimate communion with the Creator, resting serenely in the Lord's presence, lifting the mind to God, conversing openly with Christ and responding wholeheartedly to the Spirit. Authentic prayer is a dialogue in which God first addresses us through the Word which resonates in the whole of creation, throughout all of history and in every part of the Scripture. Our task is to listen attentively and to respond wholeheartedly. Our goal is to contemplate the divine beauty and to gaze upon the glory of the Lord. This kind of contemplation enables us to see ourselves more clearly, to move from the false self to the true self, and to penetrate the cultural illusions which distort our perceptions of reality.

Although Bill is a bit overwhelmed by such lofty rhetoric, he is intrigued by the possibility of learning to pray in a more mature fashion. Becoming a better prayer calls for some important moves: from repeating set prayers to speaking spontaneously with the Lord; from asking for many things to thanking God for many favors; from a great deal of talking to more silent listening; from busy meditation to restful contemplation. Growth in prayer is like developing a friendship in which we learn to listen better and trust more.

Bill knows that he will make progress in prayer only if he cooperates with God's invitation by working at it regularly and systematically. Therefore, he made a wise decision to get up earlier every morning and spend a half hour in prayerful reflection. Since he has never tried any of the traditional meditation techniques, he decided to experiment with two major types throughout the Lenten Season. He is spending the first three weeks trying the Ignatian approach of placing himself in a biblical scene and imagining, either as a participant or bystander, what it was like to see, hear and touch Jesus. He could, for example, imagine himself as Peter advising Jesus not to go to Jerusalem and then taking the full brunt of the Master's rebuke. This could lead him to offer a prayer seeking forgiveness for his own shortsighted actions and to make a resolution to be more courageous in following Christ. To put order in this whole experiment, he is following the content and method provided by the *Spiritual Exercises* of Ignatius of Loyola. This enables him to encounter Jesus in various activities (being baptized, calling the disciples, preaching and working miracles) and to reflect on the practical meaning for his everyday life.

During the last three weeks of Lent, Bill intends to use a popular form of centering prayer, a method designed to clear the mind and open the heart to God's presence within. Spiritual masters offer helpful guidance to those interested in this approach. Find a quiet place where you can sit comfortably with eyes closed. Be mindful of your breathing and repeat a mantra or short prayer, such as My Lord and My God, each time you exhale. When distractions come to mind, very gently bring your attention back to the mantra. Do not try to make something happen, such as feeling peaceful or achieving a spiritual experience. Simply stay tuned into the repetition of the mantra. This technique, which often induces physical relaxation and sharpens mental alertness, is an excellent way of setting aside distractions and preparing for contemplative prayer, which simply rests in God. Bill is not sure if he can sit still doing nothing for thirty minutes, but he is willing to try. His plan is to experiment during Lent with these two very different methods of meditation and then to choose the most effective one to use on a daily basis after Easter.

As a composite figure, Bill represents the challenges many of us face in striving to live an integrated Christian life. To meet these challenges, we all need a regular regimen of prayer which illumines and guides our daily activities. Lent provides great opportunities to deepen our prayer life and extend its influence.

11. The Metaphysics of Baseball

Baseball fans are programmed by a familiar annual rhythm. The long season begins in the spring with universal hope; moves leisurely through the summer months, gradually but relentlessly sorting out the best teams; and culminates in the fall with the always glorious and frequently dramatic World Series. In 1994 the baseball strike completely disrupted the familiar pattern for the first time in ninety years. Fans responded in various ways. A long-suffering Cleveland Indians fan, enjoying a pennant race for the first time in forty years, felt a tremendous sense of loss not unlike the death of a loved one. A passionate follower of the Detroit Tigers quickly turned his attention to football and was amazed that he hardly missed baseball until World Series time approached. Fans all over the country are still angry at both the wealthy owners and the highly paid players whose greed deprived average people of a major source of entertainment.

Unwelcome as the strike was, it did afford an opportunity to step back and reflect on the role baseball plays in American culture and the lives of individual fans. Ken Burns, creator of the acclaimed TV documentary on the Civil War, provided an excellent catalyst for this reflection with his eighteen-and-a-half-hour documentary *Baseball,* which appeared on PBS in nine segments during September 1994, just as fans were struggling with the realization that the season was over and there would be no World Series. Burns also collaborated with Geoffrey Ward on the book *Baseball: An Illustrated History* (Knopf 1994), which is filled with marvelous photos and insightful commentary.

Baseball has always attracted the attention of intellectuals and scholars who tend to see the game in metaphysical terms. Already in 1846, Walt Whitman enunciated the often repeated theme that baseball is the quintessential "American Game," our national pastime, our distinctive contribution to the world of sports. Whitman claimed that baseball was as important as the Constitution in shaping American life, in part because of its ability to enhance the physical and emotional health of the citizenry.

For the contemporary author, John Thorn, baseball's greatest contribution to America is not as a mirror reflecting our society, but as a safe haven protecting us from it. Baseball is "a providential antidote to our raging, tearing, relentless progress, an evergreen field that provides rest and recreation, myths and memories, heroes and history." We go to the ballpark to escape the rat race and to replenish our spirits. Burdened by modern life, fans are refreshed by the calm rhythms of the leisurely, slow-paced games.

From a more radical perspective, Allen Sangree sees baseball as "a national safety valve," a way of letting off steam which plays the same role in our society as political revolutions do in Central America. Some sociologists think that the enthusiasm generated by the Detroit Tigers' championship season in 1968 helped avoid riots in Detroit's simmering inner city.

The historian and biographer, Doris Kearns Goodwin, recalls when she was only seven years old her father bought her a scorebook and taught her all the intricacies of scoring a game. While watching the Dodgers play on TV on summer afternoons, she would keep score so she could tell her father every detail of the game when he came home from work. Later as an adult, when she took her own boys to Fenway Park to see the Red Sox play, she would close her eyes and recall attending games with her father. "There is magic in these moments," she says, "for when I open my eyes and see my sons in the place where my father once sat, I feel an invisible bond among our three generations, an anchor of loyalty linking my sons to the grandfather whose face they have never seen, but whose person they have come to know through this most timeless of all sports." Baseball connects the generations. Reminiscing about baseball often begins "when my dad took me to the game. . . ." Baseball gave many of us a world to share with our fathers and memories to treasure.

The astute writer Roger Angell is fascinated by the paradox that baseball looks like an easy game, but in fact makes incredible demands on players who fail more often than they succeed. The best hitters make outs more than 60% of the time. Mickey Mantle struck out over three times as often as he hit a home run. In professional football, the best teams lose only a few times a season; the best major league baseball teams know the agony of defeat over sixty times in a season. The winningest pitcher in major league history, Cy Young, lost over 300 games. Baseball highlights the mistakes of individual players like no other sport. Mention Bill Buckner's name and baseball fans do not think of his consistent play over twenty-one years, but rather of one easy groundball that went between his legs in the tenth inning of the sixth game of the 1986 World Series to cost the Red Sox the game and the world championship. Roger Angell says it is the "obdurate difficulty and the steely demands of the game that lurk beneath its sunny exterior" which entrance baseball fans.

Some people are taken by the geometry of the game. The late Bart Giamatti, who moved from the presidency of Yale University to Commissioner of Baseball, wrote a book about baseball entitled *A Free and Open Space*. He loved the open green space of the field, the precisely determined dimensions of the diamond, the many rules that govern the game, and the interplay between energy and discipline needed to excel in the sport. Focusing on the pivotal spot in the ordered space, Giamatti wrote: "Baseball is about going home and how hard it is to get there and how driven is our need. It tells us how good home is. Its wisdom says you can go home again, but that you cannot stay. The journey must always start once again, the bat, an oar over your shoulder, until there is an end to all the journeying." Not many fans would express their appreciation of the game in such lofty terms, but some of us enjoy a sweet moment of aesthetic delight when we see a perfectly executed doubleplay or a runner score from third on a sacrifice fly with a beautiful fadeaway slide into home.

Statistics have an importance in baseball not found in other sports. Football fans do not know how many yards Walter Payton gained or how many passes Joe Montana completed. Baseball fans have a remarkable memory for statistics: Roger Maris broke Babe Ruth's record by hitting sixty-one home runs in a season; Joe DiMaggio hit in fifty-six straight games; Ted Williams hit .406 in 1941; Ty Cobb had a lifetime average of .367; Cy Young won 511 games. Author Bill Somes claims that baseball stats are interesting to fans because they function as a commonly recognized standard of excellence. To say that Al Kaline got over 3,000 base hits in his career does not just mean that he got a lot of hits. To the fan it signifies that Kaline performed consistently over a long career and joined an elite group of stars who reached that high plateau – so high that no Yankee player ever made it (not Ruth,

Gehrig, DiMaggio or Mantle). Baseball statistics form a common language that bridges generations and sets standards. The strike of 1994 was especially cruel because Matt Williams and Ken Griffey had a shot at sixty-one home runs and Tony Gwynn was in range of hitting .400.

Part of the appeal of baseball is its ability to produce dramatic moments which showcase the stars and capture the imagination of the fans. Producer Ken Burns, who has a keen sense of these thrilling events, made masterful use of old films in his documentary, providing the viewer with a whole series of marvelous visual images. Game winning home runs are especially dramatic: Babe Ruth's controversial blast in the third game of the 1932 World Series against the Cubs after an ambiguous gesture which some interpreted as calling his shot; Ted Williams' long drive in the bottom of the ninth to win the 1941 All Star Game for the American League; Bobby Thompson's homer in the last of the ninth inning to give the Giants a victory over the Dodgers in the third and deciding game of the 1951 play-off series; Bill Mazeroski's home run in the bottom of the ninth to give Pittsburgh the victory over the Yankees in the seventh and deciding game of the 1960 World Series; Carlton Fisk's shot (seemingly willed fair by him and the fans) into the foul pole at Fenway Park, in the bottom of the twelfth, enabling the Red Sox to defeat the Cincinnati Reds in the sixth game of the 1975 World Series. Baseball is usually more delightful than thrilling, but these dramatic moments help make the game, in the words of poet Donald Hall, "a place where memory gathers."

All baseball memories are not happy ones. The game has its shadow side. Owners and players have always been at odds. Black players were excluded for sixty years and African Americans today see it as a white game. Gambling scandals have rocked the sport. Top stars have been poor role models. Greed threatens the future of the game. Major league games have gotten too long. Parents get carried away at Little League games. Kids are hurt emotionally by an overly competitive atmosphere. Fans do not support high school and college teams. Many parents cannot afford to take their kids to major league games.

Despite these negatives, baseball remains a delightful game. It is not a religion and should not become an idol. At its best it resonates with some noble sentiments: the drive for excellence, the need for leisure, an appreciation of physical skills, the conviction that achievement requires discipline, the hunger for special times and places, a willingness to sacrifice for the good of the group, and the desire for an ordered world where it is possible to get safely home.

12. Cal Ripken and Loyalty

As a cultural phenomenon the Cal Ripken story transcends the game of baseball and has a message for all Americans. On September 6, 1995, Ripken, the shortstop for the Baltimore Orioles for the last thirteen years, played in his 2,131st consecutive baseball game, surpassing a record for endurance held since 1939 by the immortal Yankee first baseman, Lou Gehrig. President Clinton attended the game as did many baseball celebrities, including the revered Joe DiMaggio. When the game became official in the fifth inning, the fans at Camden Yards erupted into a jubilant celebration which lasted over twenty-two minutes. About midway through the steady applause the usually reserved Ripken trotted around the stadium reaching out to the delirious crowd. The players on the visiting California Angels cheered along with the fans and greeted Ripken warmly when he got to their dugout. The TV announcers for ESPN did not say a single word for twenty-two minutes, allowing the striking visuals to tell the story. Baseball games around the country stopped when the record was broken, as players and fans stood and applauded Ripken's accomplishment. Cal Ripken breaking Lou Gehrig's record generated more national attention and excitement than any other record breaking achievement in memory, including Hank Aaron passing Babe Ruth's lifetime home-run mark and Pete Rose surpassing Ty Cobb on the all-time hit list. What accounts for the remarkable Ripken phenomenon and what does it mean for us and our culture?

Considered purely from the viewpoint of athletic achievement, the exuberant reaction appears overblown. Setting an endurance record certainly does not take as much athletic skill as the record-breaking achievements of Aaron, Rose and others. As a hitter, Ripken's statistics are not even close to those of Lou Gehrig: for example, a lifetime batting average of .278 compared to .340 for the Yankee star. Despite his great consistency as a fielder, Ripken is not considered the best fielding shortstop of his era – an honor reserved for Ozzie Smith. Even the final record-breaking game lacked the drama and suspense usually needed to ignite a crowd. None of this takes away from Ripken's truly remarkable accomplishment, but it still leaves the question of why a jaded and often cynical public got so excited about his record.

One part of the answer is that Cal Ripken fulfills the national yearning for a sports hero who can serve as a role model for the youth of today. When the former Yankee star Mickey Mantle was dying, he told young people, "Don't be like me." With an engaging honesty, he admitted that God had given him great talent and he had squandered it by his excessive drinking. By contrast, Ripken is a man of outstanding personal integrity and strong family values. He has moderate habits and stays in good shape throughout the year. No scandals mar his good name. We can embrace Cal Ripken as a sports star who is a worthy model for young people.

Many Americans also admire Ripken because he represents the ethic of hard work which governs their own lives. Like them, Cal goes to his job day after day and puts in his best effort. He is not flashy or flamboyant, but performs in an efficient and business-like way. He gets to the ballpark early, prepares himself mentally, practices diligently and plays hard. His success and recent acclaim provide striking confirmation that the American work ethic is sound and pays off. Cheering for Cal is a way of honoring all the hard working Americans who do their jobs each day without fanfare.

But an even more important factor in the Ripken phenomenon is the way he exemplifies the ideal of loyalty – a virtue in short supply in our culture today. Throughout his life Cal has been loyal to his family, his principles, his city and his team as well as to the fans and the game of baseball itself. For him loyalty has always been rooted in the family circle. Cal credits his father for teaching him as a youngster "to be there for your team and to be counted on by your teammates." He has remained close to his parents. He is happily married to his wife, Kelly, and adores his five-year-old daughter, Rachel, and his two-year old son, Ryan. One of his favorite activities is driving Rachel to school, which gives them time together. In his remarks after the record-shattering game, he obviously spoke from his heart when he said: "I thank you, Kelly, for your advice, support and joy you have brought to me, and for always being there. You, Rachel and Ryan, are my life."

Cal grew up in the Baltimore area and always wanted to play for the Orioles. After becoming a star he had opportunities to become a free agent and sign with other teams for more money, but always chose to remain in Baltimore. Cal's loyalty to the Orioles stands in sharp contrast to the "hired guns" who periodically move to a new team looking for more money or the chance to play on a championship squad. Always loyal to his fans, Cal gave them even more attention as he moved toward the record, spending many extra hours before and after games patiently and carefully signing autographs for them. Over the years he has expressed his loyalty to people in the Baltimore area by raising and donating hundreds of thousands of dollars each year for local charities.

To appreciate this aspect of the Ripken phenomenon, we need a deeper understanding of the virtue of loyalty. No one has written more extensively or wisely on this virtue than the great American philosopher, Josiah Royce (1855-1916). Royce, a friend and colleague of William James, taught at Harvard for thirty-four years until his death in 1916. Among his many published books is his 1908 Gifford Lectures, entitled *The Philosophy of Loyalty*. Worried about the rising spirit of individualism in the United States, he insisted that the old fashioned virtue of loyalty is the "center point of the moral life" and the "fulfillment of the whole moral law." Royce initially defined loyalty as "the willing and practical and thorough going devotion of a person to a cause." A martyr dying for the faith exemplifies this crucial virtue. Loyal persons choose or approve their cause and subordinate their own desires to it. The cause is larger than the private self and has value in itself. Genuine lovers, for instance, are loyal to one another and to their relationship, which they perceive as greater than themselves as individuals. Loyalty is a social virtue which unites us with others who are willing to sacrifice for the cause.

But loyalty is not simply a matter of self-sacrifice. Loyalty to a cause overcomes inner dissatisfactions and gives meaning to life. It gives us a sense of inner stability and unified purpose. Royce sees St. Augustine as an example of a person who found peace by subordinating his own volatile will to the will of God. Loyal persons do not experience a conflict between their cause and their own interests. On the contrary, they believe that loyalty to the cause will bring them fulfillment and happiness. They are engaged in fascinating projects which give them pleasure and draw forth their best efforts. Well-chosen causes activate their idealism and keep them from falling into complacency. According to Royce, loyalty manifests a belief in the Eternal. Individuals who toil and sacrifice for a worthy cause "enter the realm of spiritual truth." Guided by religious faith they can relate their particular cause, even a lost cause, to the one great project of creating the community of love in the world.

Royce argues that loyal persons are a treasure. Their virtue is contagious and their example inspiring. They help promote loyalty in a culture suffocated by individualism. Cal Ripken is a national treasure because he has won popular acclaim for the virtue of loyalty. Moreover, his good example alerts us to all the ordinary people who enrich our lives by remaining loyal to worthwhile causes.

13. Al Kaline: A Worthy Hero

"Al Kaline Voted into the Hall of Fame." When that headline appeared back in 1980, it triggered in me a flood of memories, images and associations. I recalled my own dreams to be a baseball player and make it in the big leagues. My youth was spent trying to master the game under the watchful eye of my father. I loved to practice and enjoyed the games even more. As a youngster I was able to compete with kids a few years older and this gave me encouragement.

My optimistic talk about being a ballplayer would elicit from my dad a reminder of the importance of getting a good education. He had played semi-pro ball in Pittsburgh. I loved to look at his clippings, especially the one when he helped beat Satchel Paige's Homestead Grays. People who saw my dad play told me about his great heart, determination and courage. But heart could take a 135-pound catcher only so far and my father had to direct his efforts toward another career. He continued to encourage me and seldom missed a game, but he was well aware of his son's athletic limitations. His advice to get an education was on target.

It was the summer before my senior year in high school that I began to be aware myself that I was not making the kind of progress as a player that was necessary to even consider it as a career. As this realization solidified over the next year, a great sense of disappointment took me over. For many years afterwards my night dreams suggested a connection between my failures as a baseball player and my moments of depression. But in the midst of my dark moment of recognition in high school, a ray of light appeared. Al Kaline went right from playing high school ball in Baltimore to play for my favorite team, the Detroit Tigers. Al would carry on my dream. He had all the things I admired: classic stance at the plate, grace in the field, strong and accurate arm, smart baserunner. My frustrated ambitions got attached to him. He had to carry on for me. And he did it admirably for twenty-two years. Every morning I would check the boxscore to see how many hits he got and how many runs he drove in. Two for three gave me a lift for the day; none for four put a damper on my spirits. Going to Tiger Stadium when Al was playing was a special treat. During batting practice, I would watch him intently, almost feeling as though I was taking those swings.

Kaline's steadiness was especially appealing to me. He did the job day in and day out. Year after year he piled up impressive statistics. In his twenty-second season he was playing as hard as ever. Reaching the magic number of 3,000 hits in that final year epitomized his steady and enduring excellence. But there were special moments in his career that I still treasure. I recall the fifth game of the 1968 World Series, which the Tigers eventually won in seven games over the St. Louis Cardinals. By some fortunate circumstance I was sitting with some of the Tiger brass right behind home plate. It was the seventh inning and Kaline was up in a crucial situation. The anticipation electrified me. Al singled to right and the go ahead run scored. I went crazy. We had come through in the clutch when the game and the Series was on the line.

There were disappointments also. If truth were told, Al really fell short of his early promise. He never made MVP and never won a second batting title after being the youngest to do so. He hit 399 home runs and finished his career with a .297 average, thus failing to reach some of baseball's celebrated goals. I recall the final game of his career. I joined a small crowd at Tiger Stadium on a bitterly cold day in October, to applaud the man who carried on for me all those years. He was 0 for 2 and then for some unknown reason they sent up a pinch hitter for him. A great career ended with Al in the dugout and no opportunity for the final grateful applause. It was sad and disappointing.

Ever since Kaline's retirement, my daily perusal of the Tiger boxscores has lost much of its intensity. It's not the same looking to see how many hits Melvin Nieves got. No new heroes have appeared. I guess my career is over – twenty-two years is longer than most. I wonder if other people have surrogates. I wonder if kids today have heroes. I recall Johnny Carson mentioning his failed football dreams and his enduring fantasy in which he stars as a great quarterback. Ernest Hemingway in *Old Man and the Sea* sets up Joe DiMaggio as a model of the hero who acts courageously by exhibiting grace under pressure. Santiago, the old man who is in his second day of battling the great fish says, "But I must have confidence and I must be worthy of the great DiMaggio, who does all things perfectly even with the pain of the bone spur in his heel." In commenting on this passage, one of my students in a religion and literature course said it seemed idolatrous and totally out of proportion. Is there a more benign interpretation? Is there value in having heroic figures who exemplify a particular virtue? In one of his early poems the novelist James Carroll speaks about the "thin moment, though it tries to hide, when we stopped enjoying baseball." And then he adds, "After that, life became important and everything was awful." Is this simply nostalgia for the frivolous days of youth or is it a sad commentary on adulthood that has forgotten how to play? I don't want to stop enjoying baseball. I want to keep experiencing the excitement as spring training opens, the hope that my team will finally jell, the involvement in the intense individual competition between pitcher and hitter, the satisfaction of watching graceful plays in the field, the quiet sense of the long-haul character of the season. Something would be missing. Thank goodness my father didn't lose his interest. It gave us a common language, and provided us with metaphors and images for looking at life. I can still lose myself in sports and for that I'm grateful. I wonder about those who have experienced the "thin moment" which ruled out play and ushered in unrelenting seriousness. Is everything really awful then?

Al, the truth is you weren't really great like the great DiMaggio. You should have lifted weights and gotten stronger. But you were good and steady, and always hustled, and made the plays look easy and got 3,000 hits and made it to Cooperstown. I never wanted your autograph, nor did I look for a chance to meet you personally. It was enough to check the box scores every day, and occasionally watch you get a run, throw, catch and hit.

What am I to make of these musings? Is there anything to be gleaned of general interest? Here are a few possibilities.

1. Sports are ambivalent, as are all human realities. They can become idolatrous, produce an unhealthy competitive spirit, function as escapes from reality, become too expensive and bring divisions into families. On the other hand, they can nourish our spirit, encourage a healthy competition with our own potential, foster a sense of the

limitations of life and help promote a sense of team-work.

2. At their best athletics can play a role in facilitating our human development by encouraging discipline, by testing us under pressure, by teaching us something of the harshness of life and by forcing us to deal with defeat.

3. There are people who feel vaguely guilty about their intense interest in sports. They realize that they get a bigger kick out of going to a game than to Mass, that they read the sports page before the editorials, that they would rather watch a game on TV than read the Bible or do work around the home. Some self-criticism on the part of us fans is surely in order, but these preferences are not necessarily improper. Games are inherently involving, a full life cannot be all work and God can be found outside explicit religious practices.

4. Play can function as a signal of transcendence, as Peter Berger has reminded us in *Rumor of Angels*. It can take us out of ordinary time and space, remind us that our final destiny is beyond this world. Play, when joyful and involving, is an affirmation of the triumph of creative forces over destructive ones. Our spontaneous involvement in play can speak to us of the integrated life of the Spirit.

14. Baseball and the Virtue of Eutrapelia

In a work-oriented culture, many of us struggle to keep a proper perspective on play. It is a worrisome matter that work can become all consuming and blunt our ability to enjoy the playful side of life. I recall wrestling with that concern back in 1984 after the Detroit Tigers won the World Series. My reflections, recorded then, still strike a responsive chord with me.

I need to sort out my own surprisingly muted reactions to my favorite team becoming the champions of the baseball world. There is no doubt that I was engrossed in the performance of the Tigers throughout the whole year. The early part of the season was like a dream as they moved toward a 35-5 record after one quarter of the season. I was in Tiger stadium the night they set the record for the best winning percentage after thirty games. It was the first time I experienced the cheer which became known around the country as the wave. The Detroit fans, always loyal, were responding with even greater enthusiasm and it was contagious. However, baseball is a sport which puts a premium on performance over the long haul. I kept wondering what the fans would do when the inevitable slump came and whether or not the Tigers could hold on to win in what was the toughest division in baseball.

Late in the season the Tigers went to Toronto, their closest challenger, and swept the three game series. It was obvious that the division title was locked up and it was fun to look ahead to the playoffs. In its original format the league championship series produced a special type of tension. Over the 162 game season the best teams win; in a short five game series, however, an inferior team which gets great pitching and timely hitting can beat a superior team. The fears of Tiger fans that the team with the best record in baseball would lose in a fluke proved to be unfounded as Detroit swept Kansas City in three games and moved into the World Series.

For me the Series – with its rich tradition and associated memories – has always been an important event. Its inherent appeal contrasts in my mind with the artificial, TV-inspired hype that surrounds the Super Bowl. At any rate, this Series did produce its heroes and special moments of excitement: Jack Morris pitching so well in the late innings to win the opener; Marty Castillo hitting a home run, thereby vindicating Sparky Anderson's odd decision to play him at third base against lefthanded pitching; Kirk Gibson displaying awesome power at the plate and speed on the bases in the final game. I got a special thrill out of the fourth game heroics of Alan Trammell since I was in Tiger Stadium when he belted two homers good for four runs. Being part of the hometown crowd brings an excitement that watching on TV simply cannot duplicate. In short, it was for the Tigers a great year capped by a World Series victory which produced its share of excitement.

However, despite all of the thrills of this incredible success story of the Tigers, I found my own reactions to be strangely subdued. I contrast my responses in 1984 to the delirium I experienced when the Tigers defeated the Cardinals in the 1968 World Series. I recall being in Tiger Stadium for the fifth game and going into a frenzy as Al Kaline got the key hit in the seventh inning. As I watched the seventh game of that '68 series on television in New York, I spent most of the time pacing the floor and rooting with a passion. After the Tiger victory I remember exuberant long distance phone calls to friends and a wild celebration with strangers from Detroit who suddenly appeared and acted like lifelong friends. In 1984 I joined in the cheers for Trammell's home runs but without falling into a frenzy. While watching the other games on television, I stayed relatively calm, except when Parrish threw out the speedy Wiggins without the benefit of a pitchout. After Detroit won the Series, I felt no need to join a crowd or call up Tiger fans.

I have more than a passing interest in understanding my subdued reactions. My real fear is that my reaction represents a diminishing of the scholastic virtue of *eutrapelia,* which includes the ability to enter into play wholeheartedly. It is not easy to maintain a proper sense of leisure and playfulness in a world dominated by work and serious problems. When persons can no longer enjoy such things as baseball, picnics, art and music, they have lost part of their humanity and have moved closer to a machine-like existence. While watching one of the World Series games on television, I did some routine paperwork. Afterwards I was glad the work was out of the way, but was also disappointed in myself because I failed to block out the time and to immerse myself totally in the game. The disappointment had an accompanying image in which I disappeared into the dark world of workaholism where not even the allure of the World Series could reach me.

Some serious-minded people wonder how intelligent human beings, who are aware of the great problems such as the nuclear threat and world hunger, could possibly get excited about a mere game. Perhaps we have to ask how well we will cope with any of our problems if we lose the ability to move into the world of play and fantasy. James Carroll wrote in his poem that after we stopped enjoying baseball, "Life became important and everything was awful." Play enables us to distance ourselves in a healthy way from the pressing problems of life and to return to the struggle refreshed. Play reminds us that we dare not take ourselves too seriously and that our work, important as it might be, should not become an idol. An uncle of mine, who was known for his uncomplaining attitude, died recently at the age of ninety-four. The fact that he maintained his interest in baseball until near the end of his life seemed to signal the healthy state of his spirit. His example highlights for me the importance of preserving a playful attitude, which enables us to cope better with the crises of life.

Of course, I realize that there is a far more obvious explanation for my subdued reaction to the World Series. The Series was simply not that exciting. Thanks to the surprisingly inept pitching of the San Diego starters, Detroit was always ahead early in the game. The Tigers, who were in first place the entire season, were in command of the Series from the beginning and won it in five games. The Padres did not play up to their potential. Alan Wiggins, their great baserunner, had one stolen base in five attempts. In the final game alone, Luis Salazar, who represented the tying run at first base in the eighth inning, got picked off; Tony Gwynn failed to catch a shallow fly ball by Kuntz, allowing a run to score; and Templeton, who generally played so well in the Series, failed to touch second base on a routine force play. Even the Padres' manager Dick Williams was involved in what will be remembered as a classic misjudgment. Every bit of baseball wisdom said that Gossage should intentionally walk Gibson in the eighth inning with runners on second and third base. With one out, a walk to Gibson sets up the possibility of a force play at the plate and allows Gossage to pitch to righthand-hitting Parrish, who is a definite double play possibility, and to Herndon, who is not as menacing as Gibson.

In very uncharacteristic fashion, Williams allowed Gossage to talk him into pitching to Gibson, who then hit a three-run homer icing the game and the championship. Second guessing managers is one of the joys of baseball fans, but in this case it is generally agreed that San Diego was on "self-destruct" in the final game of the Series.

Perhaps there would have been more enthusiasm for me in the Tiger victory if they had beaten the Padres at their best and in a closer Series. For the Tiger players, as they kept repeating in the post-game interviews, the victory was sweet because it was a total team effort and because they now had won respect and a place in baseball history which no one could take away from them. For fans, the thrill often comes in seeing their team come back after being down or near defeat as the 1968 Tigers did. The 1984 Detroit team was just too dominant to provide that kind of excitement. Perhaps some year the Tigers will clinch the pennant on the last day of the season and win the World Series in the seventh game after being down three games to none. Then maybe the specter of that frightening moment when baseball is no longer enjoyable will prove to be nothing more than a mildly scary illusion. In the meantime, it seems wise to cultivate the virtue of *eutrapelia*.

15. The World Series: A Rich Cultural Symbol

The 1989 World Series will be remembered more for the destructive power of the horrible earthquake that struck right before the third game than the dominance of the champion, Oakland Athletics. As a result of this tragic event, the World Series has taken on a new dimension as a cultural symbol. It will continue to capture the imagination of fans, to produce heroes and to mirror important aspects of our culture as it has done for seven decades. But because images of the Fall Classic and of the earthquake are now tied together in popular memory, the Series has acquired a new power to challenge the temptation of baseball in particular and sports in general to masquerade as an absolute and to become an idol.

By reflecting on the dramatic events surrounding the World Series of both 1988 and 1989 we can get a better understanding of the diverse ways this evolving symbol both illumines and critiques our culture.

It is game one of the 1988 World Series in Los Angeles; Oakland leading the Dodgers four to three; two outs in the bottom of the ninth inning; one man on; Dennis Eckersley, the premier relief pitcher in all baseball, on the mound; enter Kirk Gibson, the league's most valuable player who had injured his left hamstring and right knee in the championship series and was not even in the dugout during most of the game. He comes out of the training room and limps to the plate to pinch-hit. The almost 56,000 fans fall into that rare state of sports frenzy which accompanies only the most dramatic moments of athletic competition. Gibson, a powerful menacing man who played tight end at Michigan State, appears overmatched in this situation. He fouls off three straight pitches, swinging like a man in obvious pain. The count goes full. The right hander, Eckersley, throws a slider designed to break in on the outside corner to the left-handed hitting Gibson. The pitch is low, but not as far outside as Eckersley wanted it. Gibson's swing dictated by his injuries is hardly classic; but it catches the ball on the sweet part of the bat propelling it into the rightfield bleachers. As Gibson slowly limps around the bases, punctuating his progress with triumphal arm gestures, the Dodger fans break into an exuberant tribute to their hero who has suddenly assumed legendary proportions.

Kirk Gibson had duplicated the feat of the legendary hero Roy Hobbes in the fantasy baseball movie *The Natural*, only he did it by hitting an actual homerun off a real pitcher before millions of fans who will never forget it. Thus the World Series, which thrives on great individual performances, created a new hero, a courageous athlete who fulfilled the dream of every baseball player to come through in the clutch, especially when the big game is on the line.

The patterns of leisure adopted by a society reveal something of the meanings and values which hold the culture together. Particular games become popular because they resonate with the habits of the heart cultivated by the citizens of the country. Baseball captured the imagination of Americans because it reflects important aspects of our cultural ethos. The World Series brings to focus the dreams of fans all over the country. The Gibson phenomenon highlights our need for heroes who overcome adversity and get the job done.

Baseball puts a premium on individual accomplishments which benefit the team. The game is based on an isolated encounter which pits the reflexes, coordination and judgment of the batter against the speed, control and savvy of the pitcher. Baseball players cannot hide behind their teammates. Failures are clearly open to the view of all the fans. Running backs in football, even the great ones, are dependent upon their linemen for blocking. Hitters in baseball, on the contrary, are totally dependent on their own skills. It is hard to imagine a basketball team riddled with dissension winning consistently. Baseball teams can be effective on the diamond despite trouble in the clubhouse because individual performances determine the outcome. A sullen anti-social pitcher can still throw a shutout.

Baseball fans are fascinated by the record breaking accomplishments of great players: Pete Rose got more basehits than Ty Cobb; Hank Aaron surpassed Babe Ruth in the all-time home run list; Nolan Ryan struck out more batters than any other pitcher in history. The daily boxscores scrupulously record the performances of each player. Fans know the stats of their favorite players. Al Kaline hit 399 homeruns during his career.

But we admire most, the players who rise to the occasion and come through to help win games. Individual accomplishments are really for the sake of the team. The Most Valuable Player Awards go to the players who helped their team most while compiling impressive statistics. Sometime the voting sport writers give the award to a player who had less impressive personal stats then another player but who contributed more to the success of the team. Young players dream not just of making a spectacular play, but of doing it under great pressure when the game is on the line. Kirk Gibson became a mythic hero because he won a World Series game, thus realizing a dream lurking in the heart of many Americans. In our culture we have a special respect for individuals whose accomplishments benefit others or promote the well-being of the community.

The 1989 World Series produced a very different type of dramatic action. It was about a half hour before the scheduled start of the third game of the Series and most of the excited crowd was already in Candlestick Park. The earthquake hit at 5:04 PDT and the tremors lasted for about fifteen seconds. Players who had been totally focused on the game were now completely absorbed in finding and protecting their families. The 62,000 fans brought together by the Series evacuated the stadium in orderly fashion, united in a new sense of camaraderie by the quake. Residents of the afflicted area, who were waiting to watch the game on TV, suddenly found themselves players in a real life tragedy. Some fans who had expected to see their heroes play a game became heroes by risking themselves to save others. People around the country forgot about the Series and directed their attention and care to the victims of the disaster.

A new sense of proportion settled over the interrupted World Series. A player said he didn't give a damn about the game. A sports announcer noted that everything about the Series which had seemed so important now seemed so trivial. Some sports writers insisted that the Series should be canceled. The newly elected commissioner of baseball, Fay Vincent, in announcing his decision to delay the Series, called it "our modest little sporting event" which "knows its place." The tragedy reminded many of us that baseball is a game and that no athletic event, not even the World Series, is really a matter of life and death.

The decision to complete the 1989 World Series was proper and important. In the past neither the great depression nor World Wars halted the Series. To say that baseball is a game does not mean it is insignificant. Play speaks of transcendence and possesses a power to heal the spirit. As a great cultural symbol, the World Series has helped hold the country together during difficult times.

The resumption of the 1989 Series was handled with admirable decorum. The ten-day delay provided for a proper grieving period. The ceremonies before the third game were fitting, almost like a liturgy – a moment of silence for those who perished, the singing of a traditional song, and a handshake as a sign of solidarity. Replacing baseball hero Willie Mays with twelve heroes of the earthquake to throw out the ceremonial first ball was a fitting gesture which helped maintain a proper sense of perspective and priorities. The teams gathered themselves and played hard. Oakland won. With a proper sensitivity, the victors decided to show their respect for the victims of the earthquake by foregoing the traditional champagne party and celebrating in a more subdued fashion.

The World Series of 1989 added a new dimension to one of our great cultural symbols. The Series now contains a built-in critique of the enduring temptation of sports to masquerade as an idol and to claim the total allegiance of fans. The late baseball commissioner, Bart Giamatti, wrote that baseball is "designed to break your heart" because the season ends just when we need it to "buffer the passage of time" and to deal with the darkness of winter. After the 1989 earthquake, the World Series proclaims an even more significant message: baseball may provide some sense of security and freedom by ordering space and suspending time, but it has no lasting power to ward off the darkest forces. Athletic heroes delight and uplift the spirit, but cannot offer final salvation. Play is true to its nature when it points to the Gracious One who alone provides the ultimate buffer against chaos.

16. The World of Sports and the Search for Transcendence

During the 1984 Winter Olympic games some of the great moments were provided by the figure skaters. Scott Hamilton won a gold metal with a performance which was below his usual standards, but still demonstrated flashes of brilliance. It was the British pair of ice dancers, Christopher Dean and Jayne Torvill, however, who captured the imagination of the crowd with their stunning routine performed to Ravel's *Bolero*. Along with millions of people around the world, I watched the performance on TV, completely absorbed in the marvelously innovative and flawlessly performed routine. As their bodies moved in perfect rhythm and control, I found myself spontaneously cheering and applauding. It was a magnificent moment when three years of dedicated training reached a surpassing culmination. The routine, imaginatively choreographed and polished through constant repetition, became a fitting bodily expression of their own search for excellence. Scott Hamilton remarked to an interviewer that they competed not so much against others as against their own potential. The scores of the nine judges, which included a perfect set of 6.0 for artistic impression, stood as confirmation of their personal success.

Not being a particularly avid fan of ice dancing, I was intrigued by the way the performance of Dean and Torvill touched my spirit. Of course, athletics in general have a marvelous power to lift us out of ourselves, to stop ordinary clock time, to provide a liberating interlude of self-forgetfulness. We are caught up in the action, oblivious to things around us, participating vicariously in the triumphs and failures of our heroes. More specifically, the ice dancing routine spoke to me of disciplined action, controlled movement, harmonious coordination, precise bodily activity. Part of the thrill is the expectation of the next carefully planned leap or twist. And when the rehearsed movements are successfully executed, a momentary sense of repose takes over. I have a similar feeling in watching professional golfers with their grooved swings and professional bowlers with their unvarying approach, arm swing and release. The slow motion pictures and stop action shots on TV do a terrific job of highlighting this controlled bodily movement. Many sports fans enjoy watching the poetry in motion created by skilled athletes. We find the graceful movements beautiful and appreciate the discipline needed to achieve such excellence. There may be deeper reasons as well.

Graceful patterned movement reflects our own deep desire for order in the midst of chaos, for coherence in the midst of randomness, for simplicity in the midst of complexity. The enduring human struggle is to ward off chaos and to create harmony. The precise movements of the ice dancers suggests that this dream of harnessing diffused energy is not a mere utopian fantasy. Perhaps the resulting sense of repose is similar to what the music lover experiences in listening to the precise measured rhythm of Bach's music. Whatever the validity of these speculations, the fact is that the remarkable performance of Dean and Torvill provided many viewers with a few marvelous minutes of joy and exhilaration.

For believers such experiences can carry a deeper meaning. They reveal the creator God who brings order out of chaos. They suggest a world which is coherent and united by virtue of the grace of Christ. They remind us of the importance of disciplined effort in response to the promptings of the Spirit.

Another scene from the world of athletics comes to mind. Julius Erving, the outstanding forward of the Philadelphia 76ers, has the basketball. His teammates are on the other side of the court, having cleared out for him so he can go one-on-one with the defensive player. He starts left, reverses, whirls to his right along the baseline, about fifteen feet from the basket he goes airborne gliding toward the basket, and with his right arm sweeping in a long arc, he slams the ball through the hoop. The crowd goes crazy. Dr. J has once more demonstrated his famous slam dunk. He put the familiar moves on his opponent. One-on-one no defensive player can consistently stop him. As I flip through my imagination, a whole series of such spectacular maneuvers by individual players comes to mind. What marvelous athletes these great basketball players are. They move so quickly, can jump so well, have such great body control. They play with abandon, instinctively adjusting their own moves to the reaction of the defensive players. Of course, there is so much more to the game: playing solid individual and team defense, changing and controlling the tempo of the game, running a patterned offense, playing within one's capabilities, fitting into the overall structure of the team. Much of the movement is patterned and planned. Individuals spend countless hours perfecting their own standard moves. Within this framework, however, there is still the expression of raw talent, the taking of personal initiative, the spontaneous response to changing situations. In contrast to the set routines of the ice dancers, the movements of the great basketball players are free floating, responsive, reactive. In open court, heading for the basket, they do not know exactly what they are going to do. They will end up at the bucket by maneuvering in response to the defensive players. The great discipline involved in long hours of perfecting their moves frees these players to play with abandon, trusting their instinctive reactions. A fan can get a good sense of this particular skill by contrasting it with the strictly disciplined, patterned style of play used by the Soviet basketball teams in the past. Basketball seems to fit our American sense of freedom and initiative. If ice skating can remind us of Bach's music, then our brand of basketball brings jazz to mind. Jazz musicians work with a dominant theme but are free to adapt and improvise. Like jazz, basketball involves improvising, individual expression, explosive action, surprising twists. Fans thrill to the great individual moves, especially when it leads to a slam dunk. Even an opponent's spectacular play can bring a gasp of amazement. It resonates with some deep sense of appreciation for physical excellence in which human bodies break through normal restrictions.

If ice dancing can be a reminder of a God who creates order out of chaos, then basketball can speak to us of the Spirit who will not be confined or controlled. When players are performing in a tight, restricted, hesitant way, the coach may insist they let it flow, pick up the tempo, play with abandon. Talk of the Spirit reminds us that the Christian life is not simply control, or uniformity, or a defensive effort to avoid sin. It is rather a free response to a call, an attempt to celebrate diverse gifts, an adventure in pursuit of ideals. The Spirit empowers us to make creative responses, to be attentive to surprising gifts, to stand open and confident before an unknown future.

We humans need concrete experiences to serve as analogies and intimations of the presence of God in our world. For some of us fans, sports have a special power to reveal the triune God: the Creator who orders all things for our benefit; the Word who reveals the wisdom and the beauty of the divine plan; and the Spirit who calls us to use our gifts creatively in the pursuit of the highest ideals.

17. The Olympics and Healthy Competition

Barcelona, a vibrant city which combines traditional charm and modern facilities, provided an appropriate setting for the Games of the twenty-fifth Olympiad. The magnificent opening and closing ceremonies televised to an estimated 3.5 billion viewers throughout the global village celebrated some of our highest ideals, including international peace, unselfish teamwork and individual excellence. But it was the athletic competition that captured the world's attention. With no boycotts or major political incidents, sports fans were able to concentrate on the performances of amazingly skillful, welltrained athletes competing at the highest levels: Carl Lewis head-to-head with Mike Powell in the long jump; Jackie Joyner-Kersee competing in the heptathlon against the world's best female athletes, all with great skill in their favorite events; swimmers edging out an opponent for the gold medal by a mere fraction of a second; bikers competing against the field by jockeying for an advantageous position; a volleyball team with great competitive spirit managing to outperform a team with superior talent; a tiny young gymnast all alone on a balance beam competing against secret fears of a fateful misstep; the U.S. basketball team, with no serious challenge to its supremacy on the court, competing against complacency and for their country.

Many sports fans who watched the Olympics either in person or on television found themselves periodically immersed in this world of intense competition: alive with anticipation; excited by the performances of national heroes and favorite athletes; exhilarated in victory and disappointed in defeat. Those of us who felt the adrenaline flow can learn a great deal about our deepest attitudes toward competition by reflecting on the nature, intensity and motivation of our responses.

But it is not necessary to be an avid sports fan to learn something important about competition from the Olympic Games. Life in the modern Western world is inevitably competitive. Society thrusts us into competition with others on playgrounds, in schools, at the work place and even within families. It is possible to argue that our culture is overly competitive, but that does not absolve any of us of the responsibility of managing the unavoidable pressures. Moreover, we all must compete against the dark forces that assail us, such as fear, selfishness and complacency. In responding to these challenges we can gain valuable pointers by observing the way Olympic athletes respond in highly competitive situations.

Almost 11,000 athletes representing 172 countries assembled in the Olympic stadium in Barcelona for the opening ceremonies of the 1992 Games. A runner entered holding aloft the Olympic torch. A disabled Spanish archer, Antonio Rebollo, grasped a flaming arrow lit from the torch. His challenge was to shoot this arrow 200 feet to the target, thereby igniting the Olympic flame and officially beginning the Games. He was chosen over other competitors for this honor and practiced the shot over and over. Now he had to execute it before the expectant gaze of billions of people. Focusing on the fundamentals of the shot and blocking out all negative thoughts, especially fear of failure, he drew the bow and released the arrow. He hit the target and the Games began in a blaze of glory.

All of us know something of the challenge faced by the archer because we have had to perform under pressure, even if in very minor ways. We recognize the competition against negative inner voices which exaggerate our weaknesses and deflate our confidence. Some of us, mostly males, know the fear of failure in a fundamental way. It stays with us as a vague anxiety ready to take shape as pressures real or imagined mount. Under pressure, we are well-advised to concentrate on the fundamentals: our essential goodness, our God-given talents, our positive experiences. It is especially helpful to recall similar stressful situations that we have handled in the past. Let the positive messages play loud and often so that they can overwhelm the voices of fear and failure. We need to get into what some psychologists call the "flow." In this state we are absorbed in the activity, alert and concentrated so that the action flows spontaneously without being impeded by negative thoughts. Every small victory in the competition against self-doubt becomes energy for the continuing battle.

In the midst of the men's 400 meter race, Derrick Redmond, of Great Britain, suddenly went down in a heap when his right hamstring popped. Writhing in pain on the track, he said to himself that he had to get up and finish the race. At that point, he began hopping forward on one leg. Suddenly his father, Jim, rushed out of the stands past the officials and came to his son's side to help him finish the race. At first Derrick did not want his help. An inner voice told him that he should do it himself. With just the right touch, his father suggested that because they began together, they should finish together. A dedicated father who had supported his son throughout his athletic career would not abandon him in this moment of bitter disappointment. Five minutes after the race began, Derrick, assisted by his father, crossed the finish line four minutes and 16 seconds after the winner. At the end of it, Jim Redmond said, "I'm more proud of him than if he had won."

Sometimes we compete against a debilitating self-pity. External forces beyond our control have struck us down. The cross, always present, presses on our shoulders with a new intensity. The temptation is to stay down, to abandon the journey. We will show the world and get back at the perpetrators of this essentially unfair act by refusing to participate. Such pouting can last from minutes to years.

When we are competing against the demon known as self-pity, the example of courageous individuals can be helpful. The story of Derrick Redmond reminds us of the importance of perseverance in the face of adversity. So does the example of my elderly mother who, after recent surgery, could have sat around and felt sorry for herself; but instead, began taking two walks a day, on each occasion going a few yards farther until she was able to cover a block. Individuals with a gritty competitive spirit who refuse to give up reflect the Gospel wisdom that we must persevere in carrying the cross in order to live a fuller life.

Over an hour after the victor completed the men's marathon, a runner from Mongolia crossed the finish line, dead last in a field of over 80 competitors who finished the grueling race. When questioned about his performance, he said "My task is just to participate." Thus he echoed the Olympic spirit enunciated by Baron de Coubertin when he helped revive the Olympics in 1896: "The most important thing in the Olympic Games is not to win, but to take part, just as the most important thing in life is not the triumph, but the struggle."

Athletics can teach us valuable lessons about the more purposeful aspects of life. The conviction that effort has a priority over success is indeed liberating in all aspects of life. But this insight is not easily gained or maintained in our culture. After losses to Cuba and Japan, a pitcher on our Olympic baseball team commented with revealing candor, "I wouldn't have played if I had known we weren't going to win a medal." In the United States the success ethic is powerful and pervasive. To counter it we need to concentrate on finding satisfaction and even joy in simply participating, whether it is play or productive activity. A very competitive friend of mine, often frustrated by his mediocre golf game, has transformed his fundamental attitude and now enjoys playing even if his game is disappointing. Many of us would do better if we would think of competition more in terms of participating than winning.

At the 1992 Olympics, Magic Johnson was often the center of attention. His decision to play on our basketball team, despite being afflicted with the HIV virus, enabled billions of people throughout the world to experience his exuberant personality. He competed with his usual intense enthusiasm and evident delight. He spoke of the deep personal thrill of playing with the best players in the world. While attending other events as a fan, he obviously was immersed in the action and thoroughly enjoyed the competition. His famous engaging smile lit up the awards ceremony.

Without canonizing Magic Johnson or approving all his actions, we can learn from him the important notion that competitive sports are meant to be fun. Games are designed for enjoyment. Play should be involving and bring delight. Healthy competition has a power to lift us out of ourselves and to bring joy to the spirit.

When Johnson retired from the Lakers, his longtime teammate and friend Kareem Abdul-Jabbar said, "Magic taught me that I was having fun while playing professional basketball." This odd comment highlights how difficult it can be to keep fun and competitive sports in perspective. In ironic fashion, Magic Johnson supplies one of the keys to a proper outlook. Competitive games are not really a matter of life and death, although some of us experience them that way. Losing is not the end of the world. Defeat has its own lessons. Magic said that competing against Larry Bird was always fun, even if his Lakers lost to the Celtics, because Bird pushed him to a higher level of excellence. Challenge can be part of the fun of competition. Defeat does not have to erase the delight of intense and involving competition. A woman runner who failed to win a medal spoke with evident joy of being pleased that she had run her best time ever. By competing against our own potential in various aspects of life, we are more likely to enjoy the process and less likely to be decimated by the agony of defeat.

18. The Olympics and Fortitude

The Olympic Games function like a periodic retreat for the human family. During the competition billions of people around the globe, including many who do not consider themselves big sports fans, interrupt their normal patterns to enjoy watching the world's greatest athletes in action. The Games encourage us to broaden our perspectives by applauding human effort as well as achievement, and by celebrating common values which unite us despite our differences. They invite us to move beyond the routine of daily life, and to reflect on the dreams which inspire the human adventure and the virtues that we need to fulfill our deepest aspirations. Each Olympiad produces its own heroes and dramatic moments which become part of the collective memory of the human family.

The 1996 Olympics in Atlanta, which gathered 10,750 athletes from 197 countries for seventeen days of pageantry and competition, provided more than its share of memorable performances: Carl Lewis, who surprised everyone by winning the long jump for the fourth time in Olympic competition; Michelle Smith, who electrified her native Ireland by winning three gold medals and one bronze in individual swimming events; and Michael Johnson, who erased memories of previous Olympic failures by winning the 400 meters and then taking the 200 meters in world-record time. Fans in the United States took special delight in the gold medal performances of our women's teams in softball, basketball, soccer and gymnastics.

But the most dramatic moment, etched in the memory of millions by countless television replays, was supplied by the gymnast Kerri Strug in the finals of the women's team competition. With the Russian women still in contention for the gold medal, Strug, who had been previously overshadowed by her more celebrated teammates like Shannon Miller, found herself in the competitive spotlight. As the last American to perform in the final event of a long and demanding competition, she needed a good vault to secure the cherished gold medal for her team. Feeling the tremendous pressure, she did very poorly in the first of her two attempts. Worst of all, her awkward landing left her with a badly sprained ankle. With only thirty seconds allowed between vaults, she had to gather herself quickly for a final effort. Inspired by the encouraging words of her coach, Bela Karolyi, and a silent prayer for help, she sprinted down the runway, performed her vault flawlessly and landed solidly on both feet. Despite being in intense pain, she made the traditional acknowledgement to the judges while balancing on one leg, and then collapsed in tears. Later, Coach Karolyi carried the diminutive star in his arms to receive the gold medal which she had secured for the American team.

If the Olympics function like a retreat, then Kerri Strug's remarkable vault serves as an excellent catalyst for serious reflection, especially on the courage she demonstrated in performing so well despite the injury and the pressure.

Fear and anxiety are built into human nature. We all know apprehension, alarm or disquiet caused by the expectation of a particular danger, pain or disaster. Sometimes we feel caught or overwhelmed by more amorphous threats such as the loss of meaning, purpose or identity. Fears are highly personalized. Some people worry a great deal about failing or not achieving goals; others are more concerned about being alone or lacking intimacy. One person facing death agonizes over the fires of hell, while another worries about being physically cold during the dying process.

Some fears are appropriate and even useful; for example, fear of contracting AIDS can be helpful in avoiding promiscuous sex. Other fears are irrational and counterproductive; for instance, excessive worry about offending a harsh and vengeful God can lead to neurotic behavior.

Fortitude is the virtue which enables us to deal constructively with the fears and anxieties of life. It provides a reservoir of moral and spiritual strength which energizes us for action when we feel threatened or overwhelmed. The Greeks, who originated the ancient Olympic Games, prized the virtue of fortitude. Plato presented the noble Socrates as the great model of courage, a man who was willing to give his life in pursuit of wisdom and fidelity to truth. Aristotle described fortitude as the virtuous middle path between the extremes of temerity and cowardice and insisted that such courage was necessary for a productive human life.

The New Testament portrays Jesus as the supreme example of courageous behavior. He entered into spiritual combat with the demons and challenged his enemies to face the truth. Despite mortal dangers and warning from his inner circle, he bravely entered Jerusalem to promote the cause of God and humanity. Neither the religious authorities nor the Roman governor could intimidate him. Through his death and resurrection, Jesus Christ has liberated us from fear and bestowed upon us the Holy Spirit, the ultimate source of all courage. As the Apostle Paul insisted, no affliction or hardship can separate us from the love of Christ. Relying on the power of the Spirit, we can face the unavoidable dangers and sufferings of life and can unmask the irrational and imaginary threats which cause us so much unnecessary anxiety. Jesus made the point clearly: "Do not be afraid. I have overcome the world."

Kerri Strug presents a distinctive profile in courage. Small in stature, but great in spirit, she reminds us that courage is not the exclusive possession of warriors or macho males. All of us need the virtue of fortitude to be fully functioning human beings. Genuine courage is inspiring in all its diverse manifestations: political prisoners who suffer for their convictions; parents who resist societal pressures and raise their children according to Gospel values; believers who are faithful to prayer even when engulfed by the dark silence of God; young people who avoid drugs in the face of intense peer pressure; activists who continue to work for peace and justice without seeing much progress; family members who persevere in charity despite the indifference or hostility of their loved ones; professionals who maintain their integrity in a society dominated by expediency; spouses who remain faithful despite serious temptations; the sick who stay patient in the midst of physical and emotional suffering; and all those who face death with serenity and trust.

Unpredictable circumstances thrust Kerri Strug into a challenging situation under the international spotlight. Some critics argue that it was rash on her part to risk further injury and irresponsible for her coach to urge her to try again. Her mother said that, knowing Kerri, "you couldn't have stopped her unless you dragged her off." Responsive to some inner voice, Kerri asked the Lord's help and vaulted into instant fame. When she watched the video of her final vault, she could hardly believe that she showed no sign of a limp during her approach. All of her instinctive responses, developed during many years of intense training, simply took over and, despite the injury, she performed as she had thousands of times in practice. In retrospect, her courage appears as both a gift and an accomplishment.

We never know when a serious crisis or the most ordinary of situations will demand from us a courageous response. In struggling to rise to the occasion, all of our previous efforts to cultivate the virtue of fortitude will surely help. So will the inspiring profiles of courage projected both by the famous and by ordinary people. But for us Christians our greatest resource remains the gift of the Spirit of Jesus who casts out all fear.

19. Managing Our Burdensome Tasks

One of my students made an appointment to talk to me about my book *Apologetics and the Eclipse of Mystery.* I was surprised that an undergraduate was interested in discussing this difficult text which grew out of my doctoral studies and was the first book I published. It turned out that the student was not interested so much in the content of the book as in the process of writing and publishing it. His dream was to be a writer and he wanted me to tell him everything about my own experience as a beginning author. It was hard for me to remember back to 1975 when I first thought of the book, but I knew that the whole project was connected with my ministry as a priest, so I began my explanation from that perspective.

After being ordained in 1962, I served five years as an associate pastor in a large parish and then spent two years studying theology in the New York area. This led to a year of teaching at Mt. St. Mary's Seminary in Cincinnati followed by an assignment as campus minister at Bowling Green State University. It was while team-teaching a credit course on Belief and Unbelief with a brilliant agnostic, that I realized I needed a better grasp of theology to hold my own.

After studying various religious thinkers such as Paul Tillich, Bernard Lonergan, Teilhard de Chardin and, in cursory fashion, Reinhold Niebuhr, I became convinced that the theology of Karl Rahner would be most helpful to me ministering in an academic community. I decided to do my studies at the University of Oxford, convinced that a doctorate from this prestigious institution would open doors for me in the university. My motive in writing a book about Karl Rahner was clearly pastoral. At the same time I did wonder if I could make a contribution to the field of theology and if I had anything distinctive to say.

Early in our conversation, the student wanted to know if all the work that went into the book was worthwhile. For a few years after completing the book I was unable to give a straightforward enthusiastic response to such a question. I was still too close to all of the work involved – the hours spent in research, the effort to struggle through those massive German tomes written by and about Rahner, the discipline required to get the words down on paper, the long hours spent in revising the material, the search for a publisher, the editing of the material for publication, and the final proof-reading of the text. I recall that while I was writing the original manuscript I would never let myself ask whether it was worthwhile or not. I felt that if I began to speculate on that question, I would probably end up wasting a lot of my time in a fruitless effort to figure it out. In addition, I was afraid that the answer would come back, "No, nothing is worth this kind of discipline and drudgery." But now from the perspective of many years, I could tell the student honestly that the whole massive effort does seem worthwhile. Periodically this conviction becomes explicit: for example, when I realize that Rahner has given me an effective method for constructing homilies; when material from the book proves useful in teaching a class; when a Rahnerian insight helps a person I am counseling; and when I feel confident expressing my Christian faith within the academic world where I continue to minister.

I admitted to the young man that writing is a lonely business. The isolation of my years at Oxford is vivid in my memory. I am also conscious, however, of all the people who supported me during that time with countless hours of researching, duplicating, filing, typing, proof-reading and indexing. There was no way I could have finished that original manuscript in the two years I allotted myself without all of that help. Sometimes there is a tendency to forget our essentially interdependent character as human beings. Reflecting upon all the assistance I received in writing this book reminds me forcefully of the real truth of the matter – that we are indeed dependent on others, that nothing is accomplished in isolation and that the support of those who care is necessary to our psychic well being. Authors who express gratitude to others at the beginning of their books acknowledge this reality.

I told the student that I felt a deep sense of satisfaction when I actually saw the book in print. It was a quiet joy tempered by realism. There are so many books published in a given year, that one more is hardly a major event. Not many people are ever going to read it. It did not make a big splash in the theological world. It is difficult to measure any contribution it has made to the life of the church. I was gratified by the early favorable reviews and delight in positive comments periodically made by theological colleagues. Seeing the book quoted in other publications or listed among the helpful commentaries on Rahner gives me a sense of satisfaction. There is a proper pride even in limited accomplishments.

These personal reflections on writing my first book suggest some more general observations. We all have projects in life, tasks that demand sustained attention, responsibilities that call for our best efforts. Our experience includes the joyful satisfaction that comes from putting forth our best effort, the frustration that accompanies failure and the sense of liberation when burdensome tasks are completed. We also recognize the temptation to give up on our projects in the difficult times when obstacles appear, our energy fails, our motivation dims and hope of success diminishes. When threatened by such thoughts and feelings, I find it helpful to reflect on a quote from the Latin American writer Jorge Borges: "Whosoever would undertake some atrocious enterprise should act as if it were already accomplished, should impose upon himself a future as irrevocable as the past." This suggests that we set aside all speculation about whether the task will be completed or not. The strategy is to eliminate the mental loopholes which give us an easy way out. We should banish all doubts about the validity and value of the project. With confidence we proceed as though completion were a fact and success assured. The future accomplishment is as irrevocable as the past. This psychological approach suggested by Borges can be helpful in meeting our ordinary responsibilities as well as managing those tasks which appear burdensome and atrocious.

I recall a low point in writing my first book when I was exhausted emotionally and glutted mentally. It seemed that I could not continue. I described this state of affairs to my father and he gave me similar advice, but in plainer terms: "You began this job and you should finish it. Don't baby yourself. Don't feel sorry for yourself; just get down to work and complete what you set out to do." It was just what I needed to hear. The advice was sound and the fact that my advisor lived that way himself gave it moral force. Stiffened by my father's voice, I resumed my work and completed the burdensome task.

Surely there is a legitimate and important counterpoint here. At times it is proper to drop our projects, reassess their significance and check our motivation. In some situations we need to redirect our energy, take a vacation or go in a different direction. Dogged determination is not always the answer.

However, in a world that offers so many escapes, that celebrates comfort rather than struggle, many of us need the swift kick, the sharp reminder, the jolt which says "stick with it." I certainly appreciated that response from my father and suspect that we all have our moments when that is precisely what we need to hear.

All legitimate human activities are encompassed by divine grace. Worthwhile projects help spread the kingdom. Honest work has an intrinsic value and brings us closer to the Lord. A healthy pride in accomplishment includes gratitude to God and other people. Those who offer us needed support and wise advice reflect the work of the Spirit. The fatigue and failure woven into our activities unites us with the cross of Christ. Success in any of our projects can only be seen as a gift from God. As Christians, our opportunity and challenge is to share this spiritual vision of human activity with the next generation, the young people preparing to make their own contributions.

20. A Retreat by the Ocean

Teaching at the University of San Francisco during the summers, as I did for a few years, offered marvelous opportunities to encounter interesting graduate students and to participate in stimulating faculty seminars with outstanding scripture scholars and well-known theologians. I was also able to enjoy the city itself with its rich cultural life and its magnificent natural beauty – especially the ocean. Periodically, I would go the ocean for relaxation and reflection. One summer I decided to take advantage of a couple day break and spend the time in silence, recollection and prayer by the ocean. A retreat by the ocean has often fascinated me. A few years earlier a similar opportunity presented itself on the other side of the country. After giving a workshop to Navy chaplains in Norfolk, Virginia, I was able to arrange some free time and a room overlooking the ocean. The setting was spectacular and the stage was set for a few days of reflection. I contemplated the waves and walked the beaches. But nothing worked; the demons attacked me, time hurtled by, opportunities were wasted, and prayer scarcely got beyond the surface. A moment of grace had been lost; contrition was in order.

This time I was determined to do better and give the ocean a chance to speak to me of the mystery it suggests. I tried hard to get in the right mood, clear my mind, quiet my heart and pray for help against the demons who may recall a past victory and attack again. The ocean has been for many others a catalyst for reflection, a powerful symbol of the deity, a source of renewed energy. The great Lutheran theologian, Paul Tillich, said that the ocean rushing against the shore was for him a vibrant symbol of the infinite God interacting with his finite creation. Abraham Maslow, the humanistic psychologist, periodically visited a favorite place near the ocean in order to rekindle or tap again a peak experience he once enjoyed at that spot.

As part of my preparation, I read some authors who have written imaginatively about the symbolic power of the sea. In the opening chapter of Moby Dick, Herman Melville speaks glowingly of the sea. For him "meditation and water are wedded forever" and the key to the fascination of the sea is that it reflects "the image of the ungraspable phantom of life." Standing on a beach alone at night, Walt Whitman thinks of "The clef of the universes and of the future" and with mystical intuition perceives that "a vast similitude interlocks all . . . all lives and deaths, all of the past, present, future." Not only does the sea suggest to Whitman the all encompassing reality, but it speaks of immortality as it "flaunts out" a signal, "a spiritual woven signal for all nations, emblem of man elate above death." Lord Byron relates the ocean to the deity, "Dark heaving; boundless, endless, and sublime," it is "the image of eternity" and "the throne of the invisible." John Keats senses the power of the sea with its "eternal whisperings around desolate shores," to break through a brooding spirit "whose ears are dinned with uproar rude or fed too much with cloying melody." Matthew Arnold catches the more melancholy aspect of the encounter with the ocean when he points out that the waves "with tremulous cadence slow bring the eternal note of sadness in." Wallace Stevens brings back a hopeful note when he contemplates the meeting of sea and heaven and discerns "fresh transfigurings of freshest blue." My hope was that the poetry would activate some deeper levels of my psyche and make me more attentive to the God who defies logical calculations and speaks to the heart.

Blessed with free time, filled with expectation, stimulated by the poetic images, readied by preparatory prayer, I made my way to the ocean. It was evening and the sun was sinking into the horizon, producing a great crimson band which framed an apparently limitless expanse of water. A ship moved almost imperceptibly westward, like a tiny bug crawling along the crimson rim. I wondered what it was like to be on board as the land receded and firm ground was only a memory. The waves pulsated rhythmically and seemed to resonate with some point deep within producing an "almost calm." The ocean at dusk gradually gave way to the darkness of night. The shift from light to darkness suggested to me a fundamental rhythm of human existence which needed further prayer and reflection. My strategy was to alternate sitting and contemplating with walking and observing; systematic thinking with random imagining; taking hold with letting go; inner dialogue with complete quiet; wordy prayer with silent presence.

And what came of this strategy? What impact did this retreat by the ocean make? How clearly and powerfully did the Lord speak? The simple and immediate answer was that not much seemed to happen – at least nothing striking. There were no peak experiences of great inner peace and harmony, no mystical raptures where the ultimate unity of all reality was clear, no flashing insights into the human predicament, no great consolation in the presence of the Lord, no clear sense of reaching a higher stage of prayer, not even a dramatic encounter with the demons, who evidently decided to sit this one out. Given this disappointing report, it would be easy to interpret the retreat negatively, to focus on the lack of results, to consider the time spent wasted, to figure I am zero for two in oceanside retreats. I am inclined by temperament and theological orientation, however, to look for more positive ways of understanding it. Later in his life, Abraham Maslow suggested that it might be healthier to give more attention to the less intense "plateau experiences" characterized by serenity, calmness and simplicity rather than the more emotional "peak experiences" which could engender a compulsive search for artificially induced "highs." Thomas Merton offered the comforting notion that to attempt to pray even without apparent success is already to pray. Lectures I have given on the dangers of the "cult of the spectacular" and the importance of finding God in the ordinary came back to me. St. Teresa's admonition that we should not put too much emphasis on success or sensible consolations in prayer also seems to be a good corrective. From this viewpoint I can return to the retreat and discern some "whisperings of the eternal," if not shouts. Many hours peering at the "boundless endless" expanse of water combined with the general absence of consolation in prayer has reinforced my conviction that the Mystery is inexhaustible and beyond even subtle manipulation. The rhythmic waves washing over my consciousness surfaced a melancholic feeling, an "eternal note of sadness." Time is relentless and mysterious. It swallows up the joys of the past, now available only in memory, and hurtles toward a mysterious future, which certainly includes the ultimate boundary of death. Whether the Spirit produces a renewed peace over the unrepeatable past and fresh hope over the unknown future remains to be seen. My retreat by the ocean was a welcome respite from the "uproar rude" and "cloying melody" of the daily routine. It had its own subtle messages and quiet, if unspectacular, moments of grace.

In our busy and noisy world we all need to find opportunities for quiet reflection. In order to maintain a sense of balance in our lives, we must set aside time for prayer and meditation. A three day retreat may be totally impractical, but most of us can snatch from our demanding daily schedules a few moments for prayerful reflection. Some busy people are able to maintain a regular schedule of daily or weekly prayers. It also helps to have a special place for reflection. We may not have regular access to the spectacular wonders of nature, such as oceans and mountains, but we can all find beautiful settings which stir our spirits or familiar surroundings which put us in a prayerful mood. When we open our minds and hearts to God in prayer we cannot program the results. We may encounter only silence and absence. In these cases perseverance is the wise course. We all need to make regular trips into the inner silence where the gracious One resides as our illumination and strength.

21. Reading Classic Books

In our frenzied and fragmented world today, it must be counted as a blessing when we can find some satisfaction and genuine joy in our work and daily responsibilities. I recall teaching at the University of San Francisco one summer when I knew a bit of the gratification that comes to teachers when the class jells and real learning takes place. The course was for graduate students in various areas of theological studies and was entitled *The Spiritual Quest: with Guidance from Rahner*. Our purpose was to develop a personal, contemporary and indigenous spirituality making use of the framework and insights provided by Karl Rahner in his classic masterwork *Foundations of Christian Faith*.

The method was simple: we read and discussed the text chapter by chapter, from the perspective of what it meant for us in our personal spiritual quest. The eleven students in the class were a marvelous mix of background and talent, including dedicated laypersons, priests with important jobs and diverse experiences, and sisters skilled in liturgy and religious education. As the course went on, a sense of community developed. The students worked hard and had fun together. I enjoyed the periodic basketball games with some of the younger men in the class. Near the end of the course, we all shared a delightful dinner where a proper Catholic sense of celebration prevailed. After the last class we celebrated a liturgy planned by the students which incorporated material from the course into a truly prayerful experience. All of this was enjoyable and somewhat typical of the kind of pleasant experiences that often occur in such short summer sessions outside of one's ordinary environment.

The response of the students to the course was truly remarkable and gave me a great deal of satisfaction. A number of them wrote out their comments for me: 'This course is going to improve my whole approach to teaching; it gives me a new perspective on what I'm trying to do." "I'm a changed person; I feel liberated, lighter, unburdened, good about myself, ready to take on the difficult tasks waiting for me at home." "I know I'm not crazy now; I've got words to put on my experiences; I realize I'm not the only one who knows the anxiety and terror of being alone with God." "I think I'm changed; maybe it's that I feel more tolerant or open to people who seemed so different and threatening before." "I can't tell you how this course has affected me; something deep inside has been stirred up and I don't know exactly where it is going and it is scary, but it seems good to me."

Even factoring in exaggeration and bias, these responses did indeed warm my heart. They were not totally surprising to me, however, since I had received similar feedback in the past when I taught this same course.

How are we to understand the dynamics of these remarkable transformation experiences? Theories of group dynamics might help: the mix of people was enriching; an atmosphere of freedom prevailed; personal acceptance freed people to face and express their deeper thoughts and feelings; the momentum of the group encouraged extra reading and study; the encounter with others suggested viable alternative attitudes and viewpoints. No doubt many of those dynamics were at work and further exploration of them would be enlightening.

I find a deeper and more adequate explanation, however, in the analysis of reading classic texts presented by the Catholic theologian David Tracy in his erudite book *The Analogical Imagination*. Following Tracy's line of thought, we could say that the students experienced transformations because they encountered a normative, objective and compelling truth about the whole of reality in Rahner's *Foundations of Christian Faith*. In other words, it was their open and committed reading of a great book about God which unleashed the transforming power of the Spirit.

This explanation is based on two convictions: that religious classics properly read have an uncanny power to disclose hidden dimensions of life; and that Rahner's *Foundation of Christian Faith* is indeed a modern classic.

Great books, such as Plato's *Republic* or Aristotle's *Ethics*, have a life of their own which transcends the intention of the author and the historical setting in which they were produced. They say something universally and essentially true about some aspect of the human situation. These books possess fuller meaning and a compelling power that are not exhausted in a single explanation or reading. In addition, religious classics, such as Augustine's *Confessions* or Teresa of Avila's *Interior Castle*, speak to us about life as a whole and about the Mystery which envelopes us. They suggest new and better ways of living humanly in our world. We can re-read them with profit because the text always has something new and perhaps shocking or surprising to say to us. Reading the classics is like a stimulating conversation in which the subject matter engages and guides us. We should come at these texts with an inquiring attitude and with our deepest concerns in mind. We should allow the book to lead us and pull us out of our own egoism so that it can disclose new truths and suggest better ways of living freely and faithfully. When reading an important book we sometimes intuitively sense that the fundamental message is meaningful and true. After allowing its language and symbols to touch our imagination, we wrestle with the ideas in search of a deeper understanding. At the end of the process we find ourselves transformed in some significant way. I still recall the moment when I finished reading Teilhard de Chardin's *Phenomenon of Man*. Setting the book down, I said to myself: "I don't understand everything I just read, but I know for sure that I will never think the same way as before."

Something similar happened to my students as they read Karl Rahner's *Foundations*. One woman in the class wanted to give up after the first few days because the book was so hard. But with encouragement she took the risk and followed her intuition that this difficult text contained something valuable for her life. During her reading she openly sought wisdom for her own life and began to get glimmers of a response. This encouraged further reading which led to deeper insights. In her conversation with this book she was grabbed by an objective truth and carried along by a fuller meaning which proved to be liberating. She discovered a broader vision of the possibilities of human life that went beyond what Rahner could have surmised or intended as he wrote the book. This woman's experience was an intensified version of what others went through to a lesser degree. For the class as a whole, our common conversation with this text enabled us to experience a genuine, if brief, sense of community. We were collectively drawn out of ourselves by the common struggle to understand something true about our relationship to God as manifested to us by this classic work of Rahner. The classroom discussion was not just a matter of airing personal problems or expressing private opinions. We talked, rather, about something significant outside of ourselves and worked together on the common task of achieving a deeper appreciation of the divine-human relationship. In this setting individuals experienced intellectual, moral and religious transformations not in a private and sentimental way, but in a public, communal and intelligent fashion.

This whole analysis suggests that we could all benefit from a renewed conversation with our Christian classics, including the Bible and the works of the great saints and theologians. By reading them with an open and inquiring mind, we can expect to encounter authentic truths about life with a power to disclose the Mystery and transform our lives.

22. Humor: A Clue to the Spirit

Humor is connected with the playful dimension of life. It helps to keep the seriousness of work from dominating our consciousness. But does it make sense to analyze humor and to reflect on it seriously? Perhaps this will simply detract from the spontaneity and lightheartedness which are characteristics of a healthy sense of humor. Clearly, humor is an important part of a full human life. Since nothing human should be excluded from the probing searchlight of intelligence, it does make sense to think more deeply about humor, provided we respect its distinctive characteristics, especially those which defy rational analysis.

The topic has come to my attention a number of times recently. For instance, at a conference of campus ministers someone suggested that humor should be considered just as important to campus ministry as the spiritual life. The responsive laughter of the group suggested that many of the ministers found humor helpful in dealing with the abundance of failures and setbacks built into this type of ministry. As one observer noted, the definition of a campus ministry program is one in which fewer than five people show up. No doubt individuals in other fields have their own humorous ways of dealing with inevitable limitations.

During a heavy conversation in which a professional man was describing his staggering personal problems to me, he suddenly changed direction, noting that God must have a great sense of humor to have created a world with so many strange people running around behaving in such weird ways. We both laughed as some of the tension dissipated. At this point the healing power of laughter seemed more important to me than trying to introduce greater theological precision into the discussion.

While pondering the significance of this conversation, I read an article by theologian Doris Donnelly entitled "The Blessing Called Humor" (*Origins* May 5, 1988). In her insightful analysis she suggested several ways in which a sense of humor is a signal of God's grace. Although Christians influenced by Puritanical and Jansenistic attitudes may find this suggestion a bit shocking, it does seem worth exploring, provided we proceed cautiously and reverently, with emotion and imagination carefully controlled. (How easily the humorous intent of irony can fall into sarcasm.)

Self-deprecating humor reveals the essential truth that we are not gods even though we might secretly crave a bit of divine power. Humor helps provide perspective on essential aspects of the divine-human relationship, especially the crucial question of which side of the divide we are on. The ability to laugh at ourselves reflects a healthy humility, reminding us of our essential finitude. Moreover, self-deprecating humor often appears as an attractive quality. When he was seriously wounded by an assassin's bullet, President Reagan joked in characteristic fashion that he forgot to duck. On the other hand, President Carter was not able to muster a light touch in commenting on an attack by a giant rabbit while he was out in a boat. Consequently, pundits had a field day with the story of this savage attack. Public perceptions are shaped by such responses. Furthermore, in our personal relationships a light touch often makes people more at ease and opens up communication.

What I will call "cosmic humor" reminds us of the essentially mysterious depths of human existence and the imponderable character of the great questions of identity, meaning, purpose and suffering. The acknowledged expert on this topic is the great theologian W. Allen, who has clearly set forth the parameters of the debate: "Mankind faces a crossroads. One path leads to despair and utter hopelessness. The other to total extinction. Let us pray we have the wisdom to choose correctly."

Although we cannot solve the great questions, we must continue to wrestle with them. Humor enables us to appreciate the value of limited insights, while respecting the ultimately mysterious character of these crucial areas of human concern. Allen, who believes that Jesus was "extremely well-adjusted for an only child," insists that we cannot look even to Christ for final and definitive answers. Humor may not save us, but it helps keep the great issues in perspective.

Humor has a practical and utilitarian function as well. It is great for unmasking compulsions and dealing with strong passions. I recall, for example, a collegian with high standards of sexual morality who used humor to control the passionate encounters with his girlfriend. He had his standard repertoire of humorous comments, which included the statement that they both better take a cold shower. This line often proved helpful except for the time they decided to try it together. Humor does have a power to break the single-minded concentration involved in compulsive behavior and to diffuse passions of all sorts which lead to destructive behavior.

Humor can function as a healing balm in the midst of tragedy and grief. I recall the way laughter mingled with tears when my father died. While selecting a casket at the funeral home, my mother, two sisters and I all had humorous comments to make about my father's predictable and unprintable reactions to the high prices and the energetic salespitch. The shared laughter seemed to bind us together and focus our distinctive memories.

Novelist James Carroll tells the story of the time he was a passenger in a car which was headed straight for a large on-coming truck. Perplexed as to whether to offer practical advice to the driver or to say an Act of Contrition, he shouted: "O my God, I'm heartily sorry goddamnit Dave move." Evidently, humor was one way Carroll tried to deal with the precariousness of life. Tragedy which always stalks human existence can produce a paralyzing anxiety. Humor can place tragedy in a larger perspective which enables us to see light in the midst of darkness and to manage our anxiety more effectively.

To me, some tragic events which involve monstrous evil appear beyond the proper scope of humor. I recall a social situation in which I was a special guest and someone made a joke about the Holocaust. At the time I could not think of what to say so I just walked away, feeling a strong sense of revulsion over such insensitivity and probably some guilt for not speaking up. Auschwitz calls for reverent silence and repentance, not humor. Humor, like all things human, is ambivalent. It can be used to wound as well as to heal, to conceal the truth as well as to illumine it. Since a sense of humor is a gift from God, we have a responsibility to use it not as a weapon, but as an instrument of healing.

Some humor suggests the incongruities which characterize the human condition in general. In doing research for this article, I discovered some quotes from letters received by a Social Service agency. "Mrs. Jones has not had any clothes for one year and has been visited regularly by the clergy." "I cannot get sick pay. I have six children. Can you tell me why?" "I am forwarding my marriage certificate and three children, one of which is a mistake as you can see." "In answer to your letter, I have given birth to a boy weighing ten pounds. I hope this is satisfactory." Such odd juxtapositions of phrases reflect a world which is never as neat and logical as we would like. We must live in the real world, filled with strange misunderstandings, odd events, mysterious coincidences and absurd conclusions. Humor helps us manage our disjointed lives without falling into depression. When our world begins to unravel, a hearty laugh can be great therapy.

Political humor makes the important point that elected officials are human and that our cherished institutions are imperfect. Pundits throughout history have implicitly manifested the truth that all systems stand under the judgment of God. Court jesters in the past represented alternative policies which had been rejected and suffering individuals who were neglected. Today, political satirists bring out the foibles of our highest officials and point out the failures of our public policies. It is surely a great strength of our country that comedians can stand up in public and make fun of our president. Did you hear the one about the astrologer who came to the White House during the Reagan presidency?

Finally, a healthy sense of humor opens up belief in a God good enough to love us with all our foibles and limitations and powerful enough to bring our zany and often cruel history to a happy conclusion. To laugh heartily is to manifest an implicit faith that the world is more mysterious than it seems and that life can be trusted despite its absurdities. The One who sits on the throne of heaven laughing, as Psalm 2 expresses it, is indeed a gracious Lord who remains at our side through both the tears and the laughter.

23. Finding Meaning in Arduous Tasks

Since its publication in 1985 the American bishops pastoral letter *Empowered by the Spirit* has guided the development of Catholic campus ministry in the United States. It has provided a framework for the training of new campus ministers and for evaluating and improving existing ministerial programs. Over the years dedicated men and women serving on campuses around the country have found creative ways of carrying out the six major ministerial functions noted in the pastoral: forming community, appropriating the faith, forming the Christian conscience, facilitating personal development, educating for justice and preparing leaders for the future.

Early in 1995 the Catholic Campus Ministry Association held its national convention in Atlanta to celebrate the tenth anniversary of *Empowered* by reflecting on its significance today. In my keynote address to the conference, I concentrated on the new postmodern context which calls for creative approaches to the traditional task of forming community on campus. Preparing my presentation for the conference prompted me to reflect on the whole process which originally created *Empowered by the Spirit*.

For me, the project began in 1980 when a priest acquaintance from Cleveland came to Toledo with a message from the Education Committee of the United States Catholic Conference of Bishops. They wanted me to be the writer of a proposed pastoral letter on campus ministry. Before responding to this request, I tried to prevision the extent of the project and its potential problems. My imagination roamed over long meetings, conflicts with conservative bishops, hours of reading and the laborious task of getting the precise words down on paper. I also considered the opportunity to make a contribution on the national level and to learn more about my own area of ministry as well as my responsibility to the larger Church. In my mind the negatives were sharp and heavy; the positives vague and abstract.

Following an intuition which had little to do with a precise judgment of pluses and minuses, I agreed to take on the project and promised to give it my best effort. To paraphrase the Latin American author, Jorge Borges, I undertook the arduous task as though it were already accomplished and as though the future were as irrevocable as the past. I decided that for the duration of the project I would try to avoid the question of whether it was worthwhile or personally satisfying. I would immerse myself in the task like a swimmer who plunges into cold water without fretting about whether he will find it freezing or refreshing. My heavy musings were not misplaced. The arduous project weighed on my shoulders the next three years and proved to be even more demanding than anticipated.

After agreeing to take on the task, I went to Washington to be interviewed by the writing committee, which consisted of four bishops and seven campus ministers, including three priests, three sisters and one married man. I told them honestly of my liberal theological positions, my limitations as a writer and my expectations of them. We agreed that we could work together and began to discuss the purpose and content of the pastoral. Impressions of the group, which proved in the long run to be quite accurate, quickly formed in my mind. The bishops were open-minded and comfortable with honest dialogue. Bishop William Friend, the chairman, possessed amazing organizational skills and led the group with a marvelous mixture of tolerance, practical wisdom and folksy humor. The campus ministers had vast experience and broad knowledge of the national scene. Each one brought a distinctive slant to the project which enlivened the discussions and enriched the whole process. Father Joseph Kenna functioned as the convener, facilitator, reconciler, task master and liaison with the bishops conference. He became a good friend and has my lasting gratitude for supporting me during some very trying times. My role was to produce coherent drafts which reflected the consensus points in the group. I tried to do this after our initial meeting in Washington and after numerous other gatherings in places like Chicago, Boston, Denver and New Orleans. All of this blurs together in my memory as one long arduous task of trying to respond to a great variety of viewpoints and diverse interest groups. As I wrote, I felt like there were five or six distinct voices in my head clamoring for attention.

At the same time, consultations were carried on with various groups interested in campus ministry and higher education. Thus I was able to elicit the views of a group of Jesuit educators meeting in Chicago and about fifty experienced campus ministers gathering at Niagara University. We received very helpful input from a large group of students who met in Vermont. Of special note were the responses from 300 college presidents and elected faculty members who informed us of their concerns about higher education and demonstrated a remarkable openness to the views of the Church on matters of mutual concern.

With all of this input, the committee made the crucial decision to divide the pastoral into two major parts: one treating the situation of higher education as the context for campus ministry, and the other discussing the important ministerial functions carried on by the Church on campus. Following this approach I wrote a fifty-page draft entitled,

"The Quest for Wisdom: The Church in Dialogue with Higher Education," which organized the material around the theme of wisdom and offered perspectives and strategies to improve both the quality of higher education and the ministerial practice of the Church on campus. I hoped that this pastoral would spark a renewed discussion of the concerns and challenges facing higher education. However, by the time the document was finally released to the public on March 21, 1985, three major studies on higher education had already appeared and the debate was in full swing. Instead of being a lone voice calling for reform, we had joined a chorus.

Nonetheless, extensive discussions went on around the country on "The Quest for Wisdom" and many valuable criticisms and helpful suggestions were collected. On June 14, 1985, the bishops meeting in Collegeville, Minnesota, took up the document. Despite Bishop Friend's strong endorsement and my explanation of the rationale for including the first part of the letter on the educational context for campus ministry, a significant number of bishops raised objections to the first part and made it clear that they were not ready to enter the debate on higher education, at least not in this pastoral on campus ministry. The first draft, which we had worked on for two years, was now effectively dead. The bishops were calling for a total rewrite.

This posed a serious conscience problem for me. I was convinced that the Church had something important to say to higher education and that the current debate provided a good context for it. I told our committee that future historians would note that in the 1980s the Catholic bishops made constructive contributions to the national debate on the nuclear threat and the economy, but missed an important opportunity to influence the reform of higher education. It was clear to me that a pastoral letter without the explicit discussion of higher education would get almost no hearing in the academic world. My fear was that an intramural document would simply reinforce the perception that campus ministry belongs on the periphery of the academic community. On the other hand, I felt a responsibility to salvage as much of the first draft as possible. I decided to stay with the arduous

task, fully expecting to be working on it until November of
1986.

Following an outline devised by our committee, I spent
the summer drafting a totally new document. Through a
process which remains mysterious to me, a seventy-five-page
draft entitled, "Empowered by the Spirit: Campus Ministry
Faces the Future" was completed by the end of August. Our
editorial committee quickly refined and approved it, the bishops' executive committee, in a surprise move, placed it on
the agenda for their fall meeting and the full body of bishops
passed it overwhelmingly on November 15, 1985, a full year
ahead of our revised projections.

At the time of its publication the pastoral received almost no publicity in the secular media and academic officials
showed little interest in it. Within church circles, *Empowered
by the Spirit* did make more of an impact and continues to do
so. Campus ministers appreciated the bishops' strong affirmation of their service within the academic world. Many
of them used the perspective and strategies in the pastoral to
improve their ministry. The bishops' letter spawned commentaries and articles which further developed and applied its
major ideas, especially those six aspects of campus ministry
previously noted: forming community, appropriating the
faith, forming the Christian conscience, facilitating personal
development, educating for justice and preparing leaders for
the future. In 1991 The Department of Education of the
United States Catholic Conference published a handbook for
campus ministers entitled *The Gospel on Campus* which provides great practical advice for implementing all the goals
and suggestions of *Empowered by the Spirit.*

In 1995 the bishops commemorated the tenth anniversary of the pastoral by issuing a letter to college students
which recognizes their struggle and challenges them to be
faithful to their Catholic heritage. The various training
schools for campus ministers continue to structure their programs around the broad goals and major categories suggested by *Empowered.* Given the current budget and
personnel crunch, campus ministers today are using the pastoral to remind their bishops of the commitments the hierar-

chy made over a decade ago to their church on campus. All in all, *Empowered by the Spirit* has proven to be an amazingly durable guide for campus ministry in the United States.

When I reflect on these constructive uses of the pastoral, the arduous task of writing it appears in a more positive light. I have not forgotten the long meetings, the many rewrites of the text, the rejection of the first draft by the bishops, and the intense effort to complete the final text. But my memory focuses more on the great people who worked together on the project, the fun times we had and the moments when our efforts clicked and we came up with a useful insight or a workable strategy. Despite the grief he brought into my life, I am still friends with the priest who first talked me into taking on the writing assignment over fifteen years ago. Now I can laugh about the tense moments during the meetings of the writing committee and frustrating efforts to accommodate the views of liberal and conservative bishops. The opportunity to meet campus ministers from all over the country and hear about their creative ministries has proven to be a most valuable and rewarding experience for me. My memories of the bishops' meetings in Washington when they approved the final text of the pastoral letter carry a note of great satisfaction. I recently heard Joe Kenna, the principal architect of the whole process which produced the pastoral, give a talk which rehashed the history of the project. It was a fascinating experience for me to hear his perceptions of the major turning point in the process, the political intrigue that went on behind the scenes, the dark moments when the whole project seemed doomed and the sense of satisfaction he felt in the completion of the task. During his presentation, the line from Borges came back to me: take on the arduous task as though it were already completed, as though the future was as irrevocable as the past. Throughout the whole project, Joe Kenna was a good example to me of staying the course despite difficult obstacles.

All of us have to find our own ways to persevere with worthwhile tasks which are burdensome and frustrating. Our Christian faith alerts us to the deeper meaning and larger purpose present in all the activities of life, including those which weigh us down. The Gospel calls us to take up our cross daily and follow the Lord. We believe that the Spirit is at work right in the midst of ordinary tasks. This faith perspective enables us to take up those ordinary tasks with the conviction that the future is already in the hands of God.

24. Riding the Subway: an Encounter with an Unfamiliar World

We gain our sense of reality in large measure from the familiar world of relationships and activities which constitute our daily lives. The world of the familiar is necessary for our stability and well-being because it provides a sense of identity and rootedness. Limiting ourselves to the familiar can, however, restrict our vision and retard our growth, leaving us with a limited sense of what constitutes the real world. We need to encounter other worlds which challenge our easy assumptions and expand our sense of reality.

For many summers I have taught a theology course in the Graduate School of Religion at Fordham University in New York. For the most part, this keeps me in the very familiar world of academe, with its cultivated atmosphere, ordered agenda and clear preference for rational discourse. My time in New York, however, also provides an opportunity for brief but enlightening encounters with another world – the buzzing chaotic world found in the New York subway system. Vivid scenes, representing a distinctive sense of reality, remain in my memory.

The unrelieved summer heat hung heavy and oppressive. The D train, running to my residence in the Bronx, featured graffiti but no air conditioning. The late hour intensified my apprehension. Twenty years ago when living in the Bronx, I had often made this trip with no trepidation. But this summer, the scary stories about muggings, as well as the warning of friends, had activated my fears. Around 76th Street, a young fellow at the other end of the car suddenly jumped up. He had a microphone in his hand connected to a loud speaker. He announced with a great flourish that he was a stand-up comedian from the Bronx. Skillfully working around the clatter of the train and the garbled announcements, he launched into his routine, which centered on the differences between blacks, Hispanics, and whites in the way they fight and make love. My consciousness of the racial mix of the car was immediately heightened. The comedian was a black man and most of the passengers were black or Hispanic. There was one other white man besides myself. When his monologue got around to the distinctive characteristics of "white folk" in those two sensitive areas of life, I felt like a spotlight had momentarily shifted to me. Perhaps this was simply my hypersensitive imagination at work. Completing his routine before the 125th Street stop, he gathered up his props, including a large green comb which had illustrated his digression on the idiosyncrasies of Haitians. He then jumped off the train, announcing as he departed that he would be working the A train soon. It occurred to me that anyone who really wanted to catch his act should see him there since his routine will never appear on national TV.

The second scene occurred during an especially grueling three-hour battle with New York public transportation. The woman across from me looked very tired with just about enough reserve energy to make it to her dwelling place. She had her baby in the stroller well under control, offering a comforting touch during the sudden stops and the lurching starts of the train. During the relatively smooth runs, she treated the youngster to small bits of a large oatmeal cookie. Her daughter, about eight years old, was not so easily handled. She was demonstrating the kind of peevish behavior which seems to come naturally with heat and fatigue. The mother responded cleverly by engaging her daughter in a game played on a small computerized toy, seemingly designed for just such an occasion. Whether by skill or motherly indulgence the young girl managed to win the game. Her shouts of glee were met by a big smile from her mother. As the train approached their stop, I wondered how the mother would manage to gather her children and get off the train before the doors closed. Demonstrating amazing skill and dexterity that could only be born of extensive practice, she rose to her feet and pulled up the eight-year-old while grabbing the handle of the stroller. Then, anticipating the lurch of the train by bracing herself against a pole, she managed to hang on to both her children. Righting herself, she pushed the stroller off the car with one hand while pulling her daughter through the door with her other hand. As she disappeared towards the exit, my imagination followed her. She would somehow get the stroller up the stairs and out into the street. No one would help her; she would manage alone. I guessed she was a single parent who had developed the ability to cope with life on its own terms, to adapt to difficult situations with creativity and flexibility. Despite obstacles, she would find ways to care for her children. The rigors of subway travel would not keep her from taking her children to the park or exposing them to a world beyond their tenement building. Instinctively, I felt admiration for her great adaptability as well as respect for her practical skills. For me, she became a living sign of hope, witnessing to the surprising power of the Spirit.

On the subway, others were having more trouble coping. A disheveled, unwashed fellow was stretched out on the hard seats, his right leg, amputated at the knee, pointed upward. He seemed to be in a stupor, generally oblivious to his surroundings. His crutches were lying on the floor ready to support him if he could ever gather himself to take on the world again. My imagination suggested he was a veteran wounded in Vietnam. Once a young man full of life and hope, he was thrown into a dehumanizing war whose horrors still escape our full comprehension. Now he is a middle-aged man, struggling without much success to adapt to a world which has made him a victim. Whatever the truth of his past, he was surely among those living on the margins of society who find it so difficult to make their way in the mainstream. This unfortunate victim aroused in me not so much compassion as a deeper sense of the reality of social sin.

A final scene occurred while I was waiting for a train. A bearded young man with a menacing glare paced the platform shouting obscenities and curses. It was not clear if he was damning someone at the other end of the platform who has messed with him or was directing his violent outbursts at whoever was responsible for the terrible mess we call life. As he came closer to me, I backed away in fear, not even considering any response beyond avoiding his fearsome glance and horrible rage. When we finally boarded the train, he remained on the platform still venting his anger. From the safety of the car, I looked directly at his face, seeing for the first time the hurt which fueled his rage. This man needed a kind word and gentle touch. Could anyone ever get close enough to render that kind of help? Are his hurts, real and imagined, beyond the power of ordinary healing? Such intense rage not only strikes fear but raises religious questions about the relative power of good and evil in the world. Can we speak of a loving God in such a twisted and grim world? In the subway, it becomes harder to speak glibly about the triumph of good over evil.

These subway scenes present a distinctive sense of reality, adding important elements ordinarily missing in the tidy, rational, civil world of academe and suburbia. The world beneath the streets of New York has a harsher, grittier feel. The complex and intractable character of human problems is evident. Not everything can be solved by logical argument and rational discourse. The virtue of adaptability guided by practical wisdom is important for living effectively. Easy assumptions that life is fair and virtue rewarded are quickly unmasked as illusory. Small victories and ordinary virtues are treasured. Reality includes the irrational and the clutter as well as the rational and the ordered. In this world, it is difficult to deny both the reality of the cross and the need for grace.

Chapter Three

Christian Hope: Dealing with Time, Suffering and Death

1. Christian Hope and The Last Things

As we move toward the year 2,000, various dark forces continue to threaten us. *The Bulletin of the Atomic Scientists* has moved the hands of their symbolic atomic clock forward to fourteen minutes before the doomsday hour of midnight. The possibility of terrorists obtaining nuclear weapons is especially disturbing. We cannot dismiss the threat of rightwing reactionaries taking over in Russia and reviving the Cold War. Racial polarization in our country creates a climate which easily leads to violence. Our society is put at greater risk by the striking increase in teenage use of drugs, alcohol and cigarettes during the 1990s. Suicide is a major problem among young people in our country. The AIDS epidemic continues to spread around the globe. Episodic depression has increased dramatically among Americans over the past two generations. The catalogue of destructive powers which assail us is long and frightening.

How are we to cope with this depressing situation? The answer to this question is surely varied and complex. Each threat requires distinctive approaches and tactics. But in all our struggles against the dark forces, we need to maintain a spirit of hope.

154

The virtue of hope is central to the Christian outlook on life. We Christians are called to be people who hope, who have an ultimate confidence that the Absolute Future, which we call God, is drawing the whole human family and all of creation towards a final glorious fulfillment. Our faith instructs us to be on alert for the signals of hope in our world, for the intimations that the glorious future is being formed here and now in our daily experience. Christianity holds these two aspects of hope in a fruitful tension: confidence in the final triumph of good over evil, and the conviction that the mysterious power of good is at work in our world right now.

We can find signals of hope in the midst of our struggles against all the destructive forces in the world. We have apprehended some dangerous terrorists and have taken constructive steps to curb the proliferation of nuclear weapons. Despite all the social and economic problems in Russia, democracy is still in place. After the Simpson trial we have a better understanding of the depth of the racial divide in our society, and some people are working together for solutions. Now that we recognize the resurgence of addictive behavior among young people, we have renewed motivation to help them resist these temptations. In our country the AIDS epidemic has leveled off in some segments of the population. We have new drugs and better therapeutic approaches for treating depression. All of these developments offer some measure of hope that we can manage or survive the difficult personal and social problems facing us.

Our ability to recognize such signs of hope in the contemporary situation is enhanced by the Christian conviction that God is in charge of the whole historical process. We will be more alert to hopeful developments now, if we believe that good will ultimately triumph over all the forces of evil. Our belief that Christ will one day complete the work of the kingdom sharpens our perceptions of all the ways the kingdom is growing in our world today.

Theology can be an ally in the task of cultivating the virtue of hope. Especially important is the area of theology known as eschatology, which treats the last things – death, judgment, heaven, hell and purgatory. Many Christians have learned a popular version of eschatology which describes death as a separation of body and soul; judgment as a frightening revelation of our sin; heaven as a state of rest in the beatific vision; hell as a place of terrible physical and mental suffering; and purgatory as a place where temporal punishment for forgiven sin is expiated. For many believers today this portrayal is no longer helpful or credible. It is too negative and too detailed in its claims to know what the next life is like.

A viable contemporary eschatology must be more positive and more modest. It will not claim to have detailed knowledge of the future revealed by God. Its strategy will be to project out of our current grace-filled and biblically-interpreted experience a general understanding and confidence in God who brings the whole of creation to its final fulfillment. In other words, we know something of our future by reflecting on our current experience and interpreting it in the light of the New Testament. We draw conclusions about the future by meditating on the whole positive thrust of salvation history.

Contemporary eschatology begins with the conviction that we are unified, self-transcendent creatures who experience ourselves as propelled and drawn beyond our current limitations towards a mysterious future goal. Our deepest hope is that this goal is personal and will one day satisfy the longings of our heart. Our Christian tradition tells us that the future can indeed be trusted, that Christ has gone ahead of us to prepare a place for us and that the whole of creation will share in his final victory.

From this faith perspective, we can see death as an act of self-transcendence in which individuals freely and definitively hand themselves over to God and thus pass as a whole person into a new and richer existence. Perhaps our best analog for understanding death is the birth of human life in the course of the evolutionary process as the first humans emerged from animal life into the incredibly fuller existence of persons made in God's image and likeness. Death then can be viewed as an even more spectacular breakthrough into a still wider context of meaning and love.

"Heaven" is our word for describing this new mode of participation in God's life. The biblical symbols of the New Jerusalem and the heavenly banquet remind us of the communal aspect of this life as well as its joyful character. If human existence is essentially self-transcendent, then it makes sense to assume a continuing growth in our eternal life as we move into an ever closer relationship to the Inexhaustible One. The final consummation should not be confined to talk of saving one's soul, but needs to be supplemented by our understanding of the cosmic Christ who brings the whole of creation to its fulfillment and completes his body by drawing the human family into his orbit of love. Christian hope is total and comprehensive, confident that nothing good, nothing authentically human is outside of God's will to save.

The doctrine of hell respects the power of evil and safeguards human freedom. Although the success of God's overall plan is assured and made irrevocable in the resurrection of Jesus, the salvation of individuals is not. We remain free creatures and retain the root capacity to screen out God's love in a selfish act of turning in on ourselves. We should travel the path toward our final fulfillment aware that serious sin is possible, but always confident that God's love is sufficient and more powerful than all sin. Whether we think anyone actually does resist the compelling and steadfast love of God is probably a matter of temperament and training. It seems clear, however, that we Christians have every right to be optimistic that the all-powerful God who wills the salvation of all people does indeed accomplish his will.

The doctrine of purgatory, far from being an embarrassment to Catholics, is a necessary consequence of two common Christian beliefs: we are not perfect at death and we do find perfection in our life with God. Purgatory says nothing about the manner or duration of this transformation, but it does remind us that God is the one who empowers all of our growth.

Our ultimate hope is not dependent on these or any other theological speculations. It is important, however, to search creatively for more intelligible and credible ways of explaining our confidence that love is stronger than death and that the good will finally triumph over evil. We live in a cruel and brutish world which is badly in need of precisely that message of Christian hope.

2. A Meditation on Time

"How do you experience time?" The question is crucial to working out a viable spirituality. The question is not abstract or speculative. The great St. Augustine once said he knew what time was until someone asked him. Reflection on the experience of time is more personal and involving.

The time of my life is like a runaway train gradually gathering speed as it hurtles toward a dark tunnel marked death. In early years the pace was slower. At one time the tunnel was so far off in the distance that it could easily escape notice. The tracks were clear and the ride, though bumpy, felt safe and secure. When did the pace quicken? Or did it occur gradually like a spring-driven watch imperceptibly gaining time? One ordinary night a sting of the flesh mounted a sudden, not repeated, sneak attack and the tunnel suddenly moved into clear view. The train traveled more at night after that and the ride felt less secure and the speedometer periodically lurched into a red area signifying danger. A couple of passenger cars carrying loved ones broke away and disappeared into the tunnel before the date penciled into anticipation. This wrenching experience intensifies lurking questions. Do runaway trains have conductors? Do the tracks continue after the tunnel? Does the speed keep increasing until jumping off feels both desirable and impossible? Are we being pushed or drawn along the tracks or both? Is the driving force benign or malevolent? One thing is clear: Time feels different if it is surrounded by gracious purpose. The ride is just as bumpy but the soul is more focused, the spirit more integrated. The bottom, which always threatens to drop out, is more secure. Even at high speeds, train travel is manageable if we can trust the process.

The time of my days and hours takes diverse forms. Some time sounds like a metronome. It is regular, organized, routine, ordered. The points of punctuation are rhythmic: alarm, prayer, dress, eat and write, work, appointments, prayer, eat, work, exercise, eat, work, relax, prayer, sleep, alarm, etc. It sounds boring and can be; but it usually resonates with significance like a measured Bach concerto. A metronomic life can be dull or exciting; it can languish or surge, depending on perspective and attitude. The disciplined order of work and routine can bind or liberate. We do best when we accept the metronome as an unavoidable part of life, rather than attempting to banish it as though it were an intrusive stranger. The regular beat chafes not because it is regular, but because it is perceived as inimical to our freedom. When the time of our days is properly disciplined, we find new freedom and creativity. Order stores and releases energy. The real problem with metronomic days is not order, but balance. A healthy rhythm includes proper amounts of time for work and relaxation, rest and exercise, activity and sleep. We need to balance work, family and personal time. Time management techniques can help us uncover and remedy imbalances. But the metronome will provide a healthy beat only if it respects the symmetry of a full human life. God calls us to a wholeness and integrity which is more like accepting a name than following a routine.

Some days, hours and minutes feel like they are governed by a demanding clock. Pressures, stress, deadlines, demands, cut away at our calm spirit as if the core of our composure were weak and brittle. It is a sad time indeed when the watch appears as king. In this idolatrous situation, Aristotle's notion of time as numbered motion moves from an abstract definition to a concrete way of life. Then clock time thwarts, subdues and defeats human personal time. Schedules force their way up the hierarchy of values passing in the process family, friends and lovers who are descending the ladder of importance like dispossessed refugees forced out of their proper homes.

Clock time is money. Human time is love. At times choices have to be made, priorities determined. Will we honor efficiency or care? Are we to treasure punctuality or presence? Should we be governed by mechanical clocks which have no feeling for the human adventure or by the law of love which calls for concrete care of our neighbor and wholehearted commitment to our God?

Clocks make false promises that life can be totally managed. Human time refuses to be controlled by a mechanical clock, just as the last two minutes of an exciting pro football game renders irrelevant the digital watch of an excited fan. Time is what happens when friends converse, families celebrate, scholars discuss, adults play and lovers quarrel. The moment of encounter reveals both the time-bound and the time-surpassing mystery of the other person. It also serves as an intimation of the Eternal Now who is both beyond time and within time. In the contemporary world, it is true that we cannot function effectively without clock time. But more significantly, we cannot function humanly if the watch becomes an idol and we forget the abiding dignity of persons and the revelatory power of human relationships.

Sometimes it seems as if time marches on like a column of cloned soldiers on endless parade. Moment follows moment in a flat one-dimensional succession. Chronos reigns supreme; chronology makes the clearest statement; linear movement predominates. It is difficult to find surprises in chronological time, especially when we feel trapped in Nietzsche's Eternal Return, which dooms us to continual repetition. Linear time fogs the brain, and stultifies the spirit. Life becomes a continuous walk down the dreary streets of unliberated East Berlin. For all we know, we could be in Plato's cave observing shadows on the wall as though time is nothing more than a pale and distorted image of eternity. In this chronological world, zest vanishes and boredom steals in as time marches on.

Fortunately, we have other moments when time appears as opportunity and challenge. The "now" emerges from the flat world and calls us to respond vigorously and decisively. Succession is transformed from within, becoming significant moments of decision. Time takes on a rhythm, punctuated by our creative and imaginative responses. This is the *Kairos* described in the New Testament as the time of decision, the opportunity to respond to the call of Jesus without looking back. This is the moment of grace, a time to act wholeheartedly and resolutely. The *Kairos* is the place where the past and future meet in present opportunity. The past can muffle the current call of the Lord especially when it wraps us in a tight fitting hood of regret and guilt. Understanding and accepting both the light and the dark strains of our checkered past unblocks our ears and attunes us to the distinctive voice of the Lord echoing in the "now" of opportunity. The future, too, can scramble the divine message especially when our anxiety level moves into the higher decibel range. Good listeners who hear even the whispers of the Gracious One seem to be able to tune out the static and control their angst level. Dag Hammerskjold, former Secretary General of the United Nations, knew the meaning and power of living in the moment of grace. At one point in his life he answered "Yes" to the divine call and then he knew that "existence is meaningful" and that his "life in self-surrender had a goal." From that moment he understood what it means "not to look back" and "to take no thought for the morrow."

Time is not only chronology, a gray succession of minutes and hours; it is also *Kairos*, a bright sequence of challenges and opportunities. More precisely, our chronology is always more than it seems because *Kairos* inhabits its center, revealing its inner meaning. Time is what happens as we relate to the great God, whether on runaway trains or in shadowy Platonic caves; whether in the bright sunshine or near the dark tunnel. Time might feel metronomic and clockbound, but the hidden God always fills it with a deep and surprising freshness.

3. The Problem of Procrastination: Advice from Gandhi and Jesus

Procrastination is a serious problem for many people and very few of us totally escape this temptation. For some the problem is chronic, almost a way of life. They constantly put off until tomorrow things that should have been done today. Deadlines come and go unmet. Bills are paid late. Household tasks are left undone or incomplete. Birthday gifts are late and Christmas shopping put off until the last possible moment. Habitual procrastinators turn everyday life into one large delaying tactic. There is always a reason for waiting till tomorrow.

Other persons practice a more selective form of procrastination. They get most things done on time, but have difficulty in certain areas or situations. A very successful and efficient businessman is always late paying his taxes. An energetic mother is on top of things most of the year, but gets behind during the hottest days of summer. A student gets all her assignments done ahead of time except for her chemistry class, which she dislikes. A husband who generally attends to the household repair jobs quickly tends to put them off when his situation at work becomes more stressful.

Individuals who are serious about the spiritual life can benefit from a serious examination of conscience on this topic of procrastination. We need to develop a more precise picture of our own patterns of procrastination, whether habitual or selective. It is important to achieve a better understanding of exactly why we put things off, especially since unfinished tasks often leave us feeling guilty or burdened. It could be simply a problem of poor planning, which leaves blocks of wasted time. Some people fail to set priorities and so important tasks do not get done. The job might seem so overwhelming that it is hard to even think about starting it. Procrastination might be caused by the habitual pattern of doing easy and enjoyable things while neglecting more demanding and troublesome tasks. Some people put things off because they actually like to live with the pressure of impending deadlines or feel they function better under pressure.

For a couple of years I have been unable to finish a book I was writing on parish life. I wrote the first five chapters rather quickly and used them as a basis for group discussion with pastoral leaders. Then, under the pressure of time constraints, I put the project aside and have not returned to it since. Recently, I was explaining to someone that I had not gotten back to the book because I was too busy when it suddenly dawned on me that there may be another reason. At our last discussion of the book a few of the participants were quite critical of some parts of the fifth chapter. Is it possible that this criticism caused me to lose confidence in the book? Could it have engendered a subtle fear that the material is not worthwhile, that no one will want to read it, that the whole project will not succeed? Perhaps I have fallen into a type of perfectionism which is excessively fearful of failure. I still have doubts that this is really the case since I have indeed been very busy. But the possibility cannot be ignored. It certainly is true that perfectionism is one of the major causes of procrastination and deserves serious examination. Some people are paralyzed by perfectionism in obvious ways. They cannot act until everything is perfectly in order. They set unrealistically high standards which function as a roadblock to productive activity. Their fear of failure keeps them from taking the initiative on worthwhile projects. For others the temptation to perfectionism is more subtle and less encompassing. A middle-aged mother, for example, delays going back to complete her college degree because she is not sure she can compete with the younger students.

The success ethic, which pervades our culture, intensifies the psychological problems of perfectionism. Our society celebrates hard-driving efficient individuals and rewards them financially. The media lauds the political and economic winners, while assigning the losers to oblivion. Competition, the pursuit of excellence, and progress through hard work have traditionally been part of our national creed. Given our preoccupation with success, some people find it difficult to get into action, especially when their self-confidence is a bit shaky. This reluctance to get involved can happen in many ways: clamming up at a meeting; avoiding competitive games or situations; escaping from personal relationships; failing to seize opportunities for advancement at work. In these and similar situations the success ethic, which breeds fear of failure, tends to restrict individuals from engaging in constructive activity. When success is in doubt, it is hard to overcome our natural inertia and get off dead center. The tendency to procrastinate can be rooted in cultural and societal factors as well as personal psychology. Some problems with procrastination can be solved simply by employing the proper techniques. Individuals can, for example, learn time management approaches, such as doing the important but distasteful things first and breaking down overwhelming tasks into smaller units. But an effective response to procrastination rooted in perfectionism and the success ethic requires an essential change of fundamental perspectives and attitudes. In other words, it is a religious problem which requires spiritual solutions. Since this problem is so tightly woven into Western society, I find it helpful to step outside our own culture and to seek enlightenment from the Hindu religious tradition as represented by Mohandas K. Gandhi.

Gandhi is well-known for his nonviolent tactics which helped bring independence to India in 1947. The religious wellsprings of his dedicated public service are not so familiar. Throughout his long life he found enlightenment and inspiration from his Hindu religion, especially as understood in the sacred writing known as the *Bhagavad-Gita*. This book is part of the great Indian epic, the *Mahabharata*, and occupies a position in Hinduism comparable to the "Sermon on the Mount" in Christianity.

The Gita tells the story of Arjuna, who must decide whether he should enter into battle with his own kinsfolk. If he loses the battle, he will be destroyed; if he wins, he will have harmed people he cares about. In the midst of his dilemma, Krishna, an avatar or incarnation of the deity, appears and tells Arjuna that he must fight, but should do so without worrying about the outcome. Employing a version of modern biblical interpretation, Gandhi understands the story not as an historical fact, but as a commentary on the human condition. It tells us that the way to achieve salvation and self-realization is by renouncing the fruits of action. In other words, we must give up the great emphasis on success and put aside the fear of failure. Concentrate on the effort. Plan, work hard, be shrewd, but don't get hung up on the results.

The great secret of living constructively with peace of mind is to stop worrying about success or failure. Gandhi points out the distortions that occur when the success ethic is dominant: "He who is ever brooding over the result often loses nerve in the performance of his duty. He becomes impatient and then gives vent to anger and begins to do unworthy things; he jumps from action to action, never remaining faithful to any. He who broods over results is like a man given to objects of senses; he is ever distracted, he says goodbye to all scruples, everything is right in his estimation and he therefore resorts to means fair and foul to attain his end." (*Gandhi: Selected Writings*, ed. by Ronald Duncan, pp. 36-37).

On the other hand, Gandhi describes persons who have learned to renounce the fruits of action as "jealous of none, a fount of mercy, without egotism, selfless" They treat alike cold and heat, happiness and misery, friend and foe. They are "not puffed up by praise" and do "not go under" when others speak ill of them. Freed from worrying about success, they can dedicate themselves to God, forgive others and live with personal contentment.

Gandhi's key insight is rooted in an Eastern mindset that is foreign to our way of thinking. Most of us in the United States are so caught up in our own success-oriented culture with its emphasis on self-actualization that it is hard to imagine totally renouncing the fruits of action. But the main point proposed by Gandhi can serve as a helpful corrective for us. It can challenge our usual modes of thinking and force us to re-examine our priorities. It can tone down our emphasis on success and move us to concentrate on making a proper effort.

Our post-colonial world opens up the possibility of more interfaith dialogue. The world religions can indeed learn from one another. It seems to me that a Christian spirituality can accept and appropriate some of the ethical implications of Gandhi's reinterpreted Hinduism. As Christians, we recognize that human beings are a mysterious combination of infinite longings and finite capabilities. Spiritual growth demands that we accept the limitations built into this situation. Perfection is beyond our capabilities. Our hearts remain restless as we make the journey of life. Our model of full humanity, Jesus Christ, was a failure in the eyes of the world. The church gathers to remember and celebrate both the death and the resurrection of Jesus. We must continuously strive to put on the mind of Christ, even though we always fall short of this ideal. Our good efforts are more important than our failures and bear a deeper meaning than our successes. The Gospel encourages us to judge and to transform questionable cultural trends, such as our national success ethic.

These fundamental Christian teachings form a framework for interpreting Gandhi's contention that the key to life is to renounce the fruits of action. His teaching reminds us that our own Gospel encourages us to rely on the gracious God who simply asks us to keep making the effort to follow Christ. Our God calls us by name, sympathizes with our weaknesses and promises never to abandon us on the journey. But God's ways are not our ways. Our worldly successes are not really proof of divine favor. We cannot take our accomplishments before God and demand our eternal reward. We can, however, be confident that none of our good efforts are ever wasted. All the energy we expend in constructive activities, even when they seem to come to naught, is gathered up by our God and given lasting significance.

This religious perspective enables us to attack the deepest causes of procrastination. This spiritual outlook undercuts the perfectionism and challenges the success ethic which drives some individuals to frenzied activity, but leaves others paralyzed. If God is for us, we can begin our tasks without excessive fear of failure. If God is ahead of us beckoning us into the future, we can take the next step. With the conviction that our God does indeed give greater meaning to all we do, we can proceed wholeheartedly to take on all our responsibilities, even the ones we tend to put off.

4. Finding God in Natural Disasters

During the 1990s, the United States has experienced some of the worst natural disasters in our history. On August 24, 1992, Hurricane Andrew struck south Florida and Louisiana, leaving fifty-two dead and displacing 250,000 persons. Andrew, the most destructive hurricane ever to hit the U.S., caused $30 billion in property damage, destroyed or damaged 8,000 businesses and put 300,000 people out of work. The storm, which had sustained winds of 140 mph, eroded beaches, destroyed forests, damaged the coral reef and did over $35 million in damage to the Everglades and Biscayne National Parks. This immense destruction, which inflicted so much tragic suffering on the victims, gives us at least some inkling of the incredible force and energy generated by major hurricanes, such as Andrew.

Less than a year after Andrew, the Midwest had to deal with one of the worst floods our country has known. The Great Flood of 1993 contributed to forty-three deaths, devastated crops in Illinois, Iowa, Minnesota, Missouri and South Dakota and caused an estimated $10 billion in damages. For almost two months, ten times normal rain fell on eight Midwestern states, flooding over thirteen million acres of land. In Des Moines, Iowa, alone, almost thirty inches of rain fell in June, July and August leaving the city without drinkable tap water for twelve days. Along the Mississippi River anxious residents and generous volunteers worked around the clock deploying sandbags to constrain the flood. But in many places the amazingly powerful river refused to be confined and inflicted more damage on cities and countrysides.

Natural disasters invite deeper reflection. Some Christian preachers interpreted these calamities as divine punishments for the immorality rampant in our country, often basing their message on the biblical story of Noah and the flood. Other interpreters were more impressed with the great charity demonstrated by those who came to the aid of the victims of disasters. For them, the 1993 flood was not a divine punishment, but rather, an unavoidable tragedy which prompted heroic virtue and concrete acts of compassion. Reflecting on the flood, the historian Shelby Foote suggested still another approach: "I don't mean to be irreverent, but the Mississippi has a presence in life. When I think of it, I think about God Almighty himself." This close connection between the forces of nature and perceptions of the Deity deserves further exploration.

Our current environmental crisis has spawned various efforts to develop a spirituality rooted in an appreciation of the natural world. These new eco-spiritualities generally emphasize the benign aspect of nature. The ordered laws of nature speak to us of a Divine Craftsman, who has created an intelligible, structured cosmos. The fixed cycles and regular rhythms of nature suggest that God is trustworthy and provident. Through our bodies, we are inextricably tied to Mother Earth which reflects the splendor and beauty of God. As products of the evolving material world, we have a special responsibility to befriend nature and to worship its Creator. Our task is to be good stewards of the earth and to tend the earthly garden with a gentle and respectful hand. In caring for the earth we encounter the Lord of creation who guides the whole evolutionary process to its final fulfillment when there will be "a new heaven and a new earth."

This positive outlook on nature is reflected in Psalm 136 which praises God who alone "has made the heavens, set the earth firm on the waters, made the great lights, caused the sun to rule the day and the moon and stars to rule the night." Recognizing the revelatory power of nature, Jesus proclaimed God's loving care for us by pointing to the birds of the air and the lilies of the field. In contemplating nature, many of the mystics have felt intimately united with their God. A gentle rain on a day in spring moved Henry David Thoreau to recognize the presence of an "infinite and unaccountable friendliness," which was like "an atmosphere sustaining me." Teilhard de Chardin blessed nature as "the divine milieu charged with creative power, as the ocean stirred by the Spirit, as the clay molded and infused with life by the Incarnate Word." Believers with an appreciation of the order and beauty of nature can contemplate God under a variety of images: the good father who orders all things for our well-being; the comforting presence who makes us feel at home in the cosmos; the solid ground who supports all of our activities; the bright light who illumines our paths; the tender mother who nourishes our lives.

But the natural disasters, which have been so prevalent in our national consciousness of late, force us to recognize another side of nature and a different aspect of the always mysterious God. The disasters remind us that nature is not only beautiful and comforting, but also awesome and cruel. The natural world provides a sense of rhythm and regularity to our lives, but also disrupts our patterns and interrupts our routines. Nature is not only a friendly presence, but also an impersonal force which is beyond our control. The evolving material world which has produced higher forms of life also brings us earthquakes, floods and hurricanes that diminish and destroy life. As products of the evolutionary process, we have instinctual impulses which cannot be controlled by reason. We get fatigued before our work is completed. The aging process follows its own inevitable and unavoidable path. The sexual drive does not submit easily to the dictates of intellect and will. We are forced to accept the limitations of time and space which often thwart the longings of our hearts.

Scientists today tell us that the world is not as neat and ordered as Newton's mechanistic physics suggested. Popularizers of the new science insist that all natural systems have an element of randomness existing alongside the ordered predictable patterns. Analyses of the natural world must take into account random variations and chaotic turbulences. Systems function effectively not by maintaining perfect equilibrium, but by embracing the chaos and transforming it into a new ordered pattern. From this perspective a hurricane appears not simply as a tragedy, but as a random event within the order of nature which leads to a process of rebirth. Applied to human beings this theory suggests that we should embrace the irrational, disruptive, chaotic elements in our own lives as part of a process of continual personal development. It is possible, for instance, to recognize and express repressed anger directed at a friend in a way that leads to a healthier relationship. Psychic storms often have the same random, uncontrolled character as do hurricanes and floods. They both force us to reexamine our perceptions of the Ultimate Mystery which is the source and goal of the whole created world.

The mighty acts of nature point to a God whose power and energy are beyond imagination. In the presence of such majestic power, human beings feel overwhelmed, awestruck, terrified and astonished. We are limited creatures, totally dependent on the omnipotent God. To the Lord of creation we owe reverence, respect, obedience and worship. Any attempt to control or manipulate such a powerful Deity is simply out of the question.

Deeply aware of the awesome power of God, the Hebrew Scriptures warn that close personal encounters with Yahweh can be frightening and even fatal. If the Lord is passing by, it is best to cover your face. Simply touching the Ark of the Covenant, the focal point of God's glory, can bring death. When Yahweh spoke to the Israelites on Mount Sinai giving them the Ten Commandments, the people responded: "For what creature of flesh could possibly live after hearing, as we have heard, the voice of the living God speaking from the heart of the fire?" (Deut. 5:26).

In the New Testament the awesome power of God is manifested in Jesus, especially in his miracles. When Jesus calmed the great gale which came up suddenly on the Sea of Galilee, threatening to drown him and his disciples, the evangelists report that the disciples were dumbfounded, fearful and overcome with awe. They could only ask: "Who can this be that the wind and the sea obey him?" (Mk. 4:41). A God with power over storms must be awesome indeed.

Reflecting on nature, which can be violent and cruel as well as serene and beautiful, reminds us that the God of creation is both comforting and awesome. A calm lake and a gentle breeze speak to us of a God who embraces and comforts us. Hurricanes and floods reveal a powerful, majestic, supremely energetic God who inspires awe and reverential fear. A balanced Christian outlook recognizes both aspects of the one God who remains the inexhaustible Mystery.

5. Responding to Ecological Dangers: Prophetic and Mystical Approaches

The historic U.N. Conference on Environment and Development, which met during June of 1992 in Rio de Janeiro, helped many of us focus our attention on the serious environmental problems which threaten the earth. Years later it is becoming increasingly clear how difficult it is to sustain this interest in ecological problems. The individualism rampant in our culture tends to overshadow concern for the common fate of the earth. The environmental movement lacks the kind of striking catastrophic images which grab the attention of the media and move the general public. Graphic television reports of emaciated children have helped sway public opinion to assist the starving in places like Ethiopia and Somalia. It is more difficult for the average person to appreciate the dangerous long-term consequences of the depletion of the ozone layer or the destruction of the Amazon rain forest.

In order to sustain an effective response to our ecological concerns, we need a fresh act of imagination, a broader perspective and a transformation of fundamental values. The world's religious traditions can be of great service in accomplishing these fundamental shifts. Hinduism, Buddhism, Judaism, Christianity and Islam all encourage their followers to relate their own interests to the well-being of a larger whole. The monotheistic religions recognize that the lives of future human beings are as significant and valuable as our own. Biblical faith discerns the love of God manifested not only in the sweep of history, but also in the beauty of nature. Christianity teaches that the Word became flesh, that God is incarnated in our material world. Furthermore, followers of Jesus know the importance of remaining committed to good causes even when positive results are not apparent. These fundamental perspectives, drawn from the great religious traditions, form a solid basis for the effort to save the earth from destruction.

Among Christians addressing environmental concerns today, we can discern two major approaches: a prophetic ecology, which calls upon human beings to exercise responsible stewardship over the earth, and a mystical ecology, which emphasizes our deep bonds of unity with other species and the earth as a whole. Important church leaders have generally adopted a prophetic stance in addressing environmental concerns. For example, the Religious Partnership on the Environment, a coalition of Catholic, Protestant and Jewish groups, places the highest priority on establishing environmental justice. They are concerned about the effects of dump-siting on the poor and the impact of environmental decisions on workers and jobs. They call for the industrialized North to cooperate with countries in the South so that they can develop sustainable economies which fit their distinctive cultures and preserve the environment.

In their 1991 pastoral letter on the environment, "Renewing the Earth," the Catholic bishops of the United States also emphasize this prophetic approach. They insist on a consistent respect for human life which includes care for the created world. The whole human family is interdependent, and all of us must work for the common good. A contemporary "ethics of solidarity" requires an equitable use of resources and a special care for the poor and the outcasts. An authentic ecological spirituality must recognize the limits of material growth and the need for people in the industrialized countries to curb consumption. The bishops insist it is fundamentally unjust for the industrialized North, which constitutes less than 20% of the world's population, to consume 75% of the earth's natural resources.

This prophetic approach highlights the notion of stewardship. Human beings are called not to dominate the earth, but to tend the global garden as good stewards. According to Genesis 2:15, God settled Adam in the garden of Eden to cultivate and care for it. This remains the ongoing task of the human family. Prophetic ecology rejects environmental exploitation based on Genesis 1, which speaks of human mastery of the animal world and the divine command to fill the earth and conquer it. It makes stewardship rather than domination the central category. We human beings are in charge of the material world, but we must carry out this responsibility with care and respect. The prophetic approach embraces an enlightened anthropocentrism which places human beings in the center of creation, while insisting that we take responsibility for its well-being. We are not merely one of many species inhabiting the earth. We are the leading edge of the evolutionary process and have the privileged task of guiding it to its ultimate fulfillment.

Prophetic ecology supports its ethical demands with pragmatic arguments which appeal to sober realists. We must be responsible stewards in order to maintain the earth as a habitable place for the human family. We must reject consumerism, waste and exploitation so that the earth can continue to sustain coming generations. The good of all demands that the industrialized countries help the developing nations gain access to their fair share of the world's goods.

Benedict of Nursia, who founded the first Benedictine monastery at Monte Cassino, Italy in 529, can serve as a fitting patron saint of prophetic ecology. During the Middle Ages, the Benedictine monks cleared the land, developed sanitation systems and refined agricultural methods. They lived a simple lifestyle, and their communities were economically self-sustaining. Although our postmodern world is so different, the Benedictine emphasis on simplicity, practical care of the earth and sustainable economic systems can certainly help us respond constructively to the current environmental crisis.

The other major Christian approach to ecological concerns has a more mystical orientation. It stresses that we humans are essentially connected to the whole cosmos. In his provocative book, *The Dream of the Earth,* the Passionist priest, Thomas Berry, speaks of the universe as a "communion of subjects," not a collection of objects. Since rocks, plants and animals possess an intrinsic value, they are worthy of respect and cannot simply be used for our purposes. We humans are in Berry's phrase, "stardust become conscious of itself." Our roots are in the material evolving world. The mystical intuition is that our essential unity is more fundamental than what divides us. Our dualistic thinking is finally an illusion because there are deep and enduring bonds which connect us to one another, to the whole cosmos and ultimately to our God.

The mystical perception leads to a different style of theology. Sallie McFague in her book, *The Body of God: An Ecological Theology,* calls for a shift from a person-centered theology to one centered on the cosmos. Since the whole universe is God's body, we must develop an ethic of care for the world. Charlene Spretnak, the author of *States of Grace,* invites us to deeper contemplative prayer so that we can see the universe as "a glorious dance of being." Our responsibility for the earth flows out of our conviction that God is intimately present in every being. In an excellent article entitled, "The Sacrament of Creation: Toward an Environmental Theology" (cf. *Commonweal,* Jan. 26, 1990), Michael and Kenneth Himes call for a shift from the stewardship model favored by prophetic ecology to a companionship model which offers a different approach to the environmental crisis. They contend that stewardship, although a great advance over domination, still implies that the non-human creation is an object to be used rather than a subject with inherent goodness. For this reason, they have developed the companionship theme found in the second account of creation in the book of Genesis. In this story, God first creates a man and places him in the beautiful garden of Eden where he can enjoy its delights. But the man needs a companion, so God creates the animal kingdom for him. Still no companion suitable for man was found. Thus, God took a rib from the man, and made a woman, to be his true companion. The human search for companionship suggests deeper bonds with the whole of creation than first meets the eye. In the terminology of the great Jewish religious thinker Martin Buber, nature is not an "it" to be manipulated and controlled, but a "thou" to be respected and reverenced. We reverence nature not by personifying it or deifying it, but by respecting it for what it is: a limited and finite creature with marvelous power to manifest its Creator. The material world is a sacrament which can reveal the divine presence and remind us of the love of God. We are companions with the whole of creation in moving toward ultimate union with God.

In 1979, Pope John Paul II proclaimed St. Francis of Assisi as the patron saint of the environment. In his great *Canticle of the Sun*, Francis recognizes the sun and moon, earth and air, fire and water, animals and plants as our brothers and sisters. His insight is rooted in the faith conviction that all creatures are united in the essential poverty of being finite before the great God. We are all poor because we do not hold within ourselves the power of being. We do not control our own lives any more than does an animal, a plant or a rock. Christians with a contemplative heart are more attuned to this mystical ecology.

This sense of communion with the universe grounds an environmental ethic. As companions, we are responsible for the other subjects in the universe. We must develop policies which respect the earth as a fellow creature of God. We should curb consumption in our own country and help our companions in poorer countries to achieve sustainable economic development.

Our environmental crisis demands an ecological spirituality which combines the prophetic and mystical approaches. Drawing on insights from both Benedict and Francis, we can work with others to save planet earth by tending the global garden and reverencing the created world.

6. The Oklahoma City Bombing

The tragic Oklahoma City bombing is now part of our national history of suffering. For many, the human dimension of the tragedy took on an especially sad countenance in the widely disseminated picture of firefighter Chris Fields cradling a baby, Baylee Almon, in his arms. Baylee celebrated her first birthday on April 18, 1995. One day later, at 9:02 a.m., a bomb devastated the federal building and Baylee was dead. She was one of nineteen youngsters included in a death toll which reached 168. The death of innocent children brought a special poignancy to the national mourning triggered by the tragic attack.

Chris Fields was one of thousands of generous people who came to the aid of the victims. Skilled search and rescue teams from all over the United States risked their lives in a round-the-clock effort to find survivors and recover the bodies of the deceased. Many doctors and nurses volunteered to treat the wounded. Ordinary citizens stood in line for hours at the local Red Cross to donate blood. Companies supplied equipment for the rescue effort and local restaurants made food available for the volunteers. People around the country joined in prayer for the victims and their families. Once again the nation showed a remarkable capacity to focus attention on a tragedy and to respond generously. Shared suffering created a sense of solidarity which for a time eclipsed the differences which usually divide us.

As a self-contained event, the Oklahoma City bombing was a vicious and senseless assault which heaped horrible suffering on innocent victims and their families. But the bombing has a deeper and larger significance as well. It is one of many national disasters which have chipped away at the foundations of traditional American optimism, creating in the process a more somber national mood.

The eighteenth-century Enlightenment helped create the modern conviction that reason and science would ensure human progress and create a better world. In Europe the World Wars shattered this dream and set the stage for a new existential pessimism. The post-war mood in the United States, however, remained upbeat. The election of John Kennedy in 1960 heightened expectations that we could make dramatic progress on all manner of human problems, ranging from racism at home to poverty in developing countries. We could realize the American dream and extend the aura of Camelot, if only we were ready to pay the price, bear the burdens and work together for the good of the country. And then on November 22, 1963, an assassin's bullet took the life of the young president, who had come to symbolize American optimism. Violence invaded Camelot and nothing would ever be the same for us Americans. A media-enhanced strain of chaos had been unleashed and the best and the brightest could no longer keep it in check. As a nation in shock, we gathered around our television sets for President Kennedy's funeral rites, confronted with the precariousness of life and the limitations of even the most powerful among us.

Subsequent events have periodically reinforced our national sense of powerlessness in the face of aggressive attacks and random violence. The assassinations of Robert Kennedy and Martin Luther King inflicted new wounds and left the country shaken. Despite our military might we could not win the war in Vietnam and had to endure an ignominious withdrawal from Saigon. A car bomb was able to kill and wound many of our best trained and equipped marines in Lebanon. The most powerful nation on earth could not find a way to free its own citizens held hostage in Iran and for years we were unable to halt the terrible slaughter in Bosnia. The security systems installed at airports around the world were not able to prevent the explosion of the Pan Am flight over Lockerbie, Scotland. The bombing of the World Trade Center in New York brought terrorism closer to home, reminding us of how difficult it is for a free society to defend major cities against such attacks by foreign enemies. The Oklahoma City bombing extended our sense of vulnerability. No place in the country is safe from domestic terrorists who can construct powerful bombs out of readily available materials. A poll conducted shortly after the bombing indicated that 70% of Americans expected another bombing in one of our cities within the next year. Finally, our fears are fueled by daily media reports of random violence: drive-by shootings, serial killings, shooting sprees by deranged individuals and muggings in the street.

Taken together, these events of the last three decades have posed a serious challenge to traditional American optimism. They have helped create a more somber mood which reflects a heightened awareness of the essentially precarious nature of human life. The breakdown of security systems has forced us to face the radical insecurity of human existence. Our military failures have reminded us that in some situations we are utterly powerless. Repeated acts of random violence have intensified the anxiety felt by many Americans. The national disasters have set before all of us a truth known all too well by the poor and dispossessed of this world: we do not have ultimate control over our own existence. We know the temptation to escape from these painful experiences and the troubling questions they raise. But tragedies like the Oklahoma City bombing thrust them back into consciousness and challenge us to deeper reflection.

In his book *Oswald's Tale*, Norman Mailer re-examines the murder of President Kennedy which shattered the exuberant optimism of the early 1960s. He claims that if the long and agonizing national trauma unleashed by the assassination was caused by an insignificant and unhappy individual who acted alone and by sheer luck hit a moving target at eighty-eight yards, then "we live in a universe that is absurd." Mailer tries to avoid this conclusion by transforming Oswald from an absurd figure into a tragic human being. Many other Americans hold various conspiracy theories rather than accept the absurdity that one troubled man brought down the mighty and inflicted such pain on a whole nation. From a secular perspective, random violence can only appear as absurd. In a one-dimensional world, tragedies can never have any kind of ultimate meaning. In a self-contained universe, there is no final healing or redemption. In a totally secular context, the only reasonable response is to build better security systems and to find more efficient ways to deter violence. The major question is how to balance individual freedom and national security interests.

Christian faith offers another perspective and responds to deeper questions. Our Scriptures provide no simple answers to monstrous evil and horrifying tragedies. There is no easy comfort for parents who lost a child in Oklahoma City. We do believe that all human suffering is encompassed in a divine plan which assures the ultimate victory of good over all evil. At the eternal banquet every tear will be wiped away. Christian faith insists that it is possible to face and manage our deepest anxieties because the gracious God, who is our true strength, will never abandon us. The risen Christ, who cast out even the most entrenched demons, says to us, "there is nothing to fear." We can accept radical insecurity because God holds us in gracious hands. It is by recognizing our powerlessness that we can tap the strength of the Spirit. Accepting our essential vulnerability opens us to the healing touch of Christ. For believers, the assassination of President Kennedy, absurd as it might be, does not render the whole universe absurd. The tragic events of the last three decades may have tempered our optimism, but they need not lead to despair. Christianity proclaims a message of hope rooted not in security systems or military might, but in the power of God to bring good out of evil. The Christian response to tragedies like Oklahoma City is not vengeance or a fanatical pursuit of security. The Gospel calls for forgiveness, prudence and a hopeful-realism which accepts the unavoidable limitations of life, while trusting that God blesses all our efforts to construct a more humane world.

7. My Father's Death: Grieving Alone

The death of a loved one is a trauma experienced or anticipated by all of us. The commonness of the experience does not detract from the uniquely personal way in which each of us participates in the death of one whom we love. This reflection was written shortly after my father's death back on April 20, 1979. It was an expression of deep love and an important part of my grieving process.

My father enjoyed seventy-three vigorous years, had a cerebral hemorrhage, spent three days in a deep coma and died a peaceful death. Such a life must be seen as gift and blessing, especially in the light of the immense sufferings endured by so many. In my homily at the funeral Mass I tried to express the meaning of my father's life, using St. Paul's imagery from the world of athletics: "I have run the race to the finish, kept the faith, now there is for me a crown of righteousness." We are reminded of the harsh, competitive character of human life, and of the need for a persevering faith strengthened by physical and spiritual self-discipline. We need live models of these virtues – people whose aggressive temperament is tempered by love, who know that genuine competition is against one's own potential, who understand that discipline is for the sake of a richer life, who strive to earn a good living without becoming materialistic. We need the faithful Christian competitors to inspire us. I count it the greatest of gifts to have known such a man. The extent and depth of the love we shared will remain untold. His story is ordinary, but nonetheless significant. It lives on as vivid family history in the hearts of just a few – the plucky catcher on the sandlots of Pittsburgh, the hard-driving and efficient coffee plant manager, the daily Mass-goer, the volunteer worker at the Childrens' Sunshine Home. The faults of this aggressive, competitive man were glaring, but paled before his virtues. My father, George Bacik, ran the race with vigor, persevered till the end. We believe that for him is reserved the imperishable crown of victory.

Feeble words indeed (here merely summarized) for expressing sentiments deep within my heart. I longed to honor his memory with dignity and to help those who knew him less well to appreciate the distinctive features of his innate goodness. It was vitally important to me to clarify the nature of his personal struggle and to celebrate the virtues exemplified in his life. My official function at the funeral forced me to keep some of my deepest emotions in close check. The sadness and sorrow suppressed then now seeks articulation and clarification.

I began to absorb the grief from the first moment as the often rehearsed story unfolded. "It's your father; he had a stroke." My mother's voice carried its usual tone of realism even in the midst of distress. During the drive to the hospital, my mind tended to recede from the harsh fact and I tried to force it back to the painful confrontation with my worst fears – a struggle that would be repeated many times. As I entered the intensive care unit, the first sight of the stricken warrior whom I loved sliced open a gaping hole in my protected self. Through it poured a volatile sorrow which constricted my throat and numbed my brain. A shared hour with my mother and younger sister brought some measure of comfort, but then the doctor appeared with the somber report: "It is very bad; he may die tonight; there is no hope of recovery." My knees buckled slightly as I tried to support my mother. Denial was fleeting at most, as the reality bored into my mind. The sorrow then began its process of solidifying into a permanent core of sadness located somewhere near the center of my self. From then on it seemed important to me to allow that process to have free reign so that the core sadness could assume its full intensity. I suggested that we pray that the Lord take him, but my mother, operating implicitly out of a healthier theology, said we should pray that we could accept whatever happened – including the task of caring for him if he survived. A vital point became clearer to me – accepting the sorrow could not be on my own terms. The absorbing and solidifying process had to go on, but dictated by reality.

As my father lingered in a coma, I found my times to be alone with him. I expressed out loud my secret thoughts of love, respect and contrition, allowing the tears to flow. Being present for his death seemed important to me and after three days he died peacefully as my mother and I hovered and prayed over him. My instinct was to stay with the body and I helped to place it on the cart to begin the procession to the funeral home.

During the next few days my family and I had to fight periodic skirmishes against custom in order to keep the reality of death and grief in front of our eyes. My sister insisted that the mortician remove the make-up from his face. The family was present for the closing of the casket. The funeral Mass celebrated grief as well as resurrection. We gathered at the burial site and not the remote mausoleum. The family was present as the casket was lowered into the ground, and we all took a handful of dirt and dropped it on the casket. My sense was that the ritual had to be completed so that we could absorb the full measure of grief. For days afterwards, I tried to maintain a mood of mourning. My emotions, necessarily suppressed during the funeral liturgy, longed for expression. Visits to the grave, long periods of silence, serious family conversations, looking through clippings and pictures

– all those purposeful activities unleashed feelings which periodically spurted forth like a geyser.

Return to my ministerial duties afforded me further opportunities for reflection and assimilation. Strangely, as I sat writing these reflections, a student came in to tell me he just heard that his father had a heart attack and a little while later a young woman appeared who was struggling to cope with her father's impending death from cancer. I fought my way through already heightened feelings in order to be prayerfully present to these young people as they experienced their own unique encounter with grief. Facing, absorbing, accepting, assimilating, expressing, transforming – they would take their turns struggling with these tasks as we all must.

My own experience tells me they will find that grief forms bonds of human solidarity, but that it also isolates and individuates. While we suffered through my father's last days, the closeness of our family, always real and treasured, was focused and intensified by our shared sorrow. We read scripture together, celebrated the anointing of the sick, prayed together, reminisced about good times, planned for the funeral and shared something of our own confused feelings. We joked and laughed especially about the attractive foibles of the man we respected and loved. We spoke out loud to him about mutual interests and supported one another as our individual sorrow emerged. The generous support of family and friends during the whole experience was inspiring and helpful. The communal celebration of the funeral rites seemed to draw people together and provide a context of order and meaning amidst the threatening chaos. Indeed, grief has the power to produce a community of concern which, even if fleeting, provides great comfort and strength.

But at the same time grief reveals an essential aloneness. The sorrow of each person is unique. No other human being can touch the deepest level of our sadness. We finally grieve alone. Some people who have successfully negotiated their own grieving process are able to express great compassion and empathy. Even their kind words, however, fall short and we are left alone with our own unique grief. Community is

vital, presence is supportive, sympathetic words are appreciated; but the terrifying truth is that a center of sadness is
formed in the depths of our being which in its uniqueness is
unknown and unappreciated by other humans. I find a
strange comfort in the presence of people who understand
and respect this fact. It seems to provide space and scope for
an encounter with the gracious Mystery which ultimately
sustains us in our aloneness. It reminds us, as well, of our
total dependence on the One we call our Father.

8. An Anniversary Meditation

It is a rainy, dreary day – the kind that often puts me in a
reflective mood. The mystery called "death" is insistent today. It stands on the edge of my consciousness, calling for
my full attention. The intensity and timing of this summons
are not surprising. My good friends, who are dealing with
the recent tragic death of their energetic and talented twenty-
one year old son, are much on my mind. Their faith is inspiring; but their pain of loss is real and intense. It has been less
than two weeks since I found out that my mentor Karl
Rahner, the great German Jesuit theologian, died at the age
of eighty. The human family has lost an insightful interpreter
of our common experience and I feel the void. In addition,
tomorrow is the anniversary of the death of my brother
David, who died at the age of nine. He never spoke or communicated; but he did call forth a commitment of faithful
self-sacrificing love from my parents which still inspires me.
Finally, next Friday is not only Good Friday but the fifth anniversary of my father's death.

It is not surprising that death is so much on my mind
today. I must seize the opportunity to reflect more deeply on
this awesome mystery which sooner or later demands the attention of us all.

Fortunately, I had two hours until my next appointment.
From experience I knew well the best place for this reflection.
I picked up my New Testament and headed for the cemetery,
where five years ago my family and I buried the body of my

father, George Bacik. I walked to the grave site, peered down at the headstone and let my emotions and imagination run free. Spontaneously, I drifted into conversation with my father.

Dad, I miss you so much. The good times we had are so important to me – like the times we went to the Tigers game early, had our beer and hot dogs and watched batting practice. I remember when you told me I did a damn good job working for you at the coffee plant and when you said I was a major leaguer even though I was such a mediocre ballplayer. Someday I want to bring your grandchildren here and tell them what a great man their grandfather was. I want them to know the stories which mean so much to me and to pass them on to their children. Last time your five-year-old granddaughter was here she said, "Grampy must be squished down there." That still makes me laugh. I remember when your daughter got her masters degree, and we came out here and prayed and cried together before her graduation party. Dad, I miss your presence. Every time something good happens I instinctively want to tell you about it: my book got published; I shot seventy-nine on a tough course; the lecture went over real well; look at this month's column in the NCR – and always the silence, the void, the sharpened sense of loss. When a twenty-one-year-old young man dies in a senseless accident, it seems so much worse. I grieve for my friends. Seventy-three vigorous years in good health – you were lucky, George. When I visit the nursing homes and see an old man in a wheelchair staring out the window, I'm glad you went quickly. You could never have sat still that long. I am a little teary today, but not as intense as sometimes. Does the pain of loss get dulled, the edge go off the sadness? Some people worry about that as though it suggests that their love was not true or is fading. I don't worry about it. The love we shared was real and deep. As human relationships go, I haven't seen many better. I tell people that death cannot break the bonds of love. Sometimes I know that is true. Other times it is not so clear. At Mass after the Consecration I always try to think of you. Sometimes when I'm distracted I forget. I am so glad that during our years together I often told you how much I loved and respected you and appreciated what you did for me. "If you are afraid to do it, that is the best reason for doing it." That was one of the best things you taught me. That and to respect and help the underdogs in life. You seldom spoke against people, even ones who deserved it. It amazes me now to realize how strict you were about never gossiping or tearing down another person. I liked your passion, your impulsive side, your open honest way of dealing with people. My teacher, Karl Rahner, just died. One of the reasons I got along with him so well was that he was so like you. The essential goodness and care below his gruff surface was very evident to me. It all seemed very familiar. Rahner is famous and will be remembered. You are carried in the hearts of only a few; but that memory is very real and significant. Dad, I'm sorry for the bad times when I forgot that a strong man has a sensitive side as well. Strange, I don't often think about those failures or the arguments or the times I disappointed you. I like to reflect on the good times and recall those moments when we felt close and I knew you loved and respected me.

Then the spell was broken. My reflection on death had so easily and naturally turned into a dialogue with my deceased father. Mysterious are the ways of the moments of grace. Feeling the need for some perspective on such disconnected ramblings, I returned to my car, picked up the New Testament and, as planned, began to read the accounts of the passion and death of Jesus. Then suddenly, I was rousing myself from sleep. The irony struck me as I recalled the words of the Lord: "Could you not watch one hour?" I am reminded of other bits of irony in the passion story. Caiaphas says it is better to have one man die and he speaks a truth deeper than he knows, the mocking inscription "This is the King of the Jews" reveals the hidden but true identity of Jesus. Truth arrives in the midst of darkness; love triumphs precisely when wickedness seems strongest. Dialogue with a deceased loved one is not an empty monologue based on an illusion; it is rather an embodiment of the faith conviction that our loving relationships transcend the boundary of death.

I returned to reading the passion still hoping that the story of the final days of Jesus would clarify my fragmented musings and jumbled feelings. The synoptic Gospels highlight his struggle with the darkness of death: "Father, if it is possible, let this cup pass me by." "My God, my God, why have you forsaken me?" The Lord himself knew the pain of loss. After all, he had cried when his friend Lazarus died. We can learn from his example. It is a healthy exercise to face death and allow ourselves to feel the full intensity of the sense of loss. Jesus freely accepted his death and in the act of surrender achieved a paradoxical triumph over the darkness. His example encourages us to face the darkness of death with the hope that it will not swallow us up, but will serve as a passageway to a richer life.

The passion account can be read as a story of love tested but triumphant. Jesus knew better than anyone else ever has that he was loved by the Mystery which he addressed in familiar terms as "Abba." His whole life was devoted to responding to that love by sharing it with others. He wanted to gather the estranged and heal the wounded. But obstacles were everywhere. The crowds were often baffled, the religious leaders were jealous and afraid, his own disciples did not understand and the political establishment ordered him executed. Whatever the challenges, however, he remained the faithful lover. "Not my will but thine be done." "Into your hands I commend my spirit." Love, though tempted, gives all and receives all in return.

The passion of Jesus does indeed illumine this grieving process. My relationship with my father had its abrasive moments, but it was always sustained by mutual respect and love. Though tested, our love endured. Not even death can break the bonds created by true love. Anyone who has experienced the beauty and power of human love knows something of the deep truth that God is love. Sustained by this divine love, we can find the courage and strength to face death and to manage our grief.

9. Constructive Grieving

The tenth anniversary of my father's death compels reflection. At the time of my father's funeral I was deeply appreciative of the comfort and support offered by family and friends. But I was also aware that we ultimately grieve alone and in our own unique way. Since then, I have observed many individuals who have responded to the death of their loved ones in distinctive ways.

A middle-aged man has felt an abiding sense of welcomed relief ever since his long-suffering mother died many years ago. A church-going Catholic woman has struggled unsuccessfully for over five years to forgive her deceased father for the psychological abuse he heaped upon her. Parents grieving intensely over the death of their young son have used their sense of loss to come closer to God. A widow who has happily remarried seldom thinks anymore of her deceased husband. A priest who lost both parents a few years ago has continued to feel a great void in his life. A widow of almost two decades has survived by relying on the happy memories of her husband. A middle-aged man has been unable to rekindle a sense of joy since the death of his mother five years ago. It is difficult to find clear stages and patterns in these diverse experiences.

Within my own family, we find both common experiences and diverse patterns of response to my father's death. When we gather, it is still common for us to recall the familiar stories which shape our collective memory of him. We all have favorite incidents which define our unique relationships with him. All of us have noted that the feelings of grief and loss have became less intense over the years. We continue to draw strength and inspiration from his good life.

On the other hand, the experiences which trigger the memories are quite different. Throughout the whole decade my mother has been on a regular cycle, reliving the sad events of his last days every month from the seventeenth, the day he was stricken, to the twentieth, the day of his death. One of my sisters remembers him especially when using his favorite sayings and practical wisdom to instruct and encourage her children and when she has to do small household repair jobs that he used to do during his periodic visits to her home. My other sister, who is keenly aware of an ongoing relationship with her father, is especially moved by treasured objects and mementos which evoke special memories in her. My own strongest memories are spontaneously triggered by significant sporting events, especially the World Series, which symbolizes a whole world we shared. His abiding spirit is very real to me at family gatherings, especially when we pray together before meals. I also hear his harsh but forgiving voice when I have done something especially stupid or destructive. When celebrating funeral Masses, I often call on his memory to help me lead the liturgy without breaking down emotionally. My own memories seem to be related not so much to anniversaries or objects, but to events which have special emotional significance for me. Although the catalysts are different for each of the members of my family, the memory of my father remains a pervasive and enduring influence on all of us.

Beyond the emotional reactions which have a rhythm of their own, it seems vitally important to me to be faithful to my father's memory. That ideal of fidelity carries many layers of meaning for me, suggested by diverse and powerful images. In one of my fantasies I gather my nephews and favorite niece at my father's gravesite, to tell them the familiar stories which define the character of their grandfather. Then I encourage them to return to this site one day and to repeat this process with their own children, telling the stories which will pass on my father's memory to the next generation. Analyzing this fantasy, I recognize that it is connected with the thirst for immortality. It is a way of insuring continued significance for the life of the man I admired so much. My whole being rebels against the notion that my father's personal existence, filled with such an impressive accumulation of discipline, sacrifice, hard work, commitment, love and accomplishment, simply came to an end, leaving no abiding residue. In a related image, I am standing alone in an open area, my heart flooded with a sad longing for a son who will carry my memory in his heart with the same love and respect that I have for my father. Beyond its obvious meaning for a celibate priest, this fantasy represents for me an even deeper longing which cannot be fulfilled by progeny and their memories – no matter how beautiful and enduring. This deeper thirst can be satisfied only by a final fulfillment which confers eternal value and ultimate significance on me, my loved ones and all human beings. Only the eyes of faith can discern meaning in such a deep and comprehensive desire which is continually frustrated on this earth. For Christians, the resurrection of Jesus Christ grounds and strengthens our hope that our deepest longings for perpetual life and abiding significance will one day be fulfilled. The resurrection encourages us to believe what we desperately hope is true: that not even death can dissolve our being or break the deep bonds we share with our loved ones.

Fidelity to my father's memory includes for me a moral dimension. It creates an obligation to respond wisely and courageously to the messages he has imprinted on my consciousness. My sister periodically tells me I am becoming more like my father with each passing year. Her tone of voice usually suggests that this observation is not intended as an unqualified compliment. Perhaps she fears I will follow his lead and become too set in my ways and too impatient with the ordinary process of life. Given my father's conservative religious tendencies, she may fear I will end up as resident chaplain for a local chapter of "Reactionary Catholics United to Revive the Inquisition."

At any rate, her comments remind me of how often I have heard individuals say that they are becoming more like their parents. This is not surprising since we carry their genes as well as their memories. It seems important for all of us, however, to appropriate the example of our parents in a critical way. Fidelity demands that we not only emulate their virtues, but also avoid their vices. Prudence dictates that we not only act on the wise principles taught by our parents, but also learn from their mistakes. We must remain alert so that the questionable behaviors of our parents do not subtly creep into our lives. One of the things I admired most about my father was that he rose above the childrearing methods of his own father and broke a cycle of harsh practices. He never struck his children and always insisted that we reason together by talking out our differences. On occasion, he informed me that the psychologists who taught that our behavior was dictated by childhood experiences were themselves crazy. From his own experience he knew it was possible to transcend the vices of one's parents. For me, his message was clear and pointed: take hold of your own life because you are not merely a victim of fate and circumstances. It follows from this that I best honor my father's memory by trying to avoid some of his faults and failings just as he avoided some of the worst aspects of his father's behavior. We demonstrate genuine respect and love for our parents by responding in our own way to the promptings of the Spirit to become our better selves.

Sharing with others what we have learned from our parents seems an especially appropriate way to honor their memory. On many occasions I find myself spontaneously repeating bits of wisdom and advice gleaned from him. To the graduate student I say "Finish strong," recalling the decisive encouragement my father gave me when I was struggling to finish my dissertation. To the single woman despondent about her lot in life, I repeat my father's advice, "If you must compare yourself with others, think of those who have less and not more." To the shy person I say, "Push yourself a bit," thus modifying the language but retaining the sense of my father's pointed messages to his shy son.

In addition to the advice, I find myself drawing on the principles and insights implicit in his exemplary behavior: have a special care for those hurting and give those who made a mistake another chance; say prayers of thanksgiving regularly for the ordinary blessings of life like good health; never speak critically about others or hurt their reputation; place higher value on the family than on material possessions and getting ahead; do not pout or withdraw when a dispute arises, but talk it out; have respect for people who practice other religions; work hard and be responsible; play hard and be gracious in victory and defeat; keep hold of the faith because it is a source of strength; and most fundamentally, trust in the God who has given us so many blessings.

The theology I espouse today is in large part an elaboration of these principles pressed into my mind and heart by the force of my father's good example and committed life. This is clearer to me now than it was ten years ago. Even as the intensity of the sense of loss diminishes, the depth of my gratitude continues to grow.

10. Remembering the Community Builders

My sense of Holy Week this year is colored by the recent death of my cousin Mildred who has a special place in my heart since she also served as my godmother. She died suddenly at the age of sixty-nine after enjoying good health throughout her life. Although she and her wonderful husband were happily married for over four decades, they were never blessed with children. This did not prevent her, however, from exercising her maternal instincts. Rather than withdrawing into bitterness and frustration, she functioned as a second mother to numerous nieces and nephews. They often spent evenings and weekends at her home and even went on vacations with her and her husband. Their affection for their aunt was deep and genuine.

Mildred also served as the matriarch of the family after the death of her own mother. Her assumed task was to care for her brothers and sisters when they were in need, to be the reconciler in times of strife, and to gather the family for important occasions. When anyone was hurting, she was there to offer a healing touch. When important news had to be conveyed, she was the messenger. In addition to these maternal functions, she also took her role as my godmother very seriously. When I was young she took a special interest in my activities. In recent years she came with her husband to Sunday Mass at our university parish, often offering me words of encouragement. I believe that the prayers she offered regularly for me strengthened me and aided my ministry.

Mildred was a community builder who performed her good deeds with a quiet sense of dedication. Her activities never made headlines and her goodness was often taken for granted. In this regard, she was like many other good people who nurture and reconcile without receiving much recognition.

Holy Week provides an opportunity for reflection on the goodness and importance of such community builders. The death and resurrection of Jesus illumines the essential meaning of their genuine love. The interplay between Good Friday and Easter Sunday helps us interpret the significance of their lives of unselfish service. The Pascal Mystery which celebrates the emergence of new life from death prompts us not only to celebrate their contributions, but to face the pain of their absence now or in the future.

The death of a loved one always produces a sense of loss. But the distinctive character of this sense of loss is shaped by the expectations we had of the deceased person. We miss them and what they contributed to our relationship. When the communicators and reconcilers drop from our ranks, we sense a new threat to the life of the community. When those who exercise maternal care die, loved ones feel newly exposed to the harshness of life. When the nourishers no longer walk with us, we feel deprived and weakened. When a beloved spouse or lifelong friend dies, life can seem oppressive and even pointless.

The Gospel suggests that the death of Jesus produced such initial reactions among his disciples. The one who had gathered and supported them was gone. The one who cared for the outcasts and sought out the estranged was crucified. The disciples were hurt and confused. They were uprooted and at loose ends. The great dream of establishing the new Israel and building the kingdom of love was destroyed. Fear brought them together in the upper room, but the real head and heart of their community had been lost. The poignant story of the two disciples on the road to Emmaus vividly portrays this sense of loss and disappointment (Lk. 34). Fleeing Jerusalem in fear, they poured out their despair and frustration to a stranger, culminating in their sad statement of disappointment: "We were hoping that he was the one who would set Israel free."

This dark side of the Christian story encourages us to face our fears and disappointments. Good Friday cannot be glossed over in a compulsive quest for instant Easter joy. The loss of the reconcilers is especially frightening and painful. We are vulnerable in a new way. Some deep instinct to preserve, to root, to achieve solidarity is threatened. We repress such terrors at our own peril.

But for us Christians, the story cannot end with Good Friday. There is more to be said about the two disciples on the road to Emmaus. A piety which cannot get beyond the horrible sufferings of Jesus on the cross is in danger of falling into a destructive masochism. The Apostle Paul gave us a more balanced outlook by insisting that we must not grieve like those who have no hope (1 Thess. 4:13). This hope is founded on the resurrection of Christ. The man Jesus, who was crucified, has been raised to life and constituted as the Lord. The story does not end with Calvary. There are reports of an empty tomb. The risen Christ appears to Peter and 500 of his disciples. There are marvelous accounts of the Lord encountering Mary Magdalene and Thomas, the doubting twin. He appears to the disciples in the upper room in Jerusalem and eats meals with them on the shores of the sea of Tiberias in Galilee. The stranger on the road to Emmaus turns out to be Jesus himself. He dispels their confusion and ignites their hearts by his explanation of the Scriptures. They come to recognize him in the breaking of the bread and hurry back to Jerusalem to share the good news with the other disciples.

The stories of the empty tomb and the appearances of the risen Lord reveal the deepest meaning of life. They point to the most important truth: Jesus has been raised to new life by the Father. Resurrection is the key to understanding the New Testament and the whole of salvation history. It teaches us that God's justice will ultimately prevail in the world and that the demonic forces will be defeated. Jesus is revealed as the savior of the whole human family. His claim to be the bringer of the kingdom has been validated. His cause of building the community of love has been vindicated. The final triumph of the kingdom is assured. Love is stronger than all sin and the light is more powerful than all darkness. At the end time, God will be all in all.

The resurrection speaks not only of the fate of Jesus and the future establishment of the kingdom, but also inspires the community life of his followers on earth. The presence of the Spirit in the community confirms the claim that Jesus is the risen Lord. Christians now walk in the Spirit and partake of the new life won by Christ. The followers of Jesus did not seek out a new leader to take his place, but gathered around his abiding presence. Their solidarity in love was to be a sign to others that the new creation had begun and would one day be completed. The body of the risen Christ, which is destined to reach its fullness at the end time, is being formed now. Good Friday devastated the community of disciples. Easter Sunday began the process of reconstituting the community in the power of the Spirit. Sin sows disharmony; the grace of resurrection seeks to gather the whole human family into a community of love.

Thus the resurrection helps us to understand the deeper significance of the life of my godmother and all those who work to reconcile and hold together. They are doing the work of the Spirit whether they recognize this or not. The energy they expend in communicating and gathering is never wasted, but becomes part of the great project of building the kingdom of love. The concrete results of their efforts – family harmony, improved communications, healed wounds, energized individuals – all serve as indications that the risen Christ is still active in the world and that his spirit is indeed life-giving.

It is surely proper to grieve over the loss of the community builders when they pass to the richer life of heaven and join the expanding family of God. A resurrection-inspired hope, however, prompts us to transcend grief by learning from their example and carrying on their cause. We offer fitting tribute to them by expanding our own peacemaking efforts. We honor their memory by forming genuine communities built on self-sacrifice and unselfish giving. Pursuing this mission of reconciliation, we will come to know in a new way the true meaning of the death and resurrection of Jesus Christ. It is not merely an event remembered during a holy week once a year, but a living reality which provides illumination and energy for living well all the weeks of our lives.

11. Honoring a Peacemaker

In the book, *Peace Heroes in Twentieth Century America*, the editor, Dr. Charles DeBenedetti, lauded individuals "of conscience and purpose who decided to act at the risk of being wrong for what they believed was the greater good in living peace." These peace heroes were persons of hope who aspired not to power but to purpose. Borrowing a phrase, Dr. DeBenedetti described them as progenitors of "the party of humanity," an association of leaders who would move beyond nationalistic concerns and consider the well-being of the whole human family. These leaders would "depict and communicate accurately the nature and gravity of the global crisis, propose possible solutions, promulgate an inclusive sense of human solidarity, and, most of all, inspire a sense of hope that humankind might yet prevail."

The author of these insightful and inspiring words died January 27, 1987, on his forty-fourth birthday. For me and for many others, Charles DeBenedetti was himself a contemporary peace hero. As a professor of history at the University of Toledo in Ohio and author of three books, he combined extensive research with dedicated classroom teaching in his effort to further the cause of peace. His search for grassroots solutions moved him to help found the Interfaith Justice and Peace Center in Toledo, which continues to be a powerful influence for good in our area. His passion for peace thrust him out of the classroom into the world of marches, rallies and protests where he acted with both courage and intelligence. Throughout his all too brief academic career, he spoke out against the dangers of nationalism while finding his own natural home in "the party of humanity." Upon his death, the amazing outpouring of tributes testified in a graphic way to the sense of hope that he often inspired in others. Using his own criteria, we can count him among our local peace heroes.

But there is a deeper story to tell. It is the inner story of energy and motivation, of purpose and commitment, of courage and hope. At his private funeral Mass, elements of his story unfolded during the dialogue homily as members of his family spoke emotionally of their personal remembrances of the man they loved. His son recounted that, in the midst of his father's twelve- to fourteen-hour working days, he still found time to play catch with him in the front yard. Relatives described his tolerant easy-going nature, as well as his constant efforts to reconcile differences among family members and friends. A man who had drawn great inspiration from one of Chuck's books publicly dedicated himself to living out the Gospel ideals of peacemaking. His mother asked us all to continue to pray for her deceased son, while warning us not to canonize him yet – a moving reminder that even peace heroes have feet of clay and that a man can be a source of inspiration without being perfect.

Chuck and I were friends, fellow searchers and spiritual companions on the journey. It was one of the great privileges of my life to catch glimpses of the soul of this impressive man and to learn something of the mysterious well-springs of his encompassing dedication to peace. Periodically, over the course of a couple of years, we searched together for ways to manage our time, to integrate our commitments to projects and to persons and to deal with our personal limitations. In this process, we probed the meaning of the Agony in the Garden endured by Jesus. The real source of his pain, we agreed, was not so much his imminent death, but his failed mission. Totally dedicated to establishing the reign of peace and justice, Jesus sensed that his life-project was being thwarted. With death approaching, his whole mission was in shambles, his life-work still incomplete. The leaders rejected him and even his own disciples often failed to understand his message. In this situation, Jesus protested against the limits placed on his work. If possible, give me more time. "Let this chalice pass from me." But then he uttered the words which reveal the secret of his person as well as the power of his mission: "Not my will but thine be done." He placed the great cause in his Father's hands and then rested secure. Chuck and I talked about the wisdom contained in this account, as well as the tremendous challenge of appropriating and applying it.

On Friday, October 10, at 11 a.m., Chuck's daughter called me from the hospital. Her father had just been diagnosed as having an inoperable brain tumor. Seldom since my father's death seven years previous had I felt so emotionally bludgeoned. I went to the hospital to offer presence and prayer. I managed only presence as uncontrollable sobbing took me over. Grasping my hand, Chuck spoke simply but profoundly: "It is all right; it is in the hands of God." He went on to remind me of our meditation on the Agony in the Garden. The peacemaker ministered to the priest in what remains for me a significant moment of grace.

During the ensuing months, as his brilliant eloquence gradually gave way to a frustrating stammer, we had occasion to discuss the great challenges involved in facing death, transforming anger, accepting limitations and finding meaning in life. With his passion for peace still intact, he asked that I speak on the topic of peacemaking at his memorial service. I assured him that I would try to be faithful to his request as well as to his ideals. As the days went on, it was more difficult to communicate. His last words to me were, "I want to die" – a statement which seemed to me to reflect acceptance and faith. Throughout, he most treasured the intimacy and love of his family, which helped sustain him until he eventually handed over his spirit.

The many tributes at the public memorial service on our campus were not only moving, but revealed a new dimension of Chuck's personality and work. In trying to meet my commitment to a dying friend, it was not possible for me to divorce the theme of peacemaking from the man of peace, or to separate the cause from his personal witness. It seemed important that my public comments offer others a glimpse of the soul of this dedicated peacemaker.

Peacemaking was woven into the most fundamental patterns of his life. His public efforts on behalf of world peace were a natural extension of his quest for harmony in his personal relationships. His own inner peace, which appeared as both a free gift and the fruit of struggle, gave form and substance to his peace-making efforts. He lived out a simple faith which provided both an overarching framework and a profound motivation for his great outpouring of energy. His peacemaking role was solidly rooted in religious convictions and principles. He participated regularly in the Eucharist, finding nourishment in both the Gospel of peace and the sacred meal of reconciliation. Commitment to the cause of justice and peace was for him a constituent element of his Christian faith. Without making a saint out of my friend, it seems to me that his effective advocacy for peace was rooted in an uncommon degree of personal integration. He combined passion with intelligence, faith with scholarship, and personal dedication with global awareness. Although the well-springs of his personality and character remain shrouded in mystery, the importance of his personal faith shines through clearly.

His active life not only presents us with a model of wholeness, but also challenges us to rededicate ourselves to the cause of peace. His sad and untimely death raises profound questions and prompts a search for comprehensive answers. In the midst of grief and questioning, we Christians recall the saying of Jesus, "Blessed are the peacemakers." The goodness of the peacemakers lives on and their cause will one day triumph. The peace heroes, like Charles DeBenedetti, are in the hands of the God who finally wipes away every tear and ultimately establishes the reign of justice and peace.

11. Celebrating the Life of a Compassionate Priest

Fr. Ron Kurth, priest of the Toledo diocese, pastor of St. Ann Parish, advocate for the poor and dispossessed, died at the too early age of forty-nine. Two scenes dominate my memory of him. The first occurred when he gave a talk on prison reform to a group of collegians and some faculty members at

Bowling Green State University in the late 1970s. His passion for the topic was obvious. He was incensed about the horrible conditions at the Reformatory in Mansfield, Ohio. His talk drew on his personal contact with many prisoners over the years and included a slide presentation of photographs illegally taken inside the Mansfield Reformatory. He showed them for the first time on that occasion even though he had been tipped off that state officials would be in the audience. He had confided to me ahead of time that it was worth the risk since raising public awareness on the conditions in the reformatory was absolutely essential to getting the facility closed down. During the discussion period, one state official voiced strong criticism of Ron's presentation, claiming that he had exaggerated the situation at Mansfield. He also castigated him for using the illegal slides. This challenge seemed to drive Ron to a new level of intensity. Red-faced and newly energized, he thundered against a prison system which did little to rehabilitate prisoners and a great deal to dehumanize them. With his great courage and conviction, Ron reminded me that evening of the Biblical prophets who spoke out against the injustices of their own time.

The other scene fixed in my memory occurred about three weeks before his death, while he was still struggling with the cancer which eventually took his life. One evening he asked me to come to visit him at the rectory where he was enjoying the marvelous hospitality of the pastor as well as the tender love of friends and the enlightened care of the hospice nurses. With a surprising surge of energy which belied his haggard face and wasted body, he met me at the door, ushered me to a private spot, and discussed with me for almost an hour matters of deepest concern – living the faith, facing death, and especially working for justice. Demonstrating the same passion which had shaped his whole priestly life, he spoke of the importance of caring for the poor and oppressed in our world. We discussed the need for a strong and persevering faith in pursuing the work of social justice which so often proves to be frustrating. He described to me with evident satisfaction the growing network in our area of persons committed to the social apostolate. He insisted that the liturgy holds the network together, energizing those dedicated to a life of active charity. His concern was to enable more people to experience the joys and satisfactions which accompany a life lived in service to those in need. He spoke easily and naturally about the impact of Jesus Christ on his life. For him, Jesus was the one who went about doing good for others despite the consequences. His dominant image of Christ was taken from Chapter 25 of Matthew's Gospel where Jesus identifies himself with the suffering and oppressed. It was evident to me that this conviction was at the core of Ron's very being. His dedication to Jesus Christ was the fuel for his ministry, the source of the passion which drove him to give of himself so generously. The image of Jesus Christ the Liberator had fired his imagination, directing him to a life of freeing others.

Near the end of our conversation, he asked me if I would say a few words at his funeral, stressing the need for greater involvement in the work for social justice. It was important to him that the funeral proclaim in word and symbol his lifelong commitment to the poor and oppressed. With a great sense of privilege, I quickly agreed to his request. After chatting about the content of my reflections, we prayed for each other. His prayer for me and my ministry felt like a solemn commissioning. My immediate spontaneous reaction was that I had received a new and heavy responsibility to proclaim the message of social justice not only at the funeral Mass, but also in other unknown situations in the future.

I had come to give comfort to a dying priest and in the process had received new inspiration and energy. It was a privileged encounter with a man whose body was failing, but whose spirit was still strong and vibrant. I will always treasure that moment. It is easy for me to interpret the whole event as a manifestation and gift of the Spirit. Many others who encountered Ron during his long dying process found themselves moved in similar ways. The pastor, who provided warm hospitality for him, told me, with deep feeling, that he considered it a privilege to help care for such a dedicated man. A hospice nurse who helped keep him alert and comfortable during his last months spoke of his amazing inner vitality. Friends who came to offer solace often left feeling blessed in a new and very personal way. Confidants, who knew well his faults and weaknesses, became even more impressed with his deep commitment and genuine compassion. Ron Kurth remained until the very end, the priest ministering to others.

At the funeral, I carried out my charge by relating our search for comfort in the midst of grief to the story of Jesus Christ the Liberator. After his temptations in the desert, as Luke tells the story in the fourth chapter of his Gospel, Jesus, moved by the Spirit, returned to Nazareth, his hometown. Attending the synagogue on the Sabbath, as was his custom, he opened the scroll presented to him by the director and read a passage which included the phrase: "He has sent me to bring the good news to the poor, to proclaim liberty to the captives . . . to set the downtrodden free." Sitting down, Jesus identified himself and his mission with this passage by noting, "This text is being fulfilled today even as you listen."

As Jesus preached in his inaugural homily, so he lived throughout his life. He was especially attentive to the oppressed without neglecting the others. He proclaimed the poor, hungry and sorrowing to be blessed. Breaking social taboos, he spoke with women in public and included them in religious discussions. After curing the lepers, he sent them to the priest so that they could be reintroduced into the mainstream of society. Individuals imprisoned in their sins and preoccupied with their own problems were liberated by their encounters with Jesus.

In every age, the story of Jesus Christ the Liberator has captured the imagination of some Christians, usually a committed minority. Today the ranks are growing of those who appreciate the social dimension of the Gospel. They realize that sins affect institutions, producing patterns of discrimination. For them, liturgy can never be isolated from life, but must energize us in the struggle for the liberation of all. They realize that if we want peace, we must work for justice. Their dominant sense of the Christian life is shaped by Jesus who reached out to those on the margins of society and identified himself with the suffering.

At that point in my reflections, I informed the congregation crowded into St. Ann Church that I had shared this vision of the social Gospel at the solemn request of the dying priest whom they had come to honor. I quickly added that it was my privilege to do so because for me and many, Fr. Ron Kurth represented a life of commitment to the ideals of Jesus Christ the Liberator. With feet of clay but with undoubted passion, he remained faithful throughout a life of active commitment to the task of preaching the good news to the poor and liberating captives.

After the funeral I continued to reflect on the wider significance of my privileged encounter with a dying friend. Shortly afterward I used some of his ideas in my homily on the feast of Christ the King, which celebrates the triumph of a life devoted to compassionate service. A few months later I retold his story to members of the Hospice Movement, emphasizing the importance of faith in facing the reality of death. In the year of his death my Advent preaching included more attention to the liberation themes built into this season which prepares for the birth of the Prince of Peace.

Ron's influence on many of us in the Toledo diocese continues. Friends set up a lecture series in his honor for discussing the work of peace and justice. It provides an annual opportunity to reflect again on the causes which Ron represented with such passion and courage.

We all know individuals like Father Ron Kurth who demonstrate genuine compassion while working for peace and justice. My hope is that recounting his particular story will alert us all to the importance and value of these good persons who live out the ideals of Jesus Christ the Liberator. We do not have to make saints of them nor inflate their importance to discern the liberating power of the Spirit working in and through them. They remind all of us that working for justice is an essential component of the Christian life.

12. John Savage: a Profile of Practical Charity

He was uncharacteristically late for our breakfast meeting. We did not want to start without him because he was a key strategist in planning our campaign to raise funds for campus ministry at the University of Toledo. A few minutes later, John Savage, one of the most respected men in Northwest Ohio, walked in with a flourish, a stranger at his side. He sat the young man down at the table and quickly called the waitress over to take his order for breakfast. Adopting a typical academic tone, he then began to explain the situation to us. On the way to the restaurant he had picked up this Korean graduate student from Michigan State, whose car had stalled on the highway. The young man had to get back to East Lansing in a hurry for an important class. We had to figure out how to help him, John insisted. As we began to discuss the possibilities, John suddenly reached in his pocket, took out his car keys, and handed them to the young man, saying, "You take my car, drive up to East Lansing and teach your class. I will get your car fixed for you, and then you drive back to Toledo and we will exchange cars." At this point, the Korean student looked at me and said: "Why is he doing this?" And before I could answer, John said in a matter-of-fact tone, "Because I am a Christian."

It is a marvelous story which I often tell in greater detail. I repeat it here with special poignancy. John Savage died on February 8, 1993, at the age of sixty-two. For almost five years he had fought courageously against serious illnesses. Each extra day granted him, he counted a miraculous gift. Finally, even his optimistic spirit, which, according to a mutual friend, made Norman Vincent Peale look like a pessimist, could no longer counter the effects of acute leukemia. In his dying as in his life, John authored a story filled with inspiration and hope. It merits review and invites reflection.

John grew up in Toledo, Ohio, one of nine children in a deeply religious, hard-working Catholic family. As a young man, he encountered Msgr. Jerome Schmit, a highly-respected local priest, who helped him transform some of his more selfish tendencies into a genuine care for others. After graduating from the University of Toledo in 1952, John began his life of service as a high school teacher and basketball coach. After spending four years at his alma mater, Central Catholic High School, he founded, along with his brother, Bob, an extremely successful financial services firm. His personal success in the business world enabled him to multiply his contributions to society and his charity to others. He served on the boards of many companies, often combining his shrewd financial insights with principled ethical considerations. He wrote three books and lectured widely in the United States, as well as twenty other countries. People came to his talks expecting advice on managing money and improving sales techniques, but often went away with even more: renewed hope, greater confidence and a fresh challenge to reflect on their personal values, family obligations, societal responsibilities and religious commitments. John contributed generously to over sixty charities and directed or assisted in numerous fund-raising drives, including a $10 million project for a basketball and concert arena at the University of Toledo, which now bears his name. His most significant contributions, however, did not make the headlines. He formed a loving, committed partnership with his wife, Kate, and was wise enough to trust her instincts in raising their nine children. With refreshing candor he challenged those he loved to move beyond self-centeredness toward a life of service. Untold numbers benefited from his care: a word of encouragement to a despondent employee; a bit of thoughtful advice to a client; financial help to friends as well as strangers in need. I run into people all the time who tell me about the positive impact John had on them personally. His wife, Kate, was overwhelmed by the vast numbers who came to the funeral home and told her some little story of how John had helped them. Indeed, his finest moments were off center stage.

Even a brief glance at the life of John Savage sharpens and enlarges the question posed by the Korean student, "Why is he doing this?" What made him tick? Whence came his wisdom and strength? What wellsprings nourished his optimistic spirit? What moves a person to a life of generous service? Why reach out to the less fortunate? Why care about the common good?

In responding to these questions, we must explore John's own answer, "Because I am a Christian." It is at once honest, intriguing, profound and deceptively simple. We are immediately struck by the countercultural character of his response and his general approach to life. The individualism rampant in our culture bombards us with the message that we are autonomous creatures, responsible for our own happiness and well-being. Our society rewards self-sufficient individuals who can manage business affairs effectively, but it has trouble figuring out how to help those who are less fortunate and more vulnerable. Popular psychology tells us that the sky is the limit if we just learn to pull our own strings and do our own thing. The advertising world insists that having material things and acquiring more goods is the way to fulfillment and happiness. John Savage had a clear and profound understanding of the seductive power of individualism and consumerism. He was convinced that such selfishness is a major cause of depression and that caring for others is a matchless remedy.

John was less engaged with challenges to his own religious convictions. He did not take seriously any of the modern criticisms of religion, including Marx's strident claim that religion is an opiate, Nietzsche's radical suggestion that Christian charity is really a dehumanizing weakness and Freud's sweeping charge that religion keeps believers in an infantile state. Postmodern denials of normative standards for truth and goodness made no sense to him. In the midst of a serious discussion I once told John that he seemed unaffected by contemporary criticisms of faith and that he did indeed have a very simple theology. He replied, "I don't have any theology, I have a simple faith." Doubt was not part of John's religious vocabulary, even when he experienced terrible tragedies and intense personal suffering. No matter what the situation, his often repeated response was, "Remember, God is in charge."

Even within the community of faith, John's behavior seems strange or odd. Most Christians do not pick up strangers on the highway and offer them use of their car. Taking the Gospel that literally offends middle class values and violates common sense norms about personal safety. Even serious disciples of Christ might ask, "Why did you go to such extremes to help the Korean student?"

My answer to that question is that John Savage found his own radical way of appropriating the Gospel. He got to the essence of the message and made it his own. His intuitive faith enabled him to see the core of Christian wisdom and to live it out consistently in his everyday life. Sociologically, Christianity appears as a complex symbol system composed of creeds, dogmas, sacraments and other diverse institutional elements. But at a deeper level it is a total way of life, an integrated faith which coheres around dedication to Jesus Christ and his teachings. It is a comprehensive response to the deepest longings of the human heart. Christianity is a humanism which liberates persons to flourish and to contribute to the common good. John found the secret to life in his traditional Catholic faith. Before he went into the hospital the last time, I asked him about his deepest convictions, the wisdom he lived by, the core of his own faith. He understood that I was inviting him into that uncharted region called theology, but he shared his thoughts anyway. Speaking thoughtfully and very personally, he said the key word for him is "giving." Christianity calls us to give generously to others. He took seriously the words of Jesus quoted in Acts 20:35: "There is more happiness in giving than in receiving." For him, Paul's teaching that "God loves a cheerful giver" was confirmed by common experience (2 Cor. 9:7). Practical charity was his entry point into the core of the Christian message. Giving to others, especially those in need, was for him a fundamental way of following Christ. Love of neighbor and love of God were essentially connected in his mind and heart. He loved long church services and had a rich devotional life centered on the Blessed Virgin. His favorite charity was the work of the church in the central city of Toledo. For him prayer and compassion naturally went together. His last words to his wife Kate were "I love you; I love God." Authentic believers follow various routes to the center of the Gospel. John

Savage found a path which enabled him to serve others and contribute to society while placing the whole exciting journey in God's hands. This was his secret, the wisdom that guided him and the wellspring that energized him.

In his active life of charity, John often gave to others spontaneously and generously without much thought or investigation. In some situations, however, his head ruled his heart. He often said that he did not want to give his children any money. He wanted them to learn to work for it as he had. At the same time, he desperately wanted to hand on to them the Catholic heritage he treasured and the wisdom he had accumulated. In my presence, he offered one of his sons some final advice, summed up in one of the many aphorisms he constantly employed: "Remember that no success in your career can make up for a failure at home." Giving to his children meant imparting values, not doling out money.

John Savage was a human being, like all of us, with faults and failings. We do not have to make exaggerated claims of his sanctity in order to learn from him. At his best, John reveals the liberating power of Christianity and makes the wisdom of the Gospel credible. His life of giving and service exposes the limitations of individualism and consumerism. His radically hopeful spirit and his constructive contributions to society serve as a striking refutation of the influential critics who claim religion is dehumanizing. The life of John Savage challenges all of us to continue our own journey to the center of the Gospel and to live out the message wholeheartedly.

13. The Murder of a Student

The bleakness of late January turned even more foreboding as the tragic story quickly spread through the University of Toledo campus. Melissa Anne Herstrum, an attractive, popular sophomore nursing student, had been murdered in an especially brutal fashion. The type of violence we associate with urban gangs had invaded our serene campus. Our academic community, dedicated to reasoned discourse, was forced to face the kind of senseless, irrational brutality experienced all too frequently by the oppressed of the world. A flood of diverse emotions broke through the black pall thrown over the campus: fear that the killer would strike again; empathy for Melissa's parents and family; a searing sense of loss among her close friends, especially her Pi Beta Phi sorority sisters; disgust over the brutality of the crime; and rage over the injustice of it all. Many felt a vague anxiety, as if the foundation had been shaken or the bottom had dropped out. The world simply was not as safe or secure as it had been. The tragedy triggered new questions for some and revived familiar, unresolved questions for others. What meaning does life have when it can be snuffed out so easily? How can a loving God allow such evil? Can a world haunted by irrational violence still make sense? How are we to cope with the senseless death of Melissa, a young woman filled with such great potential?

That evening I went over to Melissa's sorority house on campus. My purpose was simply to offer presence and whatever support and comfort might be possible. I knew that there were no easy answers to the questions tearing at the hearts of her sorority sisters.

The grief in the house was palpable. Some of the university counselors, who did such a magnificent job attending to the emotional needs of students throughout the tragedy, had just left. I asked a couple of the young women if they wanted to pray together. They thought that was a good idea and began rounding up some of the others in the house. Before long over thirty of the sorority sisters had joined us. After an opening prayer, I read some psalms and the passage from Matthew 11 in which Jesus promises refreshment and rest for those weary and burdened. Commenting on the readings, I noted that the Jesus who claimed his burden was light did not provide any theoretical answers to the mystery of suffering. The Gospels offer no adequate explanation of why Melissa has suffered this cruel fate. Christians dare not engage in glib talk about tragedy and its causes.

I did tell the young women about my own period of deep pain when my father died many years ago. Then a wrenching grief and a disorienting sense of loss threatened to engulf my spirit. Through the pain, I learned about the uniqueness of the grieving process and the great importance of facing all of our negative emotions. There is a time to grieve deeply and thoroughly, feeling the pain in all its intensity; and then there is a time to struggle to rise above it by returning to our duties, meeting our responsibilities and getting our mind on other things. This difficult alternating process usually needs repeating, but it is far better than suffering through an extended period of low-grade grieving in which one never really faces the pain or really rises above it.

After these well-intentioned but feeble words, I asked the women if they wanted to say anything. It proved to be a moment of grace and a sign of hope for me and, I believe, for others. Out of their deep pain, some of Melissa's friends spoke words of uncommon wisdom which pressed toward constructive action.

One person spoke openly of her deep sadness and intense rage over the brutality of it all, the senseless cruelty of fourteen shots decimating her friend's body. The starkness of the comment produced the shock of reality. Melissa was dead. Dark forces assail the human family. Demonic powers named greed, hatred, domination and violence roam the world seeking victims. The image of cruel brutality opened a floodgate of emotion. I could only guess at the feelings behind the tears: rage at the killer; sadness over the loss; protest against God; anxiety over suffering; empathy for Melissa. Those who want to repress tears or even anger at God have missed the message of the psalms as well as the call for self-acceptance at the center of Christian spirituality. The release of uncensored emotion in the sorority house that evening struck me as a liberating grace. It provided space for individuals to express grief and also united the group in a deeper bond of solidarity.

As some of the emotion subsided, one of Melissa's close friends offered simple but wise advice: "We have to love one another now. We must support each other more than ever now." Indeed! When tragedy strikes it is good for us humans to huddle together. At those moments we know we are not really autonomous individuals who can make it on our own. We are social creatures, interdependent persons who were made for companionship. Love, which involves mutual giving and receiving, is what binds us together. Community happens when we work and celebrate together, but also when we cry and suffer together. Shared vulnerability often forges bonds of human solidarity with surprising depth and strength. A comforting touch which pierces our suffering is treasured and long remembered. Love which is always our calling and task is focused and directed by need and suffering. It is true: tragedy calls us to greater love and support.

This kind of extra effort at human love and care was much in evidence on our campus in the weeks following Melissa's death. President Frank Horton connected with students through his supportive presence and especially through his deeply empathetic comments at the tasteful university memorial service conducted by the Protestant chaplain, Glenn Hosman. Vice President David Meabon and other leaders in the Division of Student Affairs gave long hours of compassionate service to bring calm, order and direction to a chaotic situation. Counselors used their skills to help students deal with grief and anxiety. Individual professors and staff members offered assistance. All these good people functioned more like ministers with a vocation than employees with a job. Students also came together in mutual solidarity. Fraternities, sororities and other student groups demonstrated support for Melissa's sisters in Pi Beta Phi sorority. Religious groups offered special prayers for those hurting most. The usual tensions and divisions which characterize the academic community gave way to a greater sense of tolerance and care as we all grappled with the mystery of a violent and untimely death.

As the sorority sisters affirmed the call for greater love among themselves, one of their leaders offered another sage comment: "As bad as we feel," she said, "we have to remember that Melissa's parents feel a million times worse." Insightful words with practical import.

In any situation it is possible to think of others who are worse off; and it is often healthy to do so. One of the best ways of dealing with grief is to turn our attention to helping others. In response to the leader's comment, I told them about a very close lifelong friend of mine who had to bury his collegiate son after he died in a tragic accident. The victim's fraternity brothers all attended the funeral and many came up to my friend and his wife to say some complimentary things about their son. It meant a great deal to them and brought some measure of comfort. Subsequent comments by the sorority sisters indicated that they were not only going to attend Melissa's funeral in Rocky River, Ohio, but were also taking on the responsibility of supporting her parents, who were suffering "a million times worse."

The final comment in our group dialogue which struck me forcefully was the simple faith-filled affirmation that Melissa is in heaven now and suffers no more. The comment brought back the essential teachings of Christianity. Jesus Christ, representing the whole human race, handed himself over completely in death to the one he addressed as Abba and therefore was raised to a new and richer life which he shares with us. According to biblical imagery, he has gone before us to prepare a place for us where every tear will be wiped away. By passing through death we arrive at the heavenly Jerusalem where we enjoy the company of the saints and share in the heavenly banquet. In other words, death brings us a final fulfillment of the deepest longings of our hearts in ways beyond imagination. It is this hope for our loved ones that sustains believers throughout the grieving process. Death cannot ultimately destroy the bonds of love. Even those who die young find eternal life.

As our discussion came to a close, we began to talk about the possibility of a memorial Mass for Melissa. A number of the students quickly took hold. They picked a time and date and began writing down music suggestions and possible readings. A communion distributor said she would get other distributors to help her. A couple of people volunteered to read. They were now wholeheartedly engaged in a project to honor their friend and to deal constructively with their grief. The uncommon wisdom I discerned in their comments was now taking concrete form.

The Mass they planned drew an overflow crowd. Their personal involvement and touches gave it special poignancy. The liturgy extended the moment of grace I experienced in the sorority house and made it available to others. I believe it functioned for many as a sign of hope and a source of consolation in the midst of the dark tragedy which struck our campus and pierced the hearts of those who cared most for Melissa Herstrum.

14. Cardinal Bernardin: Befriending Death

Cardinal Joseph Bernardin, the archbishop of Chicago, died on November 14, 1996, at the age of sixty-eight. His biographer, Eugene Kennedy, called him "the most influential bishop in the history of the American church." He served as a courageous and credible spokesman for the Catholic community, especially by developing and applying the consistent ethic of life to a variety of controversial issues, ranging from nuclear weapons and welfare reform to assisted suicide and abortion. His public witness was strengthened by his own efforts to live the Gospel he preached. For example, he spent the first hour of his busy days in prayer; he visited his aging mother every day he was home in Chicago; he forgave the man who falsely accused him of sexual abuse; he took time to comfort fellow cancer patients during the last months of his life; and near the end, he spoke openly about embracing death as a friend carrying him to eternal life.

One of Cardinal Bernardin's most important initiatives became public on August 12, 1996, when he announced the formation of the Catholic Common Ground Project, which will sponsor a series of conferences designed to promote dialogue and overcome the polarization which threatens the Catholic Church and weakens its service to the world.

Work on this project first began in December of 1992 at a meeting in Detroit organized by Fr. Phil Murnion, head of the National Pastoral Life Center in New York. I was privileged to attend this meeting with the Cardinal and to be part of a group of about twenty people which has continued to meet twice a year. We eventually produced a document entitled "Called to Be Catholic: Church in a Time of Peril," which Cardinal Bernardin made public at his press conference on August 12. The statement begins by recognizing that polarization has placed the American Catholic Church in a perilous situation, inhibiting discussion, crippling leadership, confusing young people and magnifying fears. If the church is to respond effectively to the challenge of the contemporary world, it must openly and honestly discuss urgent issues, such as the changing roles of women, the meaning of human sexuality, religious illiteracy, liturgical renewal, the role of the church in political life and the relationship between Rome and the American episcopacy. To overcome the partisanship and paralysis engendered by polarization, we must rediscover our common ground "centered on faith in Jesus, marked by accountability to the living Catholic tradition, and ruled by a renewed spirit of civility, dialogue, generosity, and broad and serious consultation." Accountability to the Catholic tradition does not mean reversion to a rigid bureaucratic model of the church, nor does it rule out "legitimate debate, discussion and diversity." It does make demands on all Catholics to accept the church in all its "humanness" as a mysterious communion which foreshadows the Kingdom; to engage seriously the tradition and its authoritative representatives; and to recognize that there are boundaries which circumscribe Catholic identity, even though their formulation may at times be open to reexamination and debate. Accountability implies that church leadership engages in "wide and serious consultation," remembering that "all the faithful have a role in grasping a truth or incorporating a decision or practice into the church's life."

Effective dialogue on divisive issues requires "fresh eyes, open minds and changed hearts" as well as a willingness to abide by certain "working principles." No single group has a monopoly on the truth or the right to function as "a saving remnant" which spurns other Catholics as unenlightened. We should presume that those who hold different views are acting in good faith and should not impugn their motives or accuse them of disloyalty to the church. We do better to "put the best possible construction" on their positions, rather than trying to discredit them by emphasizing their weak points. In order to preserve the spirit of open dialogue, we must make sure that the liturgy serves not as a polarized battleground, but as a common ground which unites us. The statement ends on a hopeful note. By honestly confronting divisive issues and drawing on the charisms of all its members, "the whole church will be strengthened for its mission in the new millennium."

Cardinal Bernardin's Common Ground initiative clearly struck a nerve in the Catholic community. Many people communicated their gratitude to the Cardinal for expressing publicly some of their fears and hopes for the church. Bishop Anthony Pilla, President of the National Conference of Catholic Bishops, and Cardinal Mahoney of Los Angeles, responded favorably. The National Pastoral Life Center continues to receive numerous responses from individuals and groups around the country and the world wanting to know how they can implement the project at the local level.

Some of the strongest criticism came swiftly from Cardinals Bernard Law, James Hickey, Adam Maida and Anthony Bevilacqua. In essence, they rejected the call to dialogue about common ground found in "Called to Be Catholic." In separate statements, which are remarkably similar, they all insisted that the Church already possesses common ground in Scripture and tradition mediated through the binding teaching of the magisterium, and that the way to resolve our differences is through conversion and not dialogue which legitimates dissent.

In a written response to his critics, Cardinal Bernardin noted that the sharp criticism and immediate suspicion which greeted his "carefully framed" and "broadly supported" appeal for dialogue simply confirmed the importance of his initiative. He pointed out that "Called to Be Catholic" fully recognizes the primacy of Scripture and tradition and rejects any approach that ignores the magisterium of the church. It clearly affirms that Jesus Christ remains the normative focus of all we are and do.

While admitting the limitations and possible distortions of dialogue, the Cardinal repeated his conviction that the church today needs genuine dialogue which will help Catholics move beyond a destructive polarization and achieve greater unity by refocusing on "the fundamental principles and pastoral needs of the church." In no way does the document equate "the revitalized common ground" with the faith or call for a "least common denominator Catholicism." The goal, rather, is to create "a space of trust within boundaries" so that we can "learn to make our differences fruitful."

A couple of weeks before Cardinal Bernardin died, I wrote him a letter expressing my gratitude for the admirable way he represented the church in the public forum. I told him it was one of the great blessings of my life to have worked with him on the Common Ground Project. For me, he exemplified in his own life the high ideals envisioned by "Called to Be Catholic": open dialogue, broad consultation, principled tolerance, authentic conversion and fruitful collaboration – all solidly grounded in commitment to Christ and accountability to the Catholic heritage. He was also a politically astute leader, who carefully chose a broad based twenty-four member advisory committee to oversee the Common Ground Initiative. This helped insure the success of the March 1997 conference on the church and American culture, which modeled the kind of dialogue proposed in "Called to Be Catholic." As we await future developments, we can all honor the memory of Cardinal Joseph Bernardin by honestly facing the issues which divide us with fresh eyes, open minds and changed hearts.

15. Advice on Grieving

The grief on her face jumped out at me as I answered the door. The familiar surge of compassion added a bit of tenderness to my welcome. Susan told the story in spurts. Her boyfriend was in a car accident – killed instantly – others hurt also – just found out this morning – can't believe it – feel numb – don't know what to do. And then the agonizing question: "Why did this have to happen? He was so alive and they had such a future in front of them. Why?"

My experience told me it was time to listen and not to talk. The wrenching unanswerable question of "why" would have to wait. The important thing now was for her to face the grief and to verbalize some of her feelings. With encouragement and occasional questions, bits of the larger story came out. She told me about the history of the relationship, recent encounters with him and the last words they spoke. With flowing tears she described the total shock which struck her when she first heard the tragic news and the immense sadness which engulfed her now. In the midst of the grief, she was extremely grateful for the immediate support offered by her friends and very worried about the others who were injured.

Susan's story stirred my soul and released a great surge of empathy. I wanted to hold her and tell her that she could survive. But my feelings ranged beyond empathy for her. I was also recalling many other deaths of loved ones and friends. Susan probably did not realize that mere acquaintances of the deceased sometimes cry at the funeral home because they are reminded of the death of a loved one. But she could sense my deep feeling and it gave her some comfort and strength. It was not important or necessary to explain the origin of my more intense emotions. It was good enough that my empathy for her was genuine.

She raised the question of "why" once again. My mind silently rehearsed the classical and contemporary attempts to respond to this most vexing question. Augustine insisted that suffering and evil make sense from the higher perspective enjoyed by God. Even the worst of human tragedies are part of a divine plan that works for the good of everyone. A more contemporary approach was offered by Teilhard de Chardin who taught that suffering was an unavoidable reality in a material, evolving world groping toward its final fulfillment. But this was not the time for theological explanations, although they may be helpful to Susan in the future.

Our great teacher, Jesus, offered little by way of theoretical explanation of the problem of human suffering, beyond denying the popularly assumed connection between evil fortune and personal sin. In the revealing story about the man born blind, Jesus tells his disciples that the man's condition is not the result of his parents' sin or his own – a valuable teaching for all those who feel that their personal misfortunes are punishments from God for their sins. Although Jesus did not provide us with a comprehensive explanation of the problem of evil, he did give us inspiring examples of how he personally wrestled with the forces of evil. He cast out the demons and healed the sick. He courageously pursued his mission and obediently accepted his cross. He faced the darkness of death and commended his spirit to his Father. I tried to express all these theological thoughts to the young woman in a simple way: There are no good answers to the question of why. Not even Jesus explained that to us. But he did show us by example how to deal with the worst of suffering.

Reflecting on the life of Jesus turns the question from why to how. How do we cope with suffering, even the tragic death of a loved one. How do we keep ourselves going, face reality, gain perspective and deal constructively with grief? How do we bring faith into play when our world seems to be crumbling? Not why, but how.

Surprisingly, Susan was able to see this and openly asked for advice and direction. I knew that her grief would cloud her thinking, but I plunged in anyway. My instinct was to share with her what I had learned over the years about coping with grief. I wanted to draw on the experiences of the many people who shared their sufferings with me and told me how they handled the death of their loved ones. We are all joined together in the great struggle against the darkness of death. When our own moment of testing comes, we need support and guidance from those who have learned valuable lessons about the struggle. My desire was to gather up this collected wisdom and make it available to Susan.

My immediate advice was to stay active. Call her boyfriend's parents and try to offer comfort. Go to the wake, help plan the funeral and participate if possible. Offer to help clean out his apartment.

She should prepare herself to deal with the people who want to support her. Some will respect her unique grieving process and will provide genuine comfort; others will disappoint or aggravate her with glib answers or easy solutions. It helps to recall that many good people, especially her young friends, have not had much experience in dealing with death, and do not know how to act. Trying to make it easier for them is a good way of transforming her own grief.

Beyond surviving the next few days, Susan has to deal with her own intense and complex emotional responses. Her loss is real and permanent and sooner or later she must deal with this stark reality. She can anticipate experiencing numbness, denial, anger, depression, acceptance and peace; but perhaps not in the neat sequential packages that some claim. These feelings will probably co-exist, disappear, return and form various combinations. At particular times, one emotion might predominate, but the others will be lurking in the shadows. It would not be unusual for her to achieve an apparent victory over anger only to have it reappear suddenly and with surprising strength. The important thing is to stay in touch with these emotions, face them as they arise, and try to keep them in a proper perspective. The time will come when she should test whether her feelings are appropriate, perhaps seeking further advice if they seem out of proportion or unmanageable. A grieving widow once said to me, "It doesn't get any easier." A friend told me that occasions still arise when she has an intense longing to share good news with her father who has been deceased for over a decade. On the other hand, many persons find that time does indeed heal. The persistent sharp pain of loss gradually changes into a dull ache which only periodically breaks into consciousness. Trying to put these thoughts together, I reminded Susan that her emotions might fluctuate a great deal and suggested that we talk more about that in a couple weeks.

In the grieving process many people fall into the trap of living with a continuous, low-grade sense of sadness, without ever really experiencing the full intensity of the pain of loss and without getting back to a more normal mode of everyday living. It seems better to set aside particular times for concentrated grieving, which include intensifying the sadness and allowing the release of the deep emotions. These sessions should be followed by a determined effort to get on with life by seizing the opportunities of each day and enjoying the gifts of the moment. Susan will have to work out her own rhythms, but it is vital that she avoid that gray half-grieving attitude which never really faces the painful loss or ever quite transcends it. My capsule comment to her was: "Sometimes it helps to have a good cry and then concentrate as hard as possible on your work."

A healthy grieving process drives Christians back to the essentials of our faith. God so loved us that he sent the Son to bring us the fullness of life. Faithful to his mission, Jesus took on all the darkness of our existence, including death, and emerged the victor. Through his resurrection he has become for us the source of new life. Christ has gone ahead of us to prepare a place for us. His Spirit guides and strengthens us as we make our way toward the final boundary called death. Death is a passageway into the new and richer life of heaven. In the heavenly banquet there are no more tears. We who continue the journey on earth wait in expectant hope for the day when we will join our deceased loved ones in the final fulfillment of heaven.

Our fundamental creed includes belief in the Communion of Saints. We remain in solidarity with the good people who have gone before us into the new Jerusalem. The bonds of genuine love we shared with them cannot be broken by death. The relationship with our loved ones who have died has not been severed. It has been transformed and functions now in ways that remain mysterious. Some believers have a keen sense of the abiding presence of their deceased relatives. They feel their support and ask for their help. In this way they give expression to the common Christian conviction that the death and resurrection of Jesus has reunited the whole human family in the never-ending bonds of love.

In order to convey these essential Christian beliefs to Susan, I read the passage in the fourteenth chapter of John's

Gospel where Jesus speaks of returning to take us with him to his Father's house where there are many dwelling places. I prayed that she would find comfort in this poetic expression of our core beliefs. My hope was that this faith perspective would enable her to cope better with the grief she felt now and prepare her for our next conversation when we would talk more about long-term strategies for managing her sense of loss.

16. Inspiration from Grieving Parents

"I feel as though I have been preparing for this moment all my life." This was the poignant and revealing comment of Shelley Hoben after a memorial mass for her daughter Katie, a senior at the University of Toledo who had been killed the week before in a tragic automobile accident. A resident advisor and member of Pi Beta Phi sorority, Katie was very popular with various segments of the university community. Over 400 persons attended the memorial Mass held on campus. Reflecting the perceptions of her family and friends, I said in my homily that Katie had the marvelous gift of being able to turn tears into laughter. She encouraged people who were down, helped friends in need and generally brightened the lives of those around her. Katie was preparing to be a kindergarten teacher. Those who knew her best were convinced she would do a great job with young kids. She brought smiles to the faces of young and old alike. Turning tears into laughter was Katie Hoben's special gift, and during her all too brief time on this earth, she used it well.

Near the end of the Mass, Shelley and her husband, Charlie, addressed the assembly. He spoke directly to the collegians about the understandable tendency to rebel against the religious traditions of one's parents. He remembered his own struggles in that regard as well as those of his daughter, Katie. "But for myself," he went on to say, "it really would be impossible to face what I have in these last few days without knowing that Katie is now in God's hands." From personal experience he shared his conviction that in times of crisis

God is present as a source of strength. He concluded with the prayerful hope that we all be open to the gift of faith and learn to nurture it.

In her comments, Shelley realistically acknowledged the anger, frustration and deep sadness felt by many because Katie's promising life was cut short and she could not fulfill her dream of teaching youngsters. The grieving mother then offered a perspective suggested by a friend: even in her short life Katie had already been an effective teacher through her laughter, her kindness and her simple love of family and friends. She taught us that "we have tremendous powers to heal one another" when we heed the call of Jesus to love others as he loves us. After noting the great importance of a supportive community, Shelley expressed gratitude for the care manifested by many people at the University of Toledo: President Frank Horton and the Student Affairs staff who ministered so generously and effectively in the hours and days after the accident; the members of the Pi Phi sorority who organized the memorial Mass and managed once again, as they had when their sister Melissa Herstrum was killed, to support one another and to offer comfort to others; and the many students who sent notes and traveled to Columbus for the funeral. Shelley continued on a realistic note. Although she was now sustained in strength by the Spirit, she knew that in the coming months there would be "days without sunshine and nights without rest." On those occasions she would remember this gathering and draw strength from the memorial Mass.

After the liturgy, Charlie and Shelley continued to exemplify the faith and love they described with such deep conviction in their talks. They attended to each person who greeted them, often saying a personal word of comfort or gratitude to individual students. When the crowd dwindled, Shelley told me that this whole tragic event was the deepest spiritual experience of her life and that she felt as though she had spent her whole life preparing for it. Judging by the words and actions of these grieving parents, they must have prepared well. They are realistic about the pain of loss and the difficult process of grieving; but they remain hopeful that

Katie has gone to her reward, where all tears are turned to joy.

There is a profound truth in the notion that life is preparation. All of us are preparing for that inevitable event called death, which sets an ultimate boundary to our earthly journey. By our free decisions and actions we continually prepare ourselves for the next opportunity, great or small, that awaits us. By disciplining ourselves now, we prepare for the challenges and crises that the future surely brings. For Christians, life on earth has its deepest meaning as preparation for the life of heaven.

The question is how well we are preparing for the future challenges and opportunities built into human existence. It seems all too easy to sleepwalk through life. We can miss the essential link between preparation and performance. Poor decisions can close the doors of opportunity. Sin can blind us to possibilities for growth. Busyness can keep us from the important tasks of personal development and improved relationships. Shortsightedness can keep us from pursuing high ideals and lofty goals. Earthly cares can dominate our attention, distorting the dream of eternal life.

For Christians the season of Lent offers an annual opportunity to focus and intensify our preparations for a future open to divine grace. "Sound the trumpet, proclaim a fast, call an assembly, notify the congregation" says the prophet Joel. The apostle Paul adds "now is the acceptable time, now is the day of salvation." Lent challenges us to prepare for all the opportunities ahead of us. It calls for a disciplined effort and a clear game plan to ready us for the spiritual struggle. The season invites us to prayerful preparation for sharing in the death and resurrection of Jesus.

Traditionally, Christians have focused their Lenten penances around three Gospel practices: prayer, fasting and alms giving. All of these actions possess intrinsic value and have immediate significance; but they also help to prepare us for the continuing process of growth in the Christian life.

Prayer is at the heart of an authentic Lenten spirituality. Improving our prayer life during this season is great preparation for continued spiritual growth in all seasons of our lives.

In his classic work *Prayer*, the great twentieth-century Catholic theologian, Hans Urs von Balthasar, provides theological perspectives for developing a more contemplative spirit. We need to be supple and pliable in the hands of God, like clay in the hands of the potter. We must have a simple confidence that God is attentive to our prayers and responds to our needs, if not always in the way we would like. It is important to cultivate an attitude of habitual prayer by being alert in mind and heart to the presence of the Lord. Contemplation is nourished by listening to the word of God which echoes in the church and the world. The gracious God has already encompassed us with love even before we seek Him in prayer.

Balthasar also offers more specific advice for those seeking a deeper contemplative prayer life. Do not get bogged down in particular techniques, prescribed programs, or rigid patterns; but simply maintain a steady gaze on the glory of the Lord. Do not deliberately seek emotional highs or striking new insights. Even during dry periods persevere in prayer with a serene sense of acceptance. Use fewer words in prayer and spend more time simply resting in the presence of the Lord. Read the scriptures with an open heart rather than a critical mind. Meditate imaginatively on Jesus as depicted in the Gospel stories. Celebrate liturgy as an end in itself and not as a means of building community. Learn from the example of Mary who was open and receptive to the Word. Maintain a sense of awe and wonder before the glory of the true God revealed through Christ. A Lenten program which cultivates a contemplative spirit is great preparation for coping with the enduring pressures of contemporary life.

Fasting and other Lenten disciplines, such as working harder and drinking less, also help prepare us for future challenges and opportunities. Christian asceticism is not based on hatred of the body or a desire to inflict punishment on ourselves. On the contrary, ascetical practices are religious acts designed to promote full human development and bring us closer to God. They focus our attention and strengthen our resolve to pursue virtue rather than expediency. They help to empty our minds and hearts of self-centered concerns so that God can become the true center of our lives. There is an essential connection between asceticism and mysticism. Emptying ourselves prepares us for a closer union with God.

In the Scriptures, alms giving and all the works of justice and charity have a special prominence. "This is the fast that pleases me" says the Lord God, "to break unjust fetters" (Is. 58:6-8). Asceticism and justice are closely linked. Fasting can increase our awareness of the less fortunate, promote solidarity with the poor and move us to concrete acts of charity. Feeding the hungry during Lent attunes us to the cries of the needy who will claim our attention in the future.

As Shelley Hoben reminds us, we are all preparing for significant moments of grace that lie before us. Lent invites us to prepare well through prayer, fasting and alms giving.

In the midst of their great grief over the death of their young, vibrant daughter who had the gift of turning tears into laughter, Charles and Shelly Hoben found a remarkable strength and wisdom. Despite their deep sorrow they ministered to others and witnessed to the power of the Gospel. In mysterious ways they had been preparing all their lives for this tragic moment, as Shelley suggested. Their example proved to be inspiring and instructive. We all move toward our own moments of testing. On occasion the ever present crosses of life become heavier and more burdensome. We need to prepare well for those difficult times. Discipline, asceticism and mortification help. So do acts of charity and prayer which comes from the heart. All these practices help make us more receptive to the sustaining grace of God who never abandons us, even in times of crisis and testing.

17. Enduring Physical and Spiritual Suffering

Dear Carol,

Our recent conversation at the wedding reception continues to weigh on my heart. Aware of your willingness to share your experience, I am using this forum to continue my response. Although I was familiar with the main outline of your story through your periodic letters, my spirit was touched in a new and deeper way by hearing it face-to-face and in greater detail. Your very presence at the wedding was inspiring to me, especially when I realized how arduous the trip to Toledo was and how it would extract its toll when you returned home. Only a genuine friendship could prompt such a sacrifice. The rare opportunity it provided us to talk personally strikes me as a moment of grace.

Mercury poisoning from fillings in your teeth – what a bizarre way to have such a heavy cross thrust upon your shoulders. And to think you have been dealing with it since shortly after your marriage fifteen years ago. I recall one of your letters describing the period before it was diagnosed when you were bedridden for a year and close to death. I know you placed great significance on the remark of the doctor that it was a miracle you were alive with that much mercury in your system. It seems to me your belief that God had spared your life for a reason has been one of the main sources of your amazing perseverance.

The pattern of hope and disappointment which was established after the initial diagnosis and removal of the fillings strikes me as especially hard to handle. I thought at the time that once the source of the poison was removed you would gradually get back to your old self and function again like the energetic bubbly undergraduate student I had known.

One of your friends first told me that you were not really making the expected progress, even though you were up and around. Your upbeat letters, however, always sounded better than the reality. I wonder now how you could be so affirming of me and my ministry when you were carrying such a heavy cross.

I knew from your letters that your abiding emotional stress was relieved by periodic bouts of hope that a different doctor or a new treatment would propel you back to health. Our conversation, however, brought home to me a deeper sense of the cumulative depressing effect of going from one specialist to another, each one of whom manifested an initial confidence and ended up sadly bewildered. It does not surprise me that you found it strangely refreshing to meet the last doctor who spoke so realistically about the permanent damage done by the mercury poisoning. Your story of dashed hopes reminds me of my mother's repeated efforts to find some effective medical help for my brother who was born a victim of the R-H factor. In her case, the search was futile, but in the process she gained a deep and enduring understanding that life must be accepted realistically on its own terms. In your case, I keep thinking that something more should be done. After our conversation I considered asking some of my generous well-to-do friends if they could pay for your treatments at that center in Houston. Perhaps that is just my own fantasy floating free from important realities, such as the difficulty you have traveling and the astronomical costs involved.

Carol, the sober truth is that those of us who enjoy decent health cannot know what it is really like to suffer continuously from sickness. We cannot know the cumulative effect on body and spirit of constant pain. I am thinking about you now, but I will soon take a walk in the sun and leave those heavy thoughts behind. Still, my mind searches for some frame of reference or a concrete example which might deepen my compassion and my understanding. It is the engaging figure of Job who first appears. No routine believer or legalistic observer of the law, this sound and honest man of God represents all the genuinely good people, the upright and the Spirit-filled who have known the weight of unmerited suffering. The divine plan can seem so outrageously unfair. Job lost his oxen and servants to predatory nomads, his sons and daughters to a sudden gale, and his health to malignant ulcers. In the midst of this total deprivation accompanied by intense physical and emotional suffering, his wife yanks away one final human support as she goads him to curse God and die.

Carol, I know you can identify with parts of this story as you think about the home and children denied you and the gift of health drained away. When I reflect on your statement that you are grateful that at least you did not make from your poisoned body a baby who would have to suffer as you have, I can hear the trusting Job who rejected his wife's urging to curse God.

But as you know, Job was not always so patient and trusting. Speaking with rigorous honesty and candor, he cursed the very day he was born: "may that day be darkness, may God have no thought of it." He lamented his fate and protested his innocence demanding that God "weigh his cause in the balance." He fell into a deep depression convinced that his "eyes will never see joy again."

Perhaps the impatient Job can help you face your own intense emotional reaction to your illness. Your moments of frustration and impatience are certainly understandable. Moreover, you are not the only one who has been angry at God. Your urge to grab God around the throat and to demand some measure of comfort as well as some answers reminds me of the black protagonist in the play *The River Niger*. After a life of great suffering, he shouts vehemently at God that when he gets to heaven he is going to wrap his hand around God's throat and demand that he tell him why. When you are struggling with the spontaneous protests against God lurking in your heart, it may help to recall Job's utter honesty in expressing his feelings.

Carol, I realize that you are facing an even more distressing problem than your occasional bouts with anger. Anyone who has felt so close to God and derived so much consolation from religious practices is bound to feel horribly let down when the divine presence fades and the consolations cease. I had no idea that you have been experiencing this spiritual desolation for so many years. Your letters were always filled with such beautiful and inspiring statements of faith. Now my mind is struggling to absorb what it means to lose not only health but also spiritual consolation. One woman who has suffered greatly told me her physical and emotional pains were minor compared to the spiritual pain of loss when God suddenly seemed absent from her life. After hearing your story, a man explained to me how intense back pain has beaten down his spiritual sensibilities over a period of time.

My mind goes back to Job precisely because he refuses all easy answers. In the midst of his emotional and bodily pains, he searched for God in the east and the west and

228 \ *Christian Hope: Dealing with Time, Suffering and Death*

looked for his Lord to the north and the south; but Yahweh was nowhere to be found. And yet later the absent and invisible Lord did appear once again in the whirlwind. After warning Job to brace himself like a fighter, God said "Where were you when I laid the foundations of the earth?" And Job, responding to God's elaboration of this theme – a long discourse which really gave no clear answer or simple solution – found a new and surprising sense of acceptance and inner peace.

Carol, my concern for you put me in danger of offering glib advice. Taking the risk, I hope you follow the example of the great saints who struggled perseveringly with the "dark night of the soul" and keep up your spiritual exercises and daily prayers even if the consolation is now lacking. Find at least a few people with whom you can be yourself and can discuss openly all your feelings, even the frightening and embarrassing ones. In some of the darkest moments remember that there are individuals, myself included, who find great inspiration in your example. I hope you continue to find comfort and support from John who is as persevering and loving a husband as I know. Finally, I encourage you to let your reflection on Job flow into a more complete meditation on Christ who carried his cross and was raised to a richer life beyond all imagining.